A PRISON WITHOUT WALLS?

A Prison without Walls?

Eastern Siberian Exile in the Last Years of Tsarism

SARAH BADCOCK

OXFORD
UNIVERSITY PRESS

OXFORD
UNIVERSITY PRESS

Great Clarendon Street, Oxford, OX2 6DP,
United Kingdom

Oxford University Press is a department of the University of Oxford.
It furthers the University's objective of excellence in research, scholarship,
and education by publishing worldwide. Oxford is a registered trade mark of
Oxford University Press in the UK and in certain other countries

Published in the United States of America by Oxford University Press
198 Madison Avenue, New York, NY 10016, United States of America

British Library Cataloguing in Publication Data
Data available

Library of Congress Control Number: 2016940583

ISBN 978–0–19–964155–0

Printed in Great Britain by
Clays Ltd, St Ives plc

Links to third party websites are provided by Oxford in good faith and
for information only. Oxford disclaims any responsibility for the materials
contained in any third party website referenced in this work.

Acknowledgements

This book has had a lengthy gestation. I carried out the archival research that underpins this project between 2006 and and 2008. My research was interrupted by another kind of gestation, as I had my son Eliah in 2009, and my daughter Ava in 2011. My children have enriched and expanded my world, but may have slowed down the writing process somewhat.

This project has been financially supported by The British Academy, and the University of Nottingham provided me with invaluable sabbatical time.

I could not have completed this research without the generous help and support of staff in various archives and libraries. The National Archive of the Republic of Sakha was an exceptionally welcoming and supportive place to work. Sardana Boyakova introduced me to her knowledgable and cordial colleagues at the Institute of Humanitarian Research in Yakutsk, and generously shared her home and her local expertise with me. I would also like to thank the reading room staff in the State Archive of Irkutsk Oblast, the Irkutsk State University's Scientific Library, the Russian Archive of the Far East in Vladivostok, the State Archive of the Russian Federation in Moscow, and the Russian State Archive of Social and Political History. The Slavonic Library in Helsinki was an extraordinarily salubrious place to work, and Irina Lukka was wonderfully helpful.

Thanks to the journal *Europe-Asia Studies*, who gave me permission to reproduce material in this book from the article 'From Villains to Victims: Experiencing Illness in Siberian Exile', published in 2013. Thanks are also due to Irkutsk's regional Museum of Fine Arts in the name of V.P. Sukachev, who gave permission for me to use the image on the front cover of this book, the painting 'Pereprava cherez Angaru', by N. Dobrovol'skii.

So many colleagues and friends have helped me bring this project to fruition. Aaron Retish, Andrew Gentes, Tracy McDonald, Geoff Swain, and Jerry Surh all read substantial parts of the manuscript. Their comments and insights helped me to reshape it, and I hope, to write a better book. Peter Gatrell's incisive critique was extremely helpful. My colleagues in the department of History at University of Nottingham provided me with a convivial and supportive scholarly atmosphere in which to work. I have been lucky to work with a wonderful cohort of graduate students, who have been indulgent of my eccentricities, and whose work has helped to shape my thoughts. My undergraduate students have all also heard rather a lot about this project over the years—particular mention goes to my Special Subject 2015–2016, who renewed my faith in the joys of classroom teaching by being lovely people as well as diligent students. Any errors in the book remain, of course, my responsibility.

My friends and family, both close to home in our corner of semi-feudal Leicestershire, and scattered around the globe, have helped maintain my sanity. My husband Jonathan Kwan read this manuscript in whole and in parts. He helped me shape a broader conceptual framework, and patiently suffered the vicissitudes of the writing process with forbearance and with love. This book is dedicated to him.

Contents

List of Figures and Maps

Figures

Maps

Russian Translations, Transliterations, and Terms

Unless otherwise noted, all translations are my own. I am not a linguist, but have tried to make clear and literal translations. I have tried to translate Russian terms and terminology wherever possible, to make this book accessible to non-Russian speakers. Transliterations have been made using primarily the Library of Congress system, but in the case of names well known in English, I have followed customary practice. Where a word's translation is particularly awkward or uncertain, I have included the original Russian word italicized and transliterated in brackets. A handful of frequently used terms have been transliterated in the text, because their translation is not altogether satisfactory. These words are listed below, with explanations.

Inorodtsy—Legal term used in the Russian Empire to denote non-Russian peoples within the Russian Empire. The indigenous populations of Siberia, central Asia, and the Russian Far East were included in this category.

Katorga—hard labour

Katorzhan/Katorzhanka/Katorzhniki—hard labour prisoner

Lishents/lishentsy—person deprived of rights

I have transferred weights and measures from their Russian late Imperial terminology to their modern equivalents. Russian names for area have been translated throughout—the translations used are listed below:

Oblast	region
Guberniia	province
Uezd	district
Volost	township

Where I have referred to archival material, I have provided a short description of the document referred to, and its date where available, as well as the standard archival citation, which encompasses the abbreviated name of the archive, and the collection, file, folder, and page numbers. The archives' names have been abbreviated as follows:

GAIO—The State Archive of Irkutsk Region

GANO—The State Archive of Nizhegorod Region

GARF—The State Archive of the Russian Federation

NARS—The National Archive of the Sakha Republic

NART—The National Republic of Tatarstan

RGASPI—The Russian State Archive for Social and Political History

I try to refer to all the people mentioned in this book using their full names in the first instance, and their surname subsequently, where these names are available. Where an individual is referred to by surname only in the first instance, this indicates that I was not able to establish further biographical information about that individual.

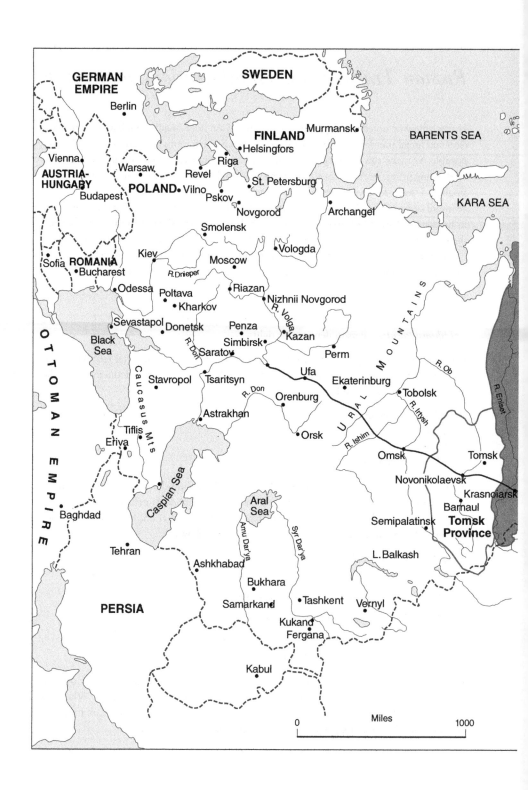

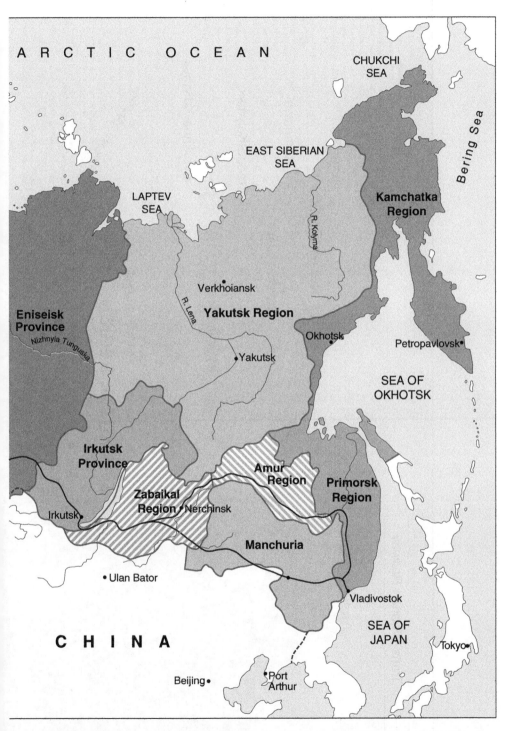

ARCTIC OCEAN

CHUKCHI SEA

EAST SIBERIAN SEA

LAPTEV SEA

Bering Sea

Kamchatka Region

Verkhoiansk

R. Kolyma

R. Lena

Yakutsk Region

Eniseisk Province

Nizhnyia Tunguska

Okhotsk

Petropavlovsk•

•Yakutsk

SEA OF OKHOTSK

Irkutsk Province

Amur Region

Primorsk Region

Zabaikal Region •Nerchinsk

Irkutsk•

Manchuria

• Ulan Bator

Vladivostok

CHINA

SEA OF JAPAN

Tokyo•

Beijing •

•Port Arthur

Map 1. Russian Empire, circa 1900. Based on map in Daniel R. Brower and Edward J. Lazzerini (eds.) *Russia's Orient: Imperial Borderlands and Peoples, 1700–1917* (Bloomington IN, 1997)

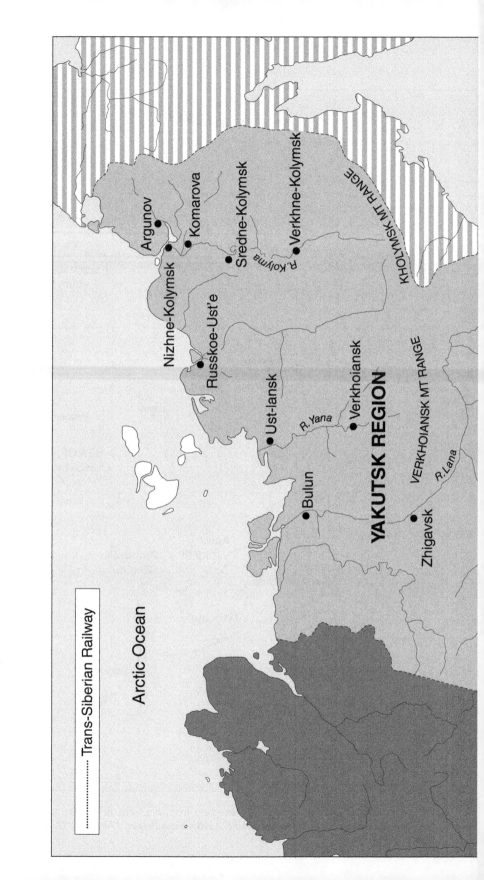

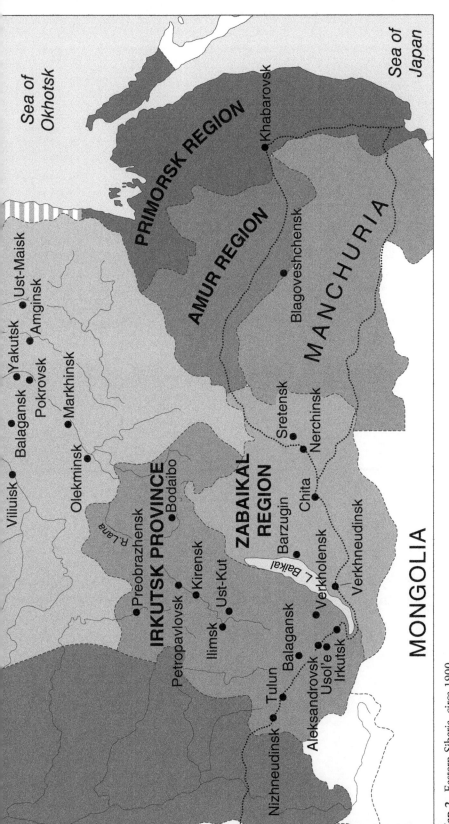

Map 2. Eastern Siberia, circa 1900

1

Introduction

A Prison without Walls?

For more than 300 years, the Tsarist regime used Siberia as its 'prison without walls'.[1] Exile was seen as fulfilling briefs of punishment, colonization, and exclusion. By the second half of the nineteenth century, this system was widely recognized to be in crisis. The Russian State ended Siberia's use as a place of exile on 12 June 1900, except for political and religious offenders.[2] The apparent end of Siberian exile reflected mounting societal and governmental unease about the failures of Siberia as a place of punishment, and was the culmination of lengthy debates from reformers and from Siberian local government demanding the end of exile. Despite the 1900 legislation, the use of Siberia to punish and to exclude unwanted elements from society actually increased significantly between 1900 and the end of the Tsarist regime in 1917. This disjoint between policy made at the centre and what actually happened in practice is a recurring theme for those studying modern Russian and Soviet history.

This book presents a snapshot of exile experience in eastern Siberia during the very last years of the Tsarist regime, from 1905 up until the February revolution of 1917. This exploration of lived experiences seeks to humanize the individuals who made up the mass of exiles, and to give a personal, human, empathetic insight into what this punishment entailed. By unravelling the threads that constituted exilic experience, we are able to comprehend why eastern Siberia was regarded as a terrible punishment, despite its apparent freedoms. There was a rift between the state's policy and intentions for eastern Siberian exile, and local conditions and practice. This book is broadly construed as a social history, so it focuses on the outcomes of policy rather than the policies themselves, but does not entirely discount state policy and practice.

Some aspects of the experience of punishment highlighted in this work confound our expectations of what state punishment involved. Siberian exile was the antithesis of Foucault's modern prison. The state did not observe, monitor, and control its exiles closely. The state often did not even know where they were. Exiles were

---

[1] The Main Prison Administration used the phrase 'a prison without walls' in 1900 to describe exile. *Ssylka v Sibir: ocherk eia istorii i sovremennago polozheniia* (St Petersburg, 1900), p. 163.

[2] Russian State Historical Archive, f. 1405, op. 88, d. 10215, ll. 304–5. From the journal of the meeting 'the commissions about the measures to abolish exile', 16 December 1899, explaining the retention of political and religious exile (reproduced in A. D. Margolis, *Tiur'ma i ssylka v Imperatorskoi Rossii. Issledovanie i arkhivnye nakhodki*, ed. N. Gal'perina (Moscow, 1995), p. 26).

free to govern their daily lives. They were free of fences, and free from close observation and supervision. Despite these freedoms, Siberian exile represented one of Russia's most feared punishments. Exile was a terrible punishment despite its absence of walls, of close supervision, of regimented life. It was terrible because it dislocated individuals and removed them from their social and intimate networks. It was terrible because making a living was a daily strain and challenge. It was terrible because of the pains of neglect—the state's oversight over exiles was nominal, but their provision of care for exiles was also nominal. It was a punishment because exile was unfree, even though the exile was beneath great skies, and surrounded by open space.

Borderland regions in the north, south, and east of the Russian Empire all figured as exile destinations in the late Imperial period, but Siberia was the main site of exile. Eastern Siberia provided a location for what was considered the Russian Empire's most stringent punishments, except perhaps for the Island of Sakhalin.[3] It was home to the infamous Nerchinsk penal district, which sprawled for 200 miles, and encompassed seven factories and twenty mines.[4] Irkutsk was an important penal location. It housed the Empire's largest katorga prison, Aleksandrovsk, and was the primary exile destination for those convicted of more serious crimes, or for those exiled administratively and perceived to be a threat to the state. Yakutsk, on the other hand, had no katorga prison, and was an altogether more marginal destination for exiles. It received little attention from the centre, and figured as a destination for those criminals considered most dangerous by the state. Its status as one of the Empire's most remote locations allows us to focus on the relationships between centre and periphery, illuminating through often extreme examples the challenges of punishment in Siberia. The problems these two regions faced as a consequence of hosting their punished residents were significant, and distinguished by the particular local conditions that they faced. Yakutsk's governors made concerted efforts to stem the tide of exiles into the region. Their dialogue with the centre provides us with an insight into regional conditions and peculiarities, and the relationship between the regional governors and the centre. This book exposes some of the conflicts that developed among different agents of state interests, and the fundamental uncertainties of state goals.

I have chosen a narrow chronological window as the focus for this book. The period from the 1905 revolution up until the collapse of the Tsarist regime in 1917 was an extraordinary period in Siberia's history as a place of punishment. There was an unprecedented rise of Siberia's penal use, and a dramatic increase in the number of exiles punished for political offences. Nicholas II's position as autocrat was fundamentally challenged by the political and social disorder that was provoked

---

[3] P. L. Kazarian, *Iakutskaia politicheskaia ssylka (istorichesko-iuridicheskoe issledovanie)* (Iakutsk, 1999), part 3, p. 68: 'Those sentenced to "remote" exile, particularly if they were from a particularly dangerous group, were sent to Yakutsk, which came to be synonymous with the "most remote place in Siberia".' For an excellent study of Sakhalin, see Sharyl M. Corrado, ' "The end of the Earth": Sakhalin island in the Russian Imperial Imagination, 1849–1906' (PhD dissertation, University of Illinois at Urbana-Champaign, 2010).

[4] Andrew A. Gentes, *Exile to Siberia, 1590–1822* (Basingstoke, 2008), pp. 124–5.

by the 1905 revolution. 1905 was marked by a series of mutinies among the army and the navy, widespread dissent and disorder among a broad strata of the urban population, and waves of rural unrest that reverberated from 1905 right up until 1907. The revolutionary movements forced the autocracy to concede some social and political freedoms, and to establish an elected parliamentary body (the State Duma). These concessions were reluctant, and the autocracy consistently resisted challenges to its monopoly on power.[5] Many of the autocracy's political reforms were half-hearted, and the government tried to curb them soon after they had been introduced. The ossifying autocratic structure of rule utilized a range of repressive measures in order to effect this resistance. Mutineers in the army and navy were weeded out and punished with hard labour sentences in Siberia. Revolt in the countryside was dealt with summarily, with court martials, death penalties, and sentences of hard labour and exile to Siberia. Participants in the urban revolutionary movement also faced systematic repression. Hard labour and exile sentences were issued for crimes ranging from terrorism and violent attacks on the state, to involvement in propaganda and membership of illegal organizations. The number of katorga prisoners increased fivefold between 1905 and 1915. Military courts were utilized extensively in the immediate crackdown against the revolutionary movement. Those deemed politically unreliable, but not guilty of significant offences were dealt with through administrative measures—many thousands of people were exiled to Siberia administratively, without having been convicted of any crime. Our period intersects with Russia's involvement in the First World War. In some respects, the war's impact on experiences of exile in eastern Siberia were minimal—far from the theatre of war, eastern Siberia continued to function as it always had. We see, though, from the activities of the imprisoned military personnel in Aleksandrovsk, and in the ways in which the state was motivated to utilize prison labour more effectively, that the war was felt in these far-off penal locations.

The exponential rise in numbers of political prisoners and exiles in our period, and the hardening of the state's attitudes towards political opponents, ensured that the experience of exile in these last years of the Imperial regime was in a number of respects distinct from the experience of exiles before 1900. First, the segregation and distinctions between political and criminal exiles were eroded. The state increasingly sought to have political offenders treated in ways comparable to those convicted of 'common' criminal offences, which meant that political prisoners were treated more punitively after 1905. The profile of political prisoners changed significantly after 1905, and this contributed to more difficult conditions for political exiles in Siberia. A survey of 15,500 administrative exiles and exile settlers, commissioned by the radical journalist Vladimir Komkov and published in 1908, gives us some useful indicators of this change in social background.[6] While

---

[5] For an incisive short treatment of the 1905 revolution, see Abraham Ascher, *The Revolution of 1905: A short history* (Stanford, California, 2004). For a useful evaluation of Russia between 1905 and 1917, see Peter Waldron, *Between two revolutions: Stolypin and the politics of renewal in Russia* (Illinois, 1998).

[6] V. Komkov, '"Sukhaia gil'otina". Ocherk sovremennoi politicheskoi ssylke v Rossii,' *Obrazovanie*, no. 8 (1908).

before 1905 there was a preponderance of exiles from the privileged classes, after 1905 the working classes and the military dominated the new political prisoner cadre. In the period 1905–8, 40 per cent (6,411) of political exiles were workers, 24 per cent (3,970) were peasants, and 34 per cent (5,502) were intelligentsia. Around 10 per cent of the political exiles between 1905 and 1908 were women.[7]

The new generation of political exiles lacked the material resources that those from wealthier classes could employ. D. Strakhov vividly recalled the workers, soldiers, sailors, and peasants crammed into his overcrowded political barrack in Aleksandrovsk transfer prison in 1908. They were hungry, having spent most of their money on their journey to Irkutsk, and that they were retaining a little for their onward journey to their final points of exile.[8] This was a sharp contrast to the background of political exiles before 1905, which were predominantly from noble or intelligentsia backgrounds, and were often well supported financially. This combination of a more punitive state and less prosperous exiles meant that the experiences of many exiles after 1905 were not easily comparable with the pre-1905 generation.

The Russian Empire was not an efficient, zealous Empire. It was a shabby and shaggy beast, which did not know its population effectively.[9] This lack of knowledge meant that it struggled to control its population, but it also meant that it struggled to define its punishments. We see the inability of the state to sharply demarcate punishment and its implications throughout this book, in different ways. Other states did not necessarily have more 'rational' punishments, and Russia was not necessarily more punitive, or more arbitrary in its punishments, than other states. Hierarchies of suffering are unhelpful to us as social historians, since such things are meaningless if we take punishment down to the level of the individual. By unravelling the intricacies of daily life, this book unpicks some of the peculiarities of the Russian case, and enables us to develop a clearer sense of what punishment entailed for individuals.

This work focuses on the region of eastern Siberia, taking the regions of Irkutsk and Yakutsk in northeastern Siberia as its focal points. It is hard to describe this region and its landscapes without resorting to the clichés of big, cold, empty, and extreme. If eastern Siberia were to declare independence, it would be ranked as the seventh largest country in the world, just behind Australia. In 1852, the Russian novelist Ivan Goncharov, who was to become famous for his depiction of the slovenly fictional nobleman Oblomov, embarked on a long sea voyage as part of a delegation commissioned to open Japan to Russian trade for the first time. His lengthy circuitous voyage took him nearly three years, around Europe and the tip of Africa to the Indian Ocean, through Singapore and Japan, and finally overland

[7] E. Nikitina, 'Ssylka 1905–1010 godov,' in *Sibirskaia ssylka: Sbornik pervyi*, ed. N. F. Chuzhak (Moscow, 1927), p. 16. Nikitina drew his statistics from Komkov, '"Sukhaia gil'otina". Ocherk sovremennoi politicheskoi ssylke v Rossii'.

[8] D. Strakhov, 'V Aleksandrovskoi peresylke,' *Katorga i ssylka* (1923).

[9] For the ways in which the state tried to 'know' her population, see Yanni Kotsonis, *States of obligation: taxes and citizenship in the Russian Empire and early Soviet Republic*, (Toronto, 2014).

through Siberia back to his home in St Petersburg.[10] The 8,000 mile Siberian section was the most physically challenging part of this epic voyage. The overweight and indolent Goncharov, who loved the comforts of a full table and sumptuous accommodation, faced his greatest challenges over the landscape of his own homeland. The otherness of eastern Siberia, and the peculiarities of its landscape and its climate, was poignantly depicted in Goncharov's wry observations. They help us to envisage what this space was like to travel through, and to live in, for a European Russian. Goncharov's depictions of the region were not clouded by unfreeness or punishment. He was a patriot and a self-styled Odysseus, making the final steps of his journey home.

> Don't forget that this is a region thought to be a complete wilderness. It is a wilderness all right. Many times you tremble on seeing the naked tops of mountains with snow on them, with snow lying in the crevasses all year round, or forests so thick that they seem to be a wall of trees, so close together are they. And when they have grown so much that the soil can't support them, they topple over and crash. You can see little animals jump between the trees, and game birds flushing out of the woods, scared by the rare appearance of man. In the distance you hear the murmur of mountain cascades, or sometimes such silence reigns that you can't bring yourself to speak or to sing, afraid of waking up the primeval silence by your own voice.[11]

Eastern Siberia is overwhelmingly dominated by taiga, a landscape characterized by coniferous forest. Eastern Siberia's forests are made up mainly of larch, which is adapted to survive the challenging continental climate. The soil in the northern parts of the region is permanently frozen. Large tracts of land turn to swamp and marsh in the short summer season, making travel slow and treacherous. The region is intersected with multiple rivers, but the most important of these is the Lena, one of the longest rivers in the world. The Lena stretches for around 2,800 miles, from lake Baikal, the world's largest and deepest freshwater lake, to the Laptev sea, an arm of the Arctic Ocean. The Lena provided the only practical trade and transport route through eastern Siberia from north to south in our period, and it remains important today.

Some parts of the region are mountainous. Two thirds of Yakutsk's area is either elevated plains or mountains, with the Verkhoiansk range the dominant mountains of the region. Stretching more than 700 miles across Yakutiia in an arc from the Lena river in the west across to the Yama river in the east, the Verkhoiansk mountains are covered in deep snow for most of the year, and are the site of some of the world's lowest recorded temperatures for areas inhabited by humans. Goncharov crossed these mountain ranges, on horseback, on foot, and sometimes carried and shoved by his Yakut guides. He recalled of the landscape:

> Sadness grabs your heart when you pass these silent regions. If you could talk to the mountains on your way, you would ask them at what time they first saw the light of day; you try to speak to some object inanimate, or to a person inanimate, the Yakut

---

[10] Ivan A. Goncharov, *The Frigate Pallade*, ed. Klaus Goetze (New York, 1987).
[11] *The Frigate Pallade*, p. 600.

guide for instance. You would ask him the question you have memorized in the Yakut language '*Kak birosta yam?*' (how far is it from here to the rest stop?) and he would answer something you wouldn't understand, or say '*gra-gra*' (far) or '*chugess*' (nearby, right away), and then you would go on for hours without saying a word.

A man of culture can't do anything in these primitive conditions. He would have to be a determined poet to enjoy a thousand miles of dreary silence, or be a savage himself to think of these mountains, rocks, and trees as the furnishings of his home, regard the bears as his comrades and the game as his sustenance.[12]

Goncharov emphasized the otherness of the landscape; 'civilised' people could not live there. The untrammelled wilderness and absence of other Russian-speaking people were common tropes in exile reminiscences of the region fifty years later.

The winters of eastern Siberia are long, dark, and frigidly cold, with temperatures down to –62°C in central Yakutiia. Spring and autumn are short and wet, and summer is short and extremely hot, with temperatures of up to 40°C. Rainfall is low, and there is persistent fog in low-lying areas, which gives the landscape an other-worldly, dream like quality. Even Russians, accustomed as they were to the long cold winters of European Russia, feared the extreme cold of eastern Siberia's winters. The climate requires special adaptations, in terms of clothing and behaviour. In order to venture out, even just walking around the shops, one must make special preparations, donning layer upon layer of insulating clothes. To stroll into Yakutsk's town centre on a cold day requires a degree of planning. Locals routinely bustle along the street for a few minutes, then duck into a shop to 'defrost' for a few minutes before continuing on their way. Late Imperial Russian officialdom fretted about Russian migrants' tendencies to adapt to local customs, rather than to import European Russian manners and customs.[13] The aspect of indigenous culture that visiting Russians were most likely to adopt was their dress; indigenous clothing layered reindeer skin and various furs, which enabled them to live and work in this forbidding climate. Goncharov described the outfit he assembled for his journey from Yakutsk to Irkutsk in the winter of 1854. He is able to give us a sense of how the outfit he was compelled to don affected not just his bodily sensations, but also his sense of self:

Now I have lying in my room a wildcat suit, an overcoat of wolf's fur, an ermine hat, a squirrel coat, a blanket of rabbit fur, boots and stockings of reindeer skin, mittens of polar fox, and several bearskins to put under me. When you put all these things on, you gradually take on the characteristics of a squirrel, a rabbit, a reindeer, a goat, or a bear; whatever in you is human vanishes by-and-by. The reindeer shirt and boots strip you of your will and permit nothing except lying down. My fur stockings make it impossible to move both my legs together, and when I put on my hat of double fur, here called a 'malakhai' my thoughts move more and more lazily in my head, and one by one fall asleep. My whole being undergoes a certain metamorphosis.[14]

[12] *The Frigate Pallade*, pp. 564–5.
[13] Willard Sunderland, 'Russians into Iakuts? "Going Native" and Problems of Russian National Identity in the Siberian North, 1870s–1914,' *Slavic Review*, no. 4 (1996); Lewis H. Siegelbaum and Leslie Page Moch, *Broad is my native land: repertoires and regimes of migration in Russia's twentieth century* (Ithaca, London, 2014), p. 31.
[14] Goncharov, *The Frigate Pallade*, p. 595.

While Goncharov's description is typically melodramatic, it does give us a sense of the degree of alienation and loss of self that could be engendered by an extreme climate. It was not only the climate and the landscape, but also the food and way of life that was unfamiliar to most European Russians. While Siberian berries were legendary for their quality and profusion, other fruits were scarce, and vegetables were limited. Eastern Siberia grew relatively low quantities of grain, because of the short growing season and scarcity of areas suitable for cultivation. This meant that bread products were more expensive, and harder to come by. Rye bread and to a lesser extent wheat bread was a fundamental part of the European Russian's daily diet.[15] Multiple Russian proverbs testified to the centrality of bread in peasant diets; 'a meal without bread is not a meal', 'a meal without bread is not worth having'.[16] Shortfalls of bread in eastern Siberia must have made European Russian incomers to the region thoroughly ill at ease.

The region was home to a large number of different indigenous peoples. There were more than 500 different tribal groups in Siberia, who spoke more than 120 languages between them.[17] The region's inhabitants included Komi, Sakha (Yakut), and Buriat ethnic groups, as well as a diverse group of twenty-six ethnic groups that were subsequently categorized as the 'small peoples of the north', and whose traditional occupations centred on reindeer herding, fishing, hunting, and trapping. These 'small peoples' were systematically 'othered' by the state.[18] Siberia had been subject to colonization by Russians from the sixteenth century onwards, but the greatest concentration of settlement occurred in the last part of the nineteenth and the early twentieth century.[19] There were fewer than 600,000 Russian settlers in the whole of Siberia in 1800. By the early twentieth century, Siberia was subject to great waves of free settlement.[20] Around five million Russian peasants officially resettled in Siberia between 1885 and 1913, and uncounted millions more migrated without permission.[21] Despite this mass migration, population density remained extremely low in eastern Siberia. The majority of migrants stayed in the fertile belt of western Siberia, just east of the Urals, and clustered around the route of the Trans-Siberian railway. Tobolsk and Tomsk provinces alone accounted for 60 per cent of the Russian population in Siberia by 1905.[22]

---

[15] R. E. F. Smith and David Christian, *Bread and salt: a social and economic history of food and drink in Russia* (Cambridge, 1984), pp. 253–60.

[16] V. I. Dal', *Poslovitsy russkogo naroda: sbornik* (Moskva, 1957), p. 180.

[17] Drawn from James Forsyth, *A history of the peoples of Siberia Russia's north Asian colony 1581–1990* (Cambridge, 1992). There is an extremely clear map of Siberia showing the distribution of Siberia's indigenous groups in Janet M. Hartley, *Siberia: a history of the people* (New Haven, 2014), p. 21.

[18] See Yuri Slezkine, *Arctic mirrors: Russia and the small peoples of the North* (Ithaca, 1994) for a wonderful treatment of the 'othered' status of northern Russia's indigenous peoples.

[19] See Aaron McGaughey, 'The Irkutsk cultural project: Images of peasants, workers and natives in late Imperial Irkutsk province, c. 1870–1905' (PhD dissertation, University of Nottingham, 2015), p. 71, for a discussion of this.

[20] For an early English language treatment of free settlement in Siberia, see Donald W. Treadgold, *The Great Siberian migration government and peasant in resettlement, from emancipation to the First World War* (Princetown N.J., 1957).

[21] Siegelbaum and Moch, *Broad is my native land*, p. 19, and for a discussion of unauthorized migration to Siberia, p. 24ff.

[22] P. Serebrennikov, 'Zaselennost Sibiri Russkimi,' *Sibirskii voprosi* no. 8 (1908), p. 25.

Eastern Siberia experienced much lower, though still significant, in-migration. Of the approximately four million settlers that came to Siberia between 1896 and 1915, around 600,000 went to Irkutsk, Transbaikal, Eniseisk, or Yakutsk regions.[23] Peasants of Russian origin accounted for three quarters of the population of Irkutsk province by 1905.[24]

The development of agriculture in eastern Siberia was gravely inhibited by the climate and short growing season, and by the unsuitability of much of the land for cultivation. Though some small-scale grain cultivation took place, most agricultural enterprise was focused around cattle-rearing in the southern and western parts of the region. The rich mineral, precious metal, and coal deposits of the region were increasingly exploited in the nineteenth and early twentieth centuries, with mining enterprises scattered across the region. Mining constituted the sole substantial industrial employment for the region, apart from infrastructure projects. The Governor General based in Irkutsk provided administrative leadership for a vast swathe of the Empire, incorporating Eniseisk province, Irkutsk province, Transbaikal, and Yakutsk. Each of these regions except Irkutsk had their own governors, all of whom answered to the Governor General.

THE PLACE OF SIBERIA IN RUSSIA

Within the Russian Empire, the division between centre and colonies was diffuse and uncertain. Russia's Empire sprawled across a single great continent, unlike the western European maritime empires. Siberia was represented both as the epitome of Russianness, and as the ultimate remote location. It was variously rich and fruitful, savage and wild, remote, and uninhabited. The place of Siberia within Russia shifted conceptually in the nineteenth century, and this shift would have important implications for the use of Siberia as a penal destination. In the eighteenth century, Russia cast herself as an empire to be compared with the great western European empires of England, Spain, and Portugal. In a conscious effort to cast Russia as an empire in a European mould, Russia's geographical space was presented as straddling two continents divided by the Ural Mountains, with the European side representing a homeland, and the Asiatic side representing a vast, foreign, colonial periphery. This crisp differentiation of Siberia as Asiatic other and western Russia as European homeland was cemented in the eighteenth century, but endured right into the twentieth century. If Siberia was a foreign colonial possession, then penal colonization was a logical move. It also legitimated the use of Siberia as a place to exclude the punished from the homeland, which could serve a triple function of

---

[23] Anatole Baikalov, 'Siberia since 1894,' *The Slavonic and East European Review*, no. 11 (1933), pp. 330–1. Another one million migrants passed through eastern Siberia on their way to the Russian Far East.

[24] K Chudovskii, 'Istoriko-etnograficheskii ocherk Irkutskoi gubernii,' *Zapiskii Sibirskogo otdel Imperatorskogo russkogo geograficheskogo obschestvo* (1865), p. 81; 'Itogi pereselencheskogo dvizheniia,' *Sibirskii voprosi*, no. 3 (1907), p. 25. By way of comparison, Eniseisk province, with its significant amounts of crown lands, accounted for 10.2% and 17.3% of settlers in those five-year periods.

punishing miscreants, colonizing empty space, and protecting the homeland by removing pernicious influences.

By the later nineteenth century, there were a series of challenges to this clear binary of homeland European and colonized Asiatic Russia, neatly divided by the Ural Mountains. Policymakers were increasingly reluctant to view Siberia as a colony.[25] The Pan-Slavic movement, which sought to distance Russia from Europe and to emphasize Russia's distinct and unique path of development, argued that Russia was not a part of Europe, but that in fact the territory of the Russian Empire was a discrete and contiguous whole. In this representation, the Urals did not signify any kind of break; the pan-Slavist and historian Vladimir Ivanovich Lamanskii declared that Russia had a 'complete absence of major internal divisions'.[26] In this vision, Siberia's history was not one of colonial conquest, but of continuous peasant settlement and expansion. These ideas were to be developed by the Eurasianist movement in the 1920s, most notably by Petr N. Savitskii, who argued that the great rivers formed natural paths, which unified the steppe and the forest, and he represented Siberia as an integral part of Russia's geography, identity, and culture.[27]

The development of the Trans-Siberian railway fed into this discourse. The construction of the railway was started in 1891, and the original route spanned more than 5,000 miles. The advent of train travel across Siberia's great southern border, into the Russian Far East, was both practically and psychologically important. The technology of movement changed the nature of Siberian space. It shrank the vast spaces of Russia's east, and made them seem more accessible and more connected with the metropole, forming an 'iron bridge' between Europe and Asia.[28] Siberia was no longer on the edge of the world, and was increasingly drawn into globalization, as the advent of train travel eased the passage of people, trade, resources, and communications.

Notions of geographical space were not just abstractions—they had important implications for the ways in which Siberia was imagined, constructed, and utilized. If Siberia was an integral part of the Russian homeland, then its use as a penal destination was extremely problematic. This unease was reflected in the later nineteenth century's growing clamour to end Siberia's use as a penal destination. The Siberian regionalist movement (*oblastnichestvo*) presented another challenge to Siberia's penal uses. The Siberian regionalists represented a growing sense of regional pride and identity, and campaigned against the subordination of Siberian interests to European Russia's interests.[29] The movement to end the use of Siberia

---

[25] Anatolii V. Remnev, 'Siberia and the Russian Far East in the Imperial geography of power,' in *Russian Empire: Space, People, Power, 1700–1930*, ed. Mark Von Hagen, A. V. Remnev, and J. Burbank (Bloomington, 2008), p. 445.

[26] In Mark Bassin, 'Russia between Europe and Asia: The Ideological Construction of Geographical Space,' *Slavic Review*, no. 1 (1991), p. 12.

[27] Marlene Laruelle, 'Conceiving the territory: Eurasianism as a geographical ideology,' in *Between Europe and Asia: The Origins, Theories, and Legacies of Russian Eurasianism*, ed. Mark Bassin, Sergei Glebov, and Marlene Laruelle (Pittsburg, 2015), p. 71.

[28] Prince E.E. Ukhtomskii employed the 'iron bridge' metaphor in *Sankt-Peterburgskie vedemosti* (Remnev, 'Russian Empire', p. 445.)

[29] There is an extremely useful short treatment of the regionalists in Steven G. Marks, *Road to Power: The Trans Siberian Railroad and the Colonisation of Asian Russia, 1850–1917* (London, 1991), chapter 3.

as a place of exile was at the heart of this discourse. Nikolai N. Iadrintsev was the regionalist movement's central figure, and he emphasized the uniqueness both of Siberia and Siberians. He published the book 'Siberia as a Colony' (*Sibir' kak koloniia*) in 1882. He deplored the exploitation of Siberia, and in particular its use as a penal colony. Iadrintsev dedicated a whole chapter of his book to the baneful influence of exiles on Siberia.[30]

The constituency of Siberia's population was an important aspect of Siberia's place within Russia. Siberia was never an uninhabited space. As we have already discussed, it was home to both indigenous peoples and to rapidly rising numbers of Russian settlers. How did penal settlement fit into the burgeoning free settlement of eastern Siberia? Free settlers increasingly fulfilled the labour needs of the region. This made the punitive settlement of Siberia look increasingly untenable—the transfer of exiles to Siberia did not meet the needs of the labour market or of agrarian settlement, both of which were met by free settlers. The perceived terrors of Siberia were seen to recede as the region became more accessible, and more culturally developed, which inhibited its punitive mission. Finally, a more populous Siberia was itself harmed by the influx of criminals.[31] The degree to which the punitive aspect of Siberian punishment diminished is difficult to quantify. Improved communications and transport networks certainly facilitated communication and escape for exiles. The daily conditions of life in exile did not however, become less onerous. The fundamentals of Siberia's efficacy as a punitive location—isolation, harsh climate, sparse population, and limited infrastructure, all endured. In fact, the large numbers of exiles sent to the region in some respects exacerbated the severity of punishment there by the early twentieth century, as pressure intensified on availability of jobs and the very limited welfare infrastructure. This point was clearly recognized by the Main Prison Administration in 1900:

> Siberia does not need colonisation (in this there can only now be in agreement), and exile is exclusively punishment—to be taken from the homeland and transferred to another place; it follows to state that Siberia becomes fuller with exiles every year, the future movement of exiles here is onerous and dangerous for the country, which actually has its own independent life and cannot any longer be considered as a 'general prison without walls'.[32]

One of the putative goals of Russian settlement in Siberia, both free and unfree, was the 'civilization' both of the Siberian space, and of Siberia's indigenous peoples by exposing them to ethnically Russian settlers' cultural influences. Peasant settlers were seen as an important tool in Russia's Imperial project.[33] Russian settlers were not distinguished culturally from European Russians in the broadest sense, despite the enthusiasm of the Siberian regionalists to identify a distinctive

---

[30] Nikolai Mikhailovich Iadrintsev, *Sibir' kak kolonii. Sovremennoe polozhenie Sibiri, ei nuzhdy i potrebnosti, ei proshloe i budushchee* (St Petersburg, 1882). See especially chapter 6.

[31] *Tiuremnyi vestnik*, 1899, no. 5, p. 188; report about the forming of a commission for the working out of measures to abolish exile.

[32] *Ssylka v Sibir: ocherk eia istorii i sovremennago polozheniia* (St Petersburg, 1900), p. 163.

[33] Remnev, 'Russian Empire', p. 442.

Siberian 'type'.[34] The cultural and ethnic Russification of Siberia was an abstract goal, which the state was unable to fulfill. The Empire's administrators evinced great anxiety that, far from Russian settlers making Siberia's indigenous peoples more Russian, in fact exposure to Siberian life made Russians live and behave more like Siberia's indigenous peoples.[35] Siberia's penal settlers were particularly ill-suited to a colonizing and civilizing mission. Criminal exiles had been convicted for a range of serious offences, and a significant proportion of them were recidivist robbers and murderers. They were disproportionately male. Exiles without families were particularly poor settler material. As the Main Prison Administration clarified,

> If we look on exile as penal settlement, then it carries in itself a fundamental block on its success; the overwhelming majority of exiles are without family, who don't have any special reason to establish themselves in the new place, constitute an unsuitable element for colonisation. They are not even suitable for simple settlement, as the peasant economy cannot work without family.[36]

Of all exiles sent to Siberia between 1892 and 1898, less than 5 per cent were women.[37] Of the 6,837 people in Irkutsk prisons in 1913, just over 2 per cent (152) were women.[38] Those family members who followed convicts into exile voluntarily were overwhelmingly women and children. Their numbers were significant in the late nineteenth century, but fell away in the early twentieth century. For the period 1892–98, 81,043 people followed exiles to Siberia, including 24,584 women and 56,459 children.[39] This shortfall of Russian women meant that it was harder for convict settlers to find partners and start families. The establishment of family life was at the heart of what the state imagined productive settlement to be.[40]

EXILE NUMBERS AND CATEGORIES
IN EASTERN SIBERIA

Who was exiled to eastern Siberia, and for what reasons? The majority of criminals in Aleksandrovsk central, Irkutsk's katorga prison, were convicted of murder, robbery, or grevious bodily harm.[41] One analysis of those convicted to serve in Siberia in 1910 found that more than 60 per cent of the convicts were exiled for serious violent crimes including murder, rape, and aggravated robbery, and nearly a

---

[34] See Hartley, *Siberia: a history of the people*, chapter 5, pp. 55–69.

[35] Sunderland, 'Russians into Iakuts? "Going Native" and Problems of Russian National Identity in the Siberian North, 1870s–1914'.

[36] *Ssylka v Sibir: ocherk eia istorii i sovremennago polozheniia* (St Petersburg, 1900), p. 163.

[37] Margolis, *Tiur'ma i ssylka v Imperatorskoi Rossii. Issledovanie i arkhivnye nakhodki*, p. 32.

[38] *Polozhenie tiuremnoi chasti i ssylki v Irkutskoi gubernii po dannym dokladov tiuremnago inspektora, 1911–1913gg* (Irkutsk, 1914), p. 17.

[39] Margolis, *Tiur'ma i ssylka v Imperatorskoi Rossii. Issledovanie i arkhivnye nakhodki*, p. 32.

[40] See Abby M. Schrader, 'Unruly felons and civilizing wives: Cultivating marriage in the Siberian exile system, 1822–1860,' *Slavic Review*, no. 2 (2007).

[41] Nina Nikolaevna Bykova, 'Istoriia Aleksandrovskago tsentrala (1900– Fevral' 1917gg.)' (Kandidatskii Nauka, Irkutsk State University, 1998), pp. 219–40.

third were sent for political crimes of various kinds.[42] The criminal code of 1903 superseded the old penal code of 1845, and significantly expanded the sections on political and religious crimes, to include preparation of seditious literature, sowing social discord, participation in collective acts of violence, and membership of illegal political parties.[43] The breadth of crimes covered by political offences occluded the possibility of a tightly defined identity for political offenders:

> There was no body of political criminals, into whose numbers fell so called 'harmful members of society', 'seditious people', 'agitators', 'agrarians', 'strikers', 'rioters', 'unreliable members of the army and navy', 'terrorists', 'expropriators', and so on and so on.[44]

Most of those convicted of political offences were convicted of participation in an illegal association or for preparation and participation in overt rebellions and revolts. A smaller, but significant number of prisoners were convicted for participation in terrorist attacks and murders. Most of those convicted for political offences were workers or in the military, while the criminals were predominantly from peasant and worker backgrounds.

There was a complex range of exile categories.[45] For the sake of clarity, I will outline the two main categories of exile to eastern Siberia in our period. First, criminal (*ugolovnyi*) exiles were exiled as a result of a sentence in a criminal court. In our period, they were usually sentenced to katorga (a period of hard labour in a designated prison), followed by exile to a named eastern Siberian destination for a set period. A sentence to eastern Siberian exile, rather than to the milder locations of western Siberia or European Russia, was usually meted out to the most serious crimes, to recidivists, and to those who were already native to Siberia. Criminal exiles were excluded from civil rights and privileges, and were referred to as *lishentsy*. *Lishentsy* were deprived of all rights of property, and lost their titles, ranks, and pensions. They lost the right to serve in state or public service, or to work in the professions of law or education. Their rights could be reinstated ten years after their sentence of exile had expired.[46] *Lishentsy* lost not only any noble privileges they may have had, but also the privileges of separation from criminals commonly accorded to politicals.[47] An unpublished memoir written in 1908 by N. Iusol'tsev recalled that the legal and material differences between administrative exiles and *lishentsy* were explicit throughout the penal system. Iusol'tsev, himself a *lishents*, recalled that when he arrived in Aleksandrovsk transfer prison, he was one of five political

---

[42] *Otchet po glavnomu tiuremnomu upravleniiu za 1910g,* (Petrograd, 1912), p. 36.
[43] Jonathan W. Daly, 'Political crime in late Imperial Russia,' *Journal of Modern History,* no. 1 (2002), pp. 71–2; *Novoe ugolovnoe ulozhenie vysochaishe utverzhdennoe 22 marta 1903 g., s prilozheniem predmetnago alfavitnago ukazatelia,* (St Petersburg, 1903).
[44] N. Takhgochlo, 'Ob usloviiakh otbyvaniia nakazaniia politicheskimi zakliuchennymi,' *Pravo,* no. 20 (1907), p. 1428.
[45] Andrew Gentes does an excellent job of detailing the multiple different types of exile sentence. (Andrew A. Gentes, 'Roads to Oblivion: Siberian exile and the struggle between state and society' (PhD dissertation, Department of History, Brown University, 2002), pp. 190–8.)
[46] *Novoe ugolovnoe ulozhenie vysochaishe utverzhdennoe 22 marta 1903 g., s prilozheniem predmetnago alfavitnago ukazatelia,* st. 25–30, pp. 5–6.
[47] *Otchet po glavnomu tiuremnomu upravleniiu za 1908g,* (Petrograd, 1910), p. 131.

prisoners in his party, but the only *lishents*. While the other four political prisoners were assigned a place in the political wing, he was assigned a place in the criminal barrack. He protested vigorously, and was granted his place on the political wing after threatening a sit-down protest in the middle of the corridor.[48]

The second category to consider was administrative exile. These exiles had not been tried in a court, but were exiled based on regional administrative orders. They were not denied civil rights and privileges, but they were required to stay within a named region for a set period. They were permitted to return to European Russia at the end of their term of exile. The proportion of administrative exiles shifted between 1906 and 1917, but made up between one third and one half of total numbers.[49] Administrative exiles had often been implicated in lesser political offences, such as distributing illegal literature, or for membership of an illegal political organization. As they were not convicted of any crime, they were not required to be shackled or to serve prison sentences, but were nevertheless transported along with the convicted criminals of every hue, and as a result spent long periods incarcerated in Russian and Siberian prisons on their route to their final points of exile.

Both the state and the exiles themselves drew crisp distinctions between political and criminal exiles. Political prisoners take the most prominent place in the literature, but made up only around 2 per cent of Siberia's exile population before 1905, and around 10 per cent after 1905.[50] While all those administratively exiled were sent for minor political offences, and could be regarded as 'politicals', a significant minority of criminal exiles was convicted for 'political' offences. How can we distinguish between the criminal and the political? The sentences that individual prisoners received provide an indication of whether the individual was regarded as a political or as a criminal. There were specific codes ascribed to political and criminal offences, and these codes were used to delineate criminal and political convicts, but were not definitive. E.N. Bril'on, for example, was listed as a criminal. He had been tried by Kiev crown court under the first and ninth parts of code 1453, for attempted murder. This seems to be a straightforward criminal case, until we add the details that he attempted to murder a regional governor, and that in his memoirs he declared an affiliation with the Socialist Revolutionary Party. If his crime had a political motive, he would have regarded himself, and have been regarded by his peers, as a political prisoner.[51]

Russia's katorga prisons were predominantly cited in eastern Siberia, and the sentence of hard labour became de rigeur for serious offences in the post 1905 period. While administrative exile for lesser political offences might well have entailed a term in a provincial European Russian location like Saratov before 1905, the vast majority of political offenders were sent to Siberian destinations

---

[48] GARF, f. 533, op. 1, d. 1178. This article was part of a published leaflet held in the archive; Oleinikov (ed.), *Pervyi literaturnyi sbornik v Yakutske.* (Yakutsk, V.V. Zharova, 1908.)

[49] V. N. Dvorianov, *Sibirskoi dal'nei storone . . . (Ocherki istorii politicheskoi katorgi i ssylki. 60-e gody XVIIIv.- 1917g.)* (Minsk, 1985), tables 8, 9, 11, pp. 270, 271, 272.

[50] As collated in Gentes, 'Roads to Oblivion: Siberian exile and the struggle between state and society', p. 523.

[51] Bykova, 'Istoriia Aleksandrovskago tsentrala', p. 71.

after 1905. There are no definitive figures for numbers and categories of exile to eastern Siberia. This is primarily because the state did not know precisely where its punished population was. I will present some summary statistics drawn from a range of sources here to give us a sense of how many exiles there were in eastern Siberia, and what crimes they had committed to get them there.

The records of Aleksandrovsk central katorga prison between 1906 and 1917 provide us with a more detailed picture of the criminals exiled to eastern Siberia. Though the records refer to prisoners serving hard labour sentences, they all went on to exile in eastern Siberia. We can get a sense of the crimes they committed, the proportion of political and criminal offenders, their social background and their ethnicity. The absolute numbers in prison varied significantly, from a low of 1,510 in 1907 to a high of 3,149 in 1916. The proportion of political prisoners varied significantly too, from 9 per cent in 1906 to 37 per cent in 1910. The majority of both political and criminal offenders were serving terms of between four and ten years.[52] Most of the politicals were young (twenty-one to thirty-one), while the criminals were spread more evenly between the ages of twenty-one and fifty-one.[53] Most of the convicts exiled to Siberia in 1910 were young. Of the 7,968 exiles sent to eastern Siberia in 1910, 64 per cent were under thirty.[54] Most were ethnically Russian.[55] The profile for exiles overall was significantly older than for prisoners, however, because some served long or life terms of exile, or completed lengthy katorga sentences before going to exile. The ageing exilic population had important implications for the Siberian region, as exiles generally required more material support in the last years of their lives.

Accurate figures about the actual numbers of exiles in Siberia were only correlated at the end of the 1890s. Government organs tried several times up until 1898 to establish the numbers of exiles in Siberia, but with limited success. There was no concrete information on death rates, on escapes, or on how many exiles had ended their sentences and left the region. Official statistics often did not include spouses and children that accompanied the exiles.[56] In 1898, the total number of exiles for all of Siberia, including Sakhalin Island, was estimated at 298,577, not including former katorga exiles, who numbered around 10,000. There were around 65,000 family members accompanying exiles, most of whom were women and children.[57] According to the 1897 census, exiles made up around 5 per cent of Siberia's population as a whole, but this varied significantly from region to region. Irkutsk

---

[52] This statistical data is drawn from Bykova, 'Istoriia Aleksandrovskago tsentrala', pp. 219–40; tables presenting statistical data on prisoners in Aleksandrovsk, 1900–1917, drawn from full information on political prisoners, and a sample of criminal records.

[53] 'Istoriia Aleksandrovskago tsentrala', pp. 219–40. This statistic indicating the extreme youth of politicals is replicated in a large-scale study of administrative exiles; Komkov, ' "Sukhaia gil'otina". Ocherk sovremennoi politicheskoi ssylke v Rossii'.

[54] *Otchet po glavnomu tiuremnomu upravleniiu za 1910g*, p. 36.

[55] 'Istoriia Aleksandrovskago tsentrala', p. 229, table 8a. 'Home regions of criminal prisoners in Aleksandrovsk central, 1900–1917'.

[56] Nikolai Mikhailovich Iadrintsev, *Statisticheskie materialy k istorii ssylki v Sibir'* (St Petersburg, 1889), volume 6, p. 331.

[57] Margolis, *Tiurma i ssylka v Imperatorskoi Rossii. Issledovanie i arkhivnye nakhodki*, p. 36.

was second only to Tobolsk in numbers of exiles, with around 24 per cent of the exile community. Yakutsk was the least populous destination for exiles, with just over 5,000 people, less than 2 per cent of the total.

Even these approximate figures did not reflect actual numbers of exiles in their places of residence. A significant number of the exiles had run away. More than 40 per cent of Irkutsk exiles were absent without permission on 1 January 1898. The Irkutsk prison inspector reported in 1897 that they did not know exactly where 67 per cent of the exiles in the region were.[58] This high proportion of exiles that had run away or were absent was reflected in other eastern Siberian regions, and it endured through our period. The number of exiles recorded in Irkutsk province on 1 January 1913 was 72,136. Of these, 83 per cent (60,183) were common criminals. Only 2.6 per cent (1927) were 'state criminals', that is, those convicted of violent resistance to the state. Forty-three per cent of the exiles (31,043) had run away or were absent without explanation.[59] These figures demonstrate that the number of exiles sent to eastern Siberia was significant. The system of exile was chaotic, however, and the numbers of exiles recorded as escaped gives us a strong indication both of the state's lack of control over its exiled population, and its lack of knowledge about the exile population.

THE IMPACT OF EXILES ON SIBERIA

Exiles constituted a massive burden on eastern Siberia in the early twentieth century. Exiles made a disproportionate contribution to Siberia's burgeoning crime rate. In 1897, exiles made up around 5 per cent of the population of Siberia as a whole, but more than 70 per cent of its imprisoned population.[60] The influx of political exiles in the early twentieth century may not have brought a crime wave with them, but they did place significant pressure on resources in the region. Most of the new wave exiles were from urban working-class backgrounds, and their trades and skills could not find a place in the sparse Siberian environment, which was characterized by little major industry, very underdeveloped towns, small urban population, scattered and unproductive agriculture, and an actual shortage of agricultural land available. Over and over again, we hear pleas and complaints from regional governors that their region could not accept more exiles.

The extensive publications of political exiles in the pre-revolutionary period, and in the years after the revolution, provided a fundament for all future work on exile. The Soviet historiography sought above all to emphasize the wealth of talent, education, and potential brought to Siberia by political prisoners, starting with the Decembrists.[61] The Menshevik exile N.A. Rozhkov commented that the

---

[58] *Tiur'ma i ssylka v Imperatorskoi Rossii. Issledovanie i arkhivnye nakhodki*, p. 37.

[59] *Otchet po glavnomu tiuremnomu upravleniiu za 1913g* (Petrograd, 1914), p. 85.

[60] Margolis, *Tiur'ma i ssylka v Imperatorskoi Rossii. Issledovanie i arkhivnye nakhodki*, pp. 22–3.

[61] For a useful guide to this massive historiography, see for example Aleksandr A. Ivanov, *Istoriografiia politicheskoi ssylki v Sibiri vtoroi polovine XIX- nachala XX veka* (Irkutsk, 2002).

significance of exile for Siberia was not only the economic development of the region, but also the formation of the region's political culture.[62] This positivist approach to exile, which reflected in part the conceits and preoccupations of political exiles, is misleading.

There were inherent conflicts in Siberia's multiple roles as a place of punishment, as a place of settlement, and as a place with an established and developing Russian community. Siberia's regional governors drew out these conflicts in their discourse with the state—all Siberian governors in the early twentieth century sought to reduce or end their region's use as a place of exile. The letters and reports of eastern Siberia's governors may have exaggerated the woes wrought by exiles in their region, in order to maximize their chances of winning the concessions that they sought. Even taking possible political manoeuvring into consideration, the tone and content of these appeals is consistent and well evidenced. While Yakutsk's governor argued that Yakutsk was uniquely ill-suited to settlement given its almost total absence of industry and urban areas, and shortage of arable land, Zabaikal's governor argued that it was precisely his region's more advanced economy, industry, and urban development that made the region unsuitable for exiles. The governor of Zabaikal wrote in 1910 that finding work in the region was impossible for exiles, and that they wandered to more populous areas searching for work, but thanks to the weak development of industry, they simply joined the ranks of the unemployed in the region, and committed crimes. Even worse, the political prisoners had their escape facilitated by this wandering, and by weak supervision over them. He concluded with a repeated request that no more exiles be sent to Zabaikal.[63]

In a further letter in 1911, Zabaikal's governor argued that the region had transformed in the last seven years, and that its large population alongside its industrial and cultural development meant that it could not be distinguished from provinces in European Russia; 'Zabaikal has lost its character and renown of empty and terrifying exile location'. The building of the Amur railway brought large numbers of workers of both sexes into the region, where they formed large settlements, further developing trade and industry. The governor argued that these changes meant the region was wholly unsuited as a place of exile. Criminals convicted of serious political offences, whose exile was intended to isolate their seditious tendencies from the rest of society as well as to punish them, 'found themselves at complete freedom in a cultured midst, and were treated as fully indentured citizens by local educated society and even by the administration'. In his account, exiles were accepted into local society and had the potential to spread their unwholesome ideas. Alongside this problem, the region's good transport links and the severe shortage of observers meant that escape was as easy as a 'simple stroll for a full citizen'. He concluded that the settlement of criminals in the region was harmful for the local population, particularly given the economic and military

[62] N.A. Rozhkov, 'Istoricheskii eksiz,' *Sibirskii student* no. 1-2 (Tomsk, 1915).
[63] GAIO, f. 25, op. 6, d. 3104, pp. 40–1, Letter from Zabaikal Military Governor to Irkutsk Military Governor, 24 June 1910.

importance of the region.[64] Despite these pleas, Zabaikal continued to be used as a key exile destination.[65]

Zabaikal governor's suggestion that the exiles be sent to the 'empty lands' of Yakutsk produced a very sore response from Yakutsk's governor meanwhile, who was at pains to point out that Yakutsk was less suitable for settlement than other regions of Siberia. Yakutsk's unsuitability for exile was, in contrast to Zabaikal, manifested in the lack both of industry and of opportunities for paid work in the region. The governor also stressed that because Yakutsk was extremely sparsely populated, the criminal exiles sent there constituted a significant proportion of the population, and exercised a thoroughly pernicious influence on the local community. Yakutsk residents had to support exiles materially through charity, and they had to endure looting, robberies, and murders committed by exiles.[66] Complaints reverberated across eastern Siberia about the high crime rates endured by the region as a result of the disproportionate numbers of serious criminals living there. This was particularly the case in Yakutsk, where the population was extremely small, but the serious crime rate high. Between 1907 and 1910, there were 16 murders and 7 attempted murders carried out by exiles in Yakutsk region.[67] The Yakutsk governor seemed to win the sympathy of the Irkutsk Military Governor, who proposed to the Ministry for Internal Affairs that exile to Yakutsk was unsustainable and harmful and should be stopped. Despite these pleas, settlement of exiles in Yakutsk continued. Yakutsk's governor from 1914, Rudol'f Eval'dovich Fon Vitte, reported to the captain of Irkutsk police administration on 12 May 1914:

> Having already witnessed around two years of regional life, I have several times asked the question of why Yakutsk region has been chosen as a place of settlement for exiles, political and criminal. It seems that the reasons are only the distance and isolation of the region from other regions of the Empire, and regional conditions and peculiarities have not been considered. In actual fact, there is nowhere in the region for exiles to live, they cannot find any means for their existence, and in actual fact, rather than on paper, there are absolutely no observations over them.[68]

This observation, and the thirty-page report on exile it is taken from, reflected the absolute frustration of eastern Siberia's regional governors about their regions' use as places of exile. It is clear from this correspondence that the governors did not recognize any advantages in hosting exiles, and repeatedly stressed that their regions were unsuitable for exile. Those that were more developed and populated, like Zabaikal region, argued that the region no longer served its punitive and isolating

[64] GAIO, f. 25, op. 6, d. 3104, pp. 47–47a; report from the captain of the gendarme's administration in Zabaikal region, 22 February 1911.

[65] GAIO, f. 25, op. 6, d. 3104, p. 49, letter from Zabaikal Military Governor to Irkutsk Military Governor, 29 April 1911.

[66] GAIO, f. 25, op. 6, d. 3104, pp. 59–61; Letter from Yakutsk governor to Irkutsk Military Governor, 3 August 1911.

[67] NARS, f. 12, op. 2, d. 5169, p. 17; information about the crimes committed by exiles in Yakutsk region, 1907–1910.

[68] NARS, f. 12, op. 21, d. 168, pp. 14–15; report from Rudolf E. Fon Vitte, Yakutsk governor, to the Captain of Irkutsk province gendarme administration, 12 May 1914.

functions. Yakutsk's governor stressed that the region lacked the infrastructure to sustain its exile population, and as a result the exiles placed an intolerable burden on the local communities.

Their narrative was adopted and supported by Irkutsk's military governor, who was their immediate superior. In a letter to the Ministry of Justice in 1909, he proposed that a new exile colony be established on Ol'khon island, which would enable the Nerchinsk katorga complex to be closed, and could end the use of Yakutsk and Zabaikal for exile settlement. Ol'khon was the biggest island on lake Baikal, at 48 miles long and 9 miles wide. It was unpopulated apart from an 'insignificant' group of Buriats. The governor proposed that a new prison with a 'tough regime' could be built on the island to house katorzhniki. Prisoners would be permitted to settle on the island when they completed their katorga term.[69] This proposal emphasized the governor's concerns about isolating exiles from Siberia's settled population, and ending the use of the region more generally as a dumping ground for exiles. His proposal was not adopted, and exiles were sent in ever increasing numbers to the region. The reasoned and passionate appeals presented by Siberia's governors did not meet their objectives. They do, though, give us an insight into local attitudes towards exile, and serve as a corrective to the contemporary and early Soviet accounts.

RUSSIAN PUNISHMENT IN COMPARATIVE CONTEXT

Siberian exile has been exceptionalized and even exoticized in treatments from George Kennan onwards.[70] Political exiles' memoirs provided a supportive mesh for international mythmaking around late Imperial Russian experience, and enabled the atrocities of the Soviet Union's penal regime to be presented as a continuity of Russian carceral horror. The British Empire presented itself as the antithesis of the Russian Empire, of western progress transposed against eastern barbarism. It was able to do this primarily because, in common with the French and Dutch Empires, it created a relatively liberally governed nation state nestled within a large and illiberal Empire.[71] If we look at the governance and care of the population within Britain, we can certainly find areas where the British state demonstrated higher levels of democratic accountability, of resourcing, of state knowledge, and of state control. If we look away from British shores, though, and direct our gaze instead towards Britain's governance of her colonial subjects, we can find a range of continuities with the Russian Empire. Russia's awkward intersection of nation state and Empire had some interesting by-products, not least of which

---

[69] GAIO, f. 25, op. 6, d. 3109, pp. 35–9; letter from Irkutsk Military Governor to the Ministry of Justice, 10 January 1909.

[70] George Frost Kennan, *Siberia and the exile system* (Chicago, 1958).

[71] For a superb exploration of this point, see Choi Chatterjee, 'Imperial Incarcerations: Ekaterina Breshko-Breshkovskaia, Vinayak Savarkar, and the Original Sins of Modernity,' *Slavic Review*, no. 4 (2015), esp. p. 870.

was that the whole population to some extent bore a colonial relationship with the state.[72]

In the British Empire, whole categories of the population were defined as criminal, using categories of race and ethnicity. These kinds of criminal categorization had more in common with the more harshly punitive carceral regimes seen in the Soviet Union, which used social or political categories to criminalize whole sections of the population, than with late Imperial Russia.[73] The British Empire's treatment of Indian revolutionaries was ruthless and severe in its penal responses. The British Empire's use of the death penalty and summary justice, highly regimented and severe prisons, and brutal and remote exile locations, place her at least on a par with the worst that the Russian Empire could offer her political offenders. But while 'the Siberian exile became a metaphor for unjust state-sponsored terror and violence', British horrors in her governance of empire were conveniently occluded by international reporting that emphasized civil unrest, mutiny, anarchy, and treason.[74] Explanations for these discrepancies in international educated opinion and press treatment are complex, but are connected to British effectiveness in managing its own international image, in contrast with the Russian state's very poor grasp on its public relations.[75]

This book aims to keep the experiences that it describes 'in historical proportion', to borrow Catriona Kelly's apt phrase.[76] This study does not set out to suggest that punishment in Russia was necessarily worse than punishment anywhere else. The experience of punishment is in itself highly subjective. Using some basic comparative frameworks, other scholars have shown that Russia's penal regime was at least comparable, and in some cases apparently more liberal than other regimes in the early twentieth century. Russia's use of the death penalty was appreciably lower than other European countries and the United States. Between 1876 and 1905, an average of four persons per million of the population were executed in Russia, as compared to 13.5 per million in England, 26.2 per million in British India, and thirty-six per million in the United States.[77] Russia's use of the death penalty rocketed between 1906 and 1910, as a result of political oppression after the 1905 revolution, when more than 9,000 people were executed. In this period, Russia's use of the death penalty was higher than England and the United

[72] Jane Burbank, 'An imperial rights regime—Law and citizenship in the Russian empire,' *Kritika-Explorations in Russian and Eurasian History*, no. 3 (2006).

[73] See for example Aidan Forth, 'Britain's Archipelago of Camps: Labor and Detention in a Liberal Empire, 1871–1903,' *Kritika: Explorations in Russian and Eurasian History*, no. 3 (2015).

[74] Chatterjee, 'Imperial Incarcerations: Ekaterina Breshko-Breshkovskaia, Vinayak Savarkar, and the Original Sins of Modernity,' p. 869.

[75] For further development of these points, see Michael J. Hughes, 'British Opinion and Russian Terrorism in the 1880s,' *European History Quarterly*, no. 2 (2011), and Chatterjee, 'Imperial Incarcerations: Ekaterina Breshko-Breshkovskaia, Vinayak Savarkar, and the Original Sins of Modernity,' p. 866.

[76] Catriona Kelly, *Children's world: growing up in Russia, 1890–1991* (New Haven, Conn.; London, 2007), p. 169.

[77] Jonathan W. Daly, 'Russian punishments in the European mirror,' in *Russia in the European context: A member of the family*, ed. Michael Melancon and Susan McCaffray (Basingstoke, 2005), p. 166.

States, but by 1910, Russia's use of the death penalty had returned to rates that compared favourably with western Europe and the United States.[78]

The second most severe means of punishment in late Imperial Russia was the imposition of a hard labour sentence (katorga). This punishment was reserved for those who had been convicted of a serious criminal offence in a court of law. Numbers of prisoners serving sentences of katorga increased rapidly in our period. There was an exponential increase in the number of katorga prisoners between 1905 and 1915. While in 1905 there were 6,123 katorga prisoners, by 1908 this number had increased to 16,450. By 1912, the number of katorga prisoners hit a peak of 31,748.[79] Siberia was the main location of hard labour prisons. It is difficult in some respects to distinguish between hard labour and exile in the Russian context, because sentences of hard labour were invariably followed by terms of exile in eastern Siberia. While an individual could be an exile but not a former katorzhan, a former katorzhan was always an exile as well.

Russia was of course not alone in utilizing hard labour as part of its penal system. The United States utilized hard labour as an integral part of its carceral system and its national economy.[80] France had historically used hard labour and exile as punishment. Between 1864 and 1897, New Caledonia, an island in the south Pacific, was used as an exile destination for French convicts. New Caledonia came to be regarded as too pleasant a destination, and was replaced with French Guiana, also known as Devil's Island, from 1897. As with the Russian system, a term of exile was bolted on to the hard labour sentence. On completion of their hard labour, convicts were required to serve a period of exile there equivalent to their hard labour sentence. French Guiana presented mortal challenges to these French convicts— the brutal prison regime, challenging tropical climate, and prevalence of tropical disease made it justifiably one of the globe's most infamous penal destinations. Of the 43,582 convicts sent to French Guiana between 1854 and 1910, more than 10 per cent died. Very few ever returned to the French mainland.[81] Eastern Siberia was a less dangerous destination, and the regime was less rigorously policed, so that exiles had far more autonomy and potential to move than in the French system.

Reminding ourselves briefly of the conditions in carceral regimes around the globe helps to de-exceptionalize the Russian case. This comparison with other states reminds us that Russia was not a rogue state or an aberrant nation in a civilized western family. Russia's use of hard labour and exile may have been a subject for condemnation in the western European and north American press, but it was in many respects less punitive, less severe, and less deadly than carceral regimes

---

[78] 'Russian punishments in the European mirror', p. 167.

[79] Statistics drawn from *Otchet po glavnomu tiuremnomu upravleniiu za 1910g; Otchet po glavnomu tiuremnomu upravleniiu za 1909g* (Petrograd, 1911), p. 36; *Otchet po glavnomu tiuremnomu upravleniiu za 1915g* (Petrograd, 1917).

[80] For an overview of the place of penal labour in America's penal system, see Rebecca M. McLennan, *The crisis of imprisonment: protest, politics, and the making of the American penal state, 1776–1941* (Cambridge; New York, 2008). For an excellent case study of penal labour in one state, see Vivien M. L. Miller, *Hard labor and hard time: Florida's 'Sunshine Prison' and chain gangs* (Gainesville, 2012).

[81] For a detailed study on French penal uses of her colonies, see Stephen A. Toth, *Beyond Papillon: the French overseas penal colonies, 1854–1952* (Lincoln, Neb.; London, 2006).

adopted in the British Empire, in France, and in the United States. The individuals that I trace in this book though, with rare exceptions, had no international comparative framework by which to judge or evaluate their own experience— they lived it on their own terms. This study aims to provide insights into individual experiences of punishment, and subjective experience is always exceptional.

APPROACHES TO SIBERIAN EXILE

The historiography on prison and exile experience in late Imperial Russia is expansive but limited. The extensive publications of political exiles in the pre-revolutionary period, and in the years after the revolution, provided a fundament for all future work on exile. These works looked exclusively at the experiences of political exiles, and almost completely ignored criminal exile, which was in fact the numerically predominant type of exile. They studied the political and social make-up of political exiles, their material conditions, their interrelations with the local population, and their part in the region's cultural and political life. The journal *Katorga i ssylka* was published by the Society for Former Political Prisoners and Exiles, which existed from 1918 until its closure in 1932, and it ran to 116 issues. This journal provides a rich repository of individuals' exile experiences, and has been drawn on extensively in this work for first person accounts. Like any sources, the memoirs published in *Katorga i ssylka* need to be read critically. The journal's brief was to remember the fallen heroes of the revolution and to record the history of revolutionaries' struggles with Tsarism.[82] Bolsheviks dominated the editorial board. Published memoirs were planned and shaped by the editorial board to follow a Bolshevik rubric. Local groups were established whose primary function was to solicit, shape, and submit memoir contributions from former political prisoners and exiles.

We can see from the stenogrammed records that exist of these local groups' meetings that while there was an element of scripting, there was also a strong degree of contestation, dispute, and individual autonomy in the shaping of memoirs. While there was a strong element of self-censorship and central direction evident at the meetings, there was also lively dispute and conflict. Participants dwelled on the person of Lenin, even when they had never met or been associated with him in any way, and by the dawn of the 1930s all the participants were Bolsheviks.[83] Despite the element of scripting that undoubtedly played a part in the construction of these narratives, some of the memoir material presents intensely personal and

---

[82] For studies of *Katorga i ssylka* as a source, see A. M. Alatortseva, 'Zhurnal "katorga i ssylka" i ego rol v izuchenii istorii revoliutsionnogo dvizhenie v Rossii,' *Istoriia SSSR*, no. 4 (1982); Larisa A. Kolesnikova, *Istoricheskie i istoriograficheskie problemy na stranitsakh zhurnala 'Katorga i ssylka'* (Nizhnii Novgorod, 2001).

[83] GARF, f. 533, op. 5. See for example d. 95, Stenogram of meetings of members of the Society for Former Political Prisoners and Exiles, 3 March 1928; d. 96, Stenogram of meetings of members of the Society for Former Political Prisoners and Exiles (1924, 1928, undated); d. 384, Stenogram of meetings of members of the Society for Former Political Prisoners and Exiles, 3 December 1931.

subjective accounts. This is particularly the case in the earlier years of the journal, which have a distinctly impromptu feel. Ultimately, despite their shortcomings, these first-person accounts of prison and exile offer us an opportunity to hear a (mediated) individual prisoner's voice, and to set it alongside other available sources.

From the beginning of the 1930s up until the mid-1950s, the role and experiences of non-Bolshevik political exiles was systematically negated or denied in Soviet historiography, and much of the scholarship constituted a history of Bolshevism in political exile. The position softened in the latter half of the 1950s, when political exiles from other parties were slowly drawn back into the picture. It was only in the post-Soviet period that more substantial studies of non-Bolshevik political exiles emerged. The narrative of lionized political prisoners, and a repressive and harsh Tsarist penal system has endured, however. The fundaments laid by the political exiles of the early twentieth century have largely survived unchallenged.

Recent western historiography has challenged these narratives, but it has focused primarily on central policy and reform, rather than on experience and the local vista. There has been no work to date which looks at the experiences of criminal prisoners and exiles in the late Imperial period, and nothing in the last fifteen years that explores political prisoners and exiles' experience. In western historiography, there have been some works on prison reform,[84] corporal punishment,[85] the police system,[86] terrorists,[87] the Trans-Siberian railway,[88] and on Siberia as a place.[89] Andrew Gentes is the only scholar to have focused on exile in Siberia, and he has made a major contribution to the scholarship of the topic. As well as his two monographs, which focused on Siberian punishment from 1590 to 1861, he has also published a number of important articles, and he has done the field a great service by translating two important primary source works on prison and exile experience, the memoirs of Petr Iakubovich, and the journalist Vlas Doroshevich's descriptions of Sakhalin.[90] While this historiography has provided a valuable

---

[84] Bruce F. Adams, *The Politics of Punishment. Prison Reform in Russia, 1863–1917* (De Kalb, 1996).

[85] Abby M. Schrader, *Languages of the Lash: Corporal Punishment and Identity in Late Imperial Russia* (DeKalb, 2002).

[86] Many, including Jonathan W. Daly, *Autocracy under siege security police and opposition in Russia, 1866–1905* (DeKalb, 1998).

[87] See for example Anna Geifman, *Thou Shalt Kill; Revolutionary terrorism in Russia, 1894–1917* (Princeton, 1993).

[88] Marks, *Road to Power: The Trans Siberian Railroad and the Colonisation of Asian Russia, 1850–1917*.

[89] Galya Diment and Yuri Slezkine, *Between heaven and hell: The myth of Siberia in Russian culture* (New York, 1993); Slezkine, *Arctic mirrors: Russia and the small peoples of the North*.

[90] Gentes, *Exile to Siberia, 1590–1822*; *Exile, murder and madness in Siberia, 1823–1861* (Basingstoke, 2010); Petr F. Iakubovich, *In the world of the outcasts: notes of a former penal laborer*, ed. Andrew A. Gentes (New York; London, 2013); Andrew A. Gentes, '"Beat the devil!" Prison Society and Anarchy in Tsarist Siberia,' *Ab Imperio*, no. 2 (2009); 'Towards a demography of children in the Tsarist Siberian Exile System,' *Sibirica: Journal of Siberian Studies*, no. 5: 1 (2006); 'Vagabondage and Siberia: Disciplinary Modernism in Tsarist Russia,' in *Cast out: vagrancy and homelessness in global and historical perspective*, ed. A. L. Beier and Paul Ocobock (Ohio, 2008); Andrew A. Gentes and Vlas Doroshevich, *Russia's penal colony in the Far East: a translation of Vlas Doroshevich's 'Sakhalin'* (London; New York, 2009).

background for state attempts at reform, and elite visions of Siberian space, its attention to grass-roots perspectives of system of punishment is limited. This study adds a new dimension to our understandings of exile by exploring how ordinary prisoners and exiles actually experienced their daily lives.

This book emphasizes the experiences of lower class and disempowered peoples on the peripheries of empire. This connects to a broader transnational historiography of punishment, migration, forced movement, and empire.[91] It also intersects with recent work on migration and movement in Russia.[92] I combine the methodologies of social history with a more cultural approach, exploring the formation of multiple identities for the punished, and the meaning and experience of displacement. I seek to present a history of individuals' punished lives, which can broaden our understandings of what it means to experience exile. This book emphasizes that all exiles, be they political or criminal, man or woman, adult or child, had their selves shaped and challenged by their experience of punishment. The regional focus of this study connects with attempts from scholars to present local and regional histories of Russia.[93] It is only by exploring the peculiarities of particular locales that we can make sense of the kaleidoscopes of individual experiences. I hope to offer the reader a sense of eastern Siberia as a place through this exploration of its use as carceral space.

With the exception of a handful of well-known political figures, the perspectives of those who were punished have generally gone unrecorded. The richest personal accounts are invariably left by political prisoners, some of whom published accounts of their experiences, or left extensive personal correspondence. These political prisoner narratives have shaped the historiography of this subject. Criminals, however, many of whom were illiterate, left little written record of their lives. This book is based on primary sources from local government, police, and prison inspector records, public and charitable organizations, private memoirs, letters and diaries, and newspapers. I have utilized archival holdings on the key eastern Siberian exile regions, Irkutsk, Yakutsk, Eniseisk, and Zabaikal. I draw on these

---

[91] The field of Subaltern studies in Colonial scholarship encapsulates this well. See for example Clare Anderson, *Subaltern lives: biographies of colonialism in the Indian Ocean world, 1790–1920* (Cambridge, 2012).

[92] Significant recent works include Siegelbaum and Moch, *Broad is my native land*; Nicholas B. Breyfogle, Abby M. Schrader, and Willard Sunderland (eds.), *Peopling the Russian periphery: Borderland colonization in Eurasian history* (London, 2007); John Randolph and Eugene M. Avrutin (eds.), *Russia in motion: cultures of human mobility since 1850* (Champaign IL, 2012); Peter Gatrell, *A whole Empire walking: Refugees in Russia during World War one* (Bloomington, 1999); Joshua A. Sanborn, 'Unsettling the Empire: Violent migrations and social disaster in Russia during World War 1,' *Journal of Modern History*, no. 2 (2006).

[93] See for example of these regional studies, see Sarah Badcock, *Politics and the people in revolutionary Russia: A Provincial History* (Cambridge, 2007); Catherine Evtuhov, *Portrait of a Russian province: Economy, society, and civilization in nineteenth-century Nizhnii Novgorod* (Pittsburgh, Pa, 2011), Corinne Gaudin, *Ruling Peasants: Village and State in Late Imperial Russia* (DeKalb, 2007); Donald J. Raleigh (ed.) *Provincial landscapes: Local dimensions of Soviet power, 1917–1953* (Pittsburg, 2001); Aaron B. Retish, *Russia's Peasants in Revolution and Civil War: Citizenship, Identity, and the Creation of the Soviet State, 1914–1922* (Cambridge, 2008); Sarah Badcock, Liudmila G. Novikova and Aaron B. Retish (eds.) *Russia's home front in war and revolution, 1914–22 vol. 3, book 1: Russia's revolution in regional perspective* (Bloomington, Indiana, 2015).

sources to recreate details of everyday life for exiles and to trace the extraordinary relationship of dependence, surveillance, and reprisal between exiles and regional governors. This study draws on the rich political prisoner literature, but tries to challenge and contextualize it, in order to include the criminal exiles who were punished alongside the politicals, but who are often occluded or demonized in the political prisoner accounts. At the same time, these first-hand accounts can be read as attempts to make sense of criminals' experience and to express their identities.

I will study political prisoners alongside common criminals. As we have discussed, the proportion of political prisoners increased significantly after 1905, but they remained a tiny minority among the punished population. Both the state and prisoners themselves were keen to distinguish those convicted of political crimes and those convicted of criminal offences. This has been reinforced by the historiography, which has been concerned almost exclusively with political prisoners. This study represents an important divergence from this tendency. Criminal voices are often difficult to find. With the exception of the memoirs of Petr Iakubovich written in the 1880s, there are no substantial ego-documents produced by criminal prisoners, but very many produced by political prisoners. Criminal exiles did not utilize the written word in exploring and recording their selves. There is evidence from later studies of prison culture that tattoos formed a personal narrative and an ego-document for criminals.[94] My study has not enabled me to access more than fragmentary glimpses of these body adornments. There are fragmentary written sources that present criminal voices and inner lives, and I use these where I can, in particular archival letters and petitions.

A collection of prison songs was compiled in 1908 by V.N. Gartevel'd, a musician who travelled around Siberia. They provide a first-person voice for criminals. These songs are of course mediated and shaped by the intentions and desires of Gartevel'd himself, but they are nevertheless a rare example of where the criminal voice was actually prioritized over the political voice. Gartevel'd noted that a significant proportion of the 1908 *katorzhniki* were politicals, and not criminals, but that 'they didn't have musical significance, as their motifs were almost all adopted from western European songs'.[95] The words of these songs dwell on familiar themes, of a mother's love, of hope for an easier life, and of love known and lost. They hint at the criminals' inner world, but ultimately they offer us only a tantalizing glimpse of criminal lives. Gartevel'd subsequently staged performances of the prison songs in concert halls in St Petersburg and Moscow, to great popular acclaim.[96]

---

[94] Arkady Bronnikov, *Russian criminal tattoo police files, volume 1*, ed. Murray and Sorrell FUEL (London, 2014). This work is a compilation of photographs taken by Arkady Bronnikov, a professor of Criminology at the University of Perm, who interviewed and photographed large numbers of convicts between 1963 and 1991. These photographs hint at the subjects' inner lives and representations of self. As the extremely limited commentary on the images indicates, though, they offer only glimpses into a complex and multifaceted world, and cannot be read straightforwardly, as they are layered with different veneers of meaning.

[95] V.N. Gartevel'd, *Pesni katorgi: Pesni Sibirskikh katorzhan, beglikh i brodiag* (Moskva, 1910).

[96] *Katorga i brodiagi Sibiri* (Moskva, 1913). See also J. Von Geldern and L. McReynolds, *Entertaining Tsarist Russia: Tales, Songs, Plays, Movies, Jokes, Ads, and Images from Russian Urban Life, 1779–1917* (1998), p. 285.

The experiences of family members that accompanied exiles to Siberia are incorporated into this work throughout. Though followers, as they were known, were not targeted for punishment by the state, and in the case of children in particular, were actually the targets of benefaction and amelioration from the state, their experiences and treatment meant that the lines between those who had been judicially punished by the state and the innocents were profoundly blurred. I regard the followers as an integral part of eastern Siberia's punished population. By studying the punished population without particular distinction between those whose punishment was intended by the state, and those whose punishment was incidental, we can explore the human cost of punishment more effectively, and get a more penetrating insight into interactions between native Siberians and the punished population.

This book is structured in a broad narrative arc, that moves from travel to exile, life and communities in exile, work and escape, and finally illness in exile. Throughout, I try to draw out individual stories and reimagine the lived experience of exile. I try, despite the limitations of the sources, to focus on how individuals perceived and represented their own lives, and to give my reader a sense of how it might have felt to experience exile.

2

The Journey
Travel and Prisons

On 18 March 1908 we left Irkutsk transfer prison for Aleksandrovsk. There was nothing special about the journey, it was all as usual—feet slipping in the melting snow, great pain from the leg irons that chafed and chilled, the occasional crunch of a blow from a gun butt on the shoulder. It was nothing special, all as usual... We were really close to Aleksandrovsk central, a *verst*, maybe only half a *verst*, when my strength failed me. Someone nearby picked me up and dragged me so that I wasn't trampled underfoot...

(Dmitrii Strakhov, 1908)[1]

Strakhov's dramatic account of his arrival at Aleksandrovsk prison exemplifies memoirs' accounts of travel to exile. He speaks of long, frozen journeys and squalid transfer prisons. He speaks of brutality from guards. He speaks of shackles, and illness, and support from comrades. The journey to exile had a hold on the popular imagination, and was repeatedly represented in popular fiction and art. The Russian landscape painter Issac Levitan happened upon the old Vladimirka highway in 1892 as he was returning from a hunting trip. This stretch of road between Moscow and Vladimir was infamous for its use as the route for prisoners on their way to Siberian exile. As Levitan reportedly described it,

It's the Vladimirka road, the Vladimirka along which convoys of countless unhappy souls with chained feet formerly made their way towards the prisons of Siberia.[2]

Levitan returned to the spot the next day with a large canvas, and produced his masterpiece, *The Vladimirka Tract* over several sittings, directly from nature.[3] The painting was an emotional evocation of solitude and loss, with a single figure walking in the distance under leaden skies. The Trans-Siberian railway was to make that tract largely redundant as a means of transporting prisoners, but the painting encapsulates popular imaginings of a long, desolate, empty journey.[4]

---

[1] Strakhov, 'V Aleksandrovskoi peresylke'.
[2] As recounted by Levitan to the painter Kouvchinnikova, cited in P. Leek, *Russian Painting* (London, 2005), p. 199.
[3] Averil King and Isaak Il'ich Levitan, *Isaak Levitan: Lyrical landscape* (London; New York, 2006), p. 67.
[4] On the importance and peculiarities of Russian landscape painting, see Christopher David Ely, *This meager nature: landscape and national identity in Imperial Russia* (DeKalb, 2002).

Lev Tolstoy's last novel, Resurrection, devoted its final sections to his protagonists' journey to Siberia, a journey that was both penal and transformative.[5]

Travel to exile was an integral part of the prisoner experience, and should be considered as part of a penal arc from imprisonment, through travel, to exile. Studies of the Gulag have also focused on the conditions and particularities of travel to place of punishment as an integral part of the prisoner experience, and there are some comparable features in the late Imperial experience.[6] Geography was used as punishment in late Imperial Russia. Siberia's remote location necessitated lengthy and dislocating travel, and this travel shaped prisoners' experiences.[7] The Trans-Siberian railway facilitated much quicker and more effective movement of prisoners from European Russian centres to Siberia. It did not however supersede the need for foot stages and barge travel. Eastern Siberia had few tertiary railways, and final destinations for prisoners were never adjacent to the railway, because the railway was regarded as an escape risk. In order to get to their final destinations, prisoners had to walk, and take barges along the great river routes, mainly the Angara and the Lena.

Irkutsk province from west to east constituted the main exile tract along the line of the Trans-Siberian railway. Aleksandrovsk prison, near Irkutsk, was the central staging point for exile parties moving on to destinations in Irkutsk province, and to Yakutsk and Zabaikal regions. Prisoners were escorted along the way by convoy commands on the main routes. There were nineteen convoy commands in Siberia, and an additional five escort convoy commands serving the Nerchinsk *katorga* complex.[8] Officers of the convoy commands were members of the regular army infantry, though in more remote locations irregular guards drawn from the local population sometimes escorted prisoners. These convoys were responsible for escorting prisoners on rail, water, and on foot to their places of punishment.

Foot stage tracts (*Peshe-yetapnyi trakti*) connected towns with other population points and also towns with their nearest railway or port. As Russia's railway network developed, the number of exile foot stages was reduced. Eastern Siberia was the exception to this. The lack of other means of transport in much of eastern Siberia beyond Irkutsk meant that prisoner parties still went on foot and by barge, often for hundreds of miles, moving from one town to the next. This means of transport necessitated long periods of time set aside for journeys, and long periods in transit prisons along the way. Long foot stages were problematic for the prison administration because they were expensive to administer, offered opportunities for escape, and tended to worsen conditions for those in transit. A baggage train followed every party, carrying baggage, invalids, prisoners from the privileged classes, the sick,

---

[5] Leo Tolstoy, *Resurrection* (Oxford, 1994), pp. 341–483.

[6] See for example Anne Applebaum, *Gulag: A History* (Westminster, MD, 2004), chapter 9, pp. 159–79.

[7] See Judith Pallot and Laura Piacentini, *Gender, geography and punishment: The experience of women in carceral Russia* (Oxford, 2012).

[8] NARS, f. 12, op. 2, d. 1260, ll. 120–4, letter from the Chancery of Irkutsk Military governor to Yakutsk governor, 1 August 1902.

women with young children, and children under the age of twelve.[9] Although the journeys in eastern Siberia were very arduous, they tended to involve lengthy journeys by river, which reduced the foot stages significantly. Eastern Siberia did not have the longest foot stages in the Empire. Semirechensk in Kazakhstan, Semipalatinsk in Turkestan, Archangelsk and Tobolsk headed the Main Prison Administration's shame list of provinces with the longest foot stages.[10]

The memoir accounts are sometimes ambivalent about prisoners' attitudes to transit. While some regarded transit as central to their pains of imprisonment, others, particularly those who had served out katorga sentences, looked forward to the open spaces and freedom that they imagined awaited them in exile, and their more positive attitudes coloured their depictions of transit. The process of travel was in itself a punishment, but it was also a transformative state, of movement from the known to the unknown, and from a place of belonging and statehood to a place of otherness and alienation. Prison was integral to the experience of transit, as all exiles spent substantial periods in transfer prisons on their journey to exile, regardless of their crimes or their sentence.

All exile memoirs emphasized the importance of relationships developed between prisoners on their journey to exile, which provided a network of cooperation, support, and friendship that made transit more bearable. These relationships often endured in prison and in exile destinations. Such relationships were an integral part of most prisoners' experiences, and created a support network to substitute for the social framework of friends, neighbours, workmates, and family that prisoners lost when they were exiled. Travel to exile provided a shared experience of stress and deprivation that provided prisoners with some common bonds and helped them to forge a new social framework. Aleksei Sysin, a political prisoner who was exiled to Siberia between 1901 and 1906, stressed the importance of travel to exile and prison as a forum for forging relationships.[11] For many prisoners, the prospect of being denied the social support network that prisoners developed was the most fearful prospect of all. Mariya Shkol'nik, who used the pen name Marie Sukloff, was exiled for involvement in revolutionary activities in 1903, when she was just eighteen years old. Sukloff recalled breaking down hopelessly when she was told that she would be exiled alone to the village of Aleksandrovsk in Yeniseisk province. Her travelling companions were sent to other villages.[12]

Russia's penal system suffered from acute overcrowding in the period between 1905 and 1917. The number of inmates in Russian prisons doubled between 1906 and 1908 because of political oppression, but there was no corresponding increase in penal capacity.[13] The absolute number of individuals sent to eastern Siberia

[9] *Otchet po glavnomu tiuremnom uupravleniiu za 1908g*, p. 132.
[10] *Otchet po glavnomu tiuremnomu upravleniiu za 1909g*, p. 127.
[11] A. Sysin, 'Ubiistvo konvoinogo ofitsera Sikorskogo,' *Katorga i ssylka*, no. 6 (1924), p. 190.
[12] Marie Sukloff, *The life story of a Russian exile* (New York, 1914), p. 95. Sukloff returned to Russia in 1918, and a Bolshevized version of her memoir was printed in Russian in 1927.
[13] Adams, *The Politics of Punishment. Prison Reform in Russia, 1863–1917*, p. 133; Stephen G. Wheatcroft, 'The crisis of the late Tsarist penal system,' in *Challenging traditional views of Russian history*, ed. Stephen G. Wheatcroft (Basingstoke, 2002), pp. 39–42.

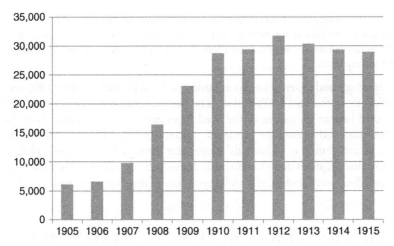

Figure 2.1. Number of katorga prisoners, 1905–15

increased significantly year on year after 1905, because of the political crackdown and because of the increased use of katorga sentences by the courts. There was an exponential increase in the number of katorga prisoners between 1905 and 1915, from 6,123 in 1905 to a peak of 31,748 in 1912. This is clearly illustrated in Figure 2.1.

The majority of katorga prisons were in Siberia, though the increase in the number of katorga prisoners necessitated the building of two European katorga prisons, in Shlisselburg in 1907, and in Orlovsk in 1908.[14] Overcrowding worsened conditions in prisons for all prison inmates. Marie Sukloff recalled her train journey in 1904 from Kishinev to Kansk with horror, 'filthy and crowded to its upmost capacity'.[15]

Though criminal convicts made up the bulk of the prisoners travelling to eastern Siberia, political prisoners provide the overwhelming majority of sources for this chapter, because it was they, and not the largely illiterate and marginalized criminals, that wrote voluminous descriptions of their experiences in transit. Taking these memoirs as a basis for exploring the experience of transit more generally is problematic, not least because political prisoners sought to explicitly distance themselves from the criminals they travelled alongside. The criminals are written out of most of these memoirs, and rarely mentioned except in brief pejorative terms. Transit was however the period of exile where prisoners of all categories, political, criminal, and administrative, shared close living space, conditions, food, and daily life. Political exiles were mixed with prisoners of other categories in transit from the 1880s onwards.[16] Marie Sukloff recalled,

[14] M. H. Gernet, *Istoriia tsarskoi tiur'mi v piatikh tomakh* (Moscow, 1953), volume 5, pp. 21–2, 252–4.
[15] Sukloff, *The life story of a Russian exile*, p. 89ff.
[16] Pavel L. Kazarian, *Iakutiia v sisteme politicheskoi ssylki Rossii 1826–1917 gg* (Yakutsk, 1998), p. 241.

...my comrades and I were lined up with a party of convicts who were being transported to Siberia for robbery and murder. Our wrists were chained to theirs, and in this fashion we were marched four abreast, in the middle of the dusty road, to the railway station.[17]

Any privileges and differentiations accorded political prisoners before 1905 receded significantly in the post-1905 period. The political prisoners' memoir material has been used here to get a sense of the lived experience for all prisoners. This chapter will be structured around the prisoners' trajectory of experience. While the overall theme of the chapter is individuals' movement through Russia's geographic space, much of this chapter is dedicated to stasis as well. The experience of not moving, and incarceration, was paradoxically an integral part of the journey to eastern Siberia.

THE FIRST STAGES: GETTING TO ALEKSANDROVSK

The distance of 40 miles had to be negotiated in two days, the guards pushing the men on with their bayonets and rifle-butts. The party stopped but once a day for fifteen minutes to snatch a bit of rest. And only upon arriving in the sleeping quarters, filthy and unheated barracks along the road, did the convicts warm themselves with a little hot tea... After travelling for twelve consecutive days in a prison car, I had bidden goodbye to the railroad at Irkutsk. When our party of 260 people reached Aleksandrovsk, the guards ordered us to await the opening of the prison gates. The entire party, like one man, dropped to the ground. In spite of the intense cold, we all lay in the snow, silently and long, until we recovered somewhat from the fatigue of the march. (Vladimir Zenzinov, in 1910)[18]

...the guards hurried us and drove us on, and I remember when, at last, the walls of Irkutsk prison were seen, the whole party, like one man, lay on the ground, right in the dirt, in the puddles. (Andrei Sobol, in 1906)[19]

Aleksandrovsk served as Siberia's penal hub in our period. The arrival at Aleksandrovsk was the culmination of a long and varied journey from European Russia to eastern Siberia. Both Sobol and Zenzinov, writing four years apart, used nearly the same words to describe their arrival at Aleksandrovsk. Aleksandrovsk incorporated the transfer prison for prisoners travelling onwards to eastern Siberian exile, but was also a katorga prison in its own right. Most of the journey to Irkutsk was travelled on the Trans-Siberian railway. For those prisoners whose final exile destination was eastern Siberia, their journey was invariably routed through Aleksandrovsk. The journeys began in transfer prisons in the European urban centres of the Empire. Butyrka in Moscow was one of the most important, and infamous, transfer hubs serving the penal transportation network.

---

[17] Sukloff, *The life story of a Russian exile*, p. 89.
[18] Vladimir Zenzinov, *The road to oblivion* (New York, 1931), p. 5.
[19] Andrei Sobol', '"Kolesukha",' *Katorga i ssylka* (1921), p. 96.

Up until the 1880s, epic foot stages and crowded barges transferred convicts from central Russia to Siberia.[20] Ekaterina Breshkovskaia, recalling her journey to Kara near Irkutsk in 1878, described a long and squalid barge journey on the Volga, and, rather thrillingly, an extraordinary ride by troika across 3,000 miles from Perm to Kara.[21] Petr Iakubovich wrote a seminal account of the journey to Irkutsk in 1887.[22] In our period, the development of rail travel made the stages of travel from European Russia to Aleksandrovsk much faster and more consistent than they had been in the earlier period. The development of the Trans-Siberian railway from the 1890s onwards transformed convicts' journeys from European Russia to destinations up to Irkutsk.[23] The railway provided a cheaper, more rapid, and more humane means of transport. Despite these improvements in transport systems, the logistics of travel over huge distances across sparsely populated countryside meant that travel continued to be a physically weakening and emotionally dislocating experience. Until 1912, convicts went on foot from Irkutsk along the Angara tract under military convoy to Aleksandrovsk village, where the katorga and transfer prisons were situated. This journey of around forty-seven miles is what Sobol and Zenzinov recounted.

On the railways, specially strengthened prisoners' wagons were designated for prisoners' use. The prisoners' wagons were meant to have double floors, barred windows, and locks on the doors, but many were very old, and only the newer ones were built to plan.[24] In practice, there were only 490 prisoner wagons available, so in many cases prisoners were moved in passenger wagons. Iadov, a political prisoner travelling in 1912 from his *katorga* term in Butyrka, Moscow, to 'cold but long awaited Siberia', recalled that the journey to Irkutsk by train passed relatively quickly, with only two stops, in Samara and in Krasnoiarsk. The only real inconvenience was that in his wagon all but four of the men had their arms and legs shackled, and 'they sweated as if in a sauna'.[25]

A. Dobrokhotin-Baykov, a Moscow worker who was sent to Yakutsk exile in 1911, recalled his journey to Irkutsk vividly:

We left Butyrka prison (in Moscow) on a hot day in June, and set off for Siberia in a 'protected' prisoners' wagon. After a long and distressing journey in sealed dirty wagons, with stops for several days in prisons of towns en route... we arrived in Irkutsk in the middle of August, where we were imprisoned in the regional prison. Sitting in the dirty, wooden, relatively large general barrack, together with criminal trash, was a nightmare. Filth, stench, the appalling swearing of the criminals—all this acted on us badly. After two weeks we were directed on foot, a party of 200, to

---

[20] For an excellent discussion of this, see Daniel Beer, 'Penal Deportation to Siberia and the Limits of State Power, 1801–1881,' *Kritika: Explorations in Russian and Eurasian History*, no. 3 (2015).

[21] Ekaterina K. Breshko-Breshkovskaia, *Hidden Springs of the Russian Revolution* (London, 1931), pp. 181–9. Kara was a gold mine located east of Irkutsk, which was closed in 1898.

[22] Iakubovich, *In the world of the outcasts: notes of a former penal laborer*, volume 1, pp. 5–21.

[23] The building of the Trans-Siberian railway began in 1892. The stretch from Krasnoiarsk to Irkutsk was completed in 1899.

[24] *Otchet po glavnomu tiuremnomu upravleniiu za 1908g*, p. 129ff.

[25] Iadov, 'Iz angarskikh perezhivanii,' in *Sibirskaia ssylka: Sbornik pervyi*, ed. N. F. Chuzhak (Moscow, 1927).

Aleksandrovsk central. The journey around the hills was an absolute Golgotha. Physically exhausted by sitting and bad food, several of us, me included, could not walk far and fell from incapacity. Rough handling and blows from the soldier convoy forced us to get up and moving again. And then again we fell, and again gun butts. Somehow we dragged ourselves forward. We were no more than a week in [Aleksandrovsk] central.[26]

Like the account from Dmitrii Strakhov that opened this chapter, and the accounts from Zenzinov and Sobol that opened this section, this memoir emphasized squalid conditions, overcrowding, brutality from guards, and exhausting marches. It adds the writer's distaste for sharing close quarters with 'common' criminals to the picture. This sentiment emerges in many political prisoners' accounts of transit. In 1912, the walk to Aleksandrovsk central that Dobrokhotin-Baikov, Sobol, and Zenzinov described was shortened by the use of a train station at Usol instead, which reduced the foot journey to prison to around ten miles. A new building to house transfer prisoners was established in 1913 near Usol station.[27]

Whether they were sentenced to exile or to hard labour, prisoners often faced a lengthy stay at Aleksandrovsk. This was because the routes on from Aleksandrovsk to more remotely located exile points, or to the Nerchinsk katorga complex, were only passable between April and September, when the waterways were navigable. For the rest of the year, frozen rivers and impassible roads made many journeys impracticable. In the summer months, convoys left the prison regularly, but there were sometimes backlogs of prisoners awaiting transit, so even a summer arrival at Aleksandrovsk could necessitate a lengthy wait. Prisoners got to know each other and developed their own distinctive subcultures in Aleksandrovsk prison. The communities that developed in prison could form a basis for the networks of support that developed in exile.[28]

The prison administration sought to operate a rational and controlled model of prison population management. In practice, the levels of overcrowding and the limited facilities and resources available made a mockery of these ambitions. There was a constant stream of prisoner groups arriving and leaving the prison, with the numbers usually peaking around August. While we can give indications of the numbers of prisoners in Aleksandrovsk, these are very imprecise, because there were significant fluctuations in the population from month to month. Between April and December 1909, for example, the number of prisoners fluctuated from 1,457 (on 20 May), to 2,181 (on 25 September).[29] We can state with confidence that both katorga and transfer prisons were severely overcrowded by 1909. At the end of

[26] A. Dobrokhotin-Baikov, 'V Yakutskoi ssylke (zapiski rabochego),' in *Sibirskaia ssylka: Sbornik pervyi*, ed. N. F. Chuzhak (Moscow, 1927).

[27] *Polozhenie tiuremnoi chasti i ssylki v Irkutskoi gubernii po dannym dokladov tiuremnago inspektora, 1911–1913gg.*

[28] For an example of the importance of prison stages in subsequent formation of exile community, see this description of the pre-exile activities that took place in Krasnoiarsk transfer prison; E. Tsingovatov-Korol'kov, 'Organizatsiia vzaipomoshchi Eniseiskoi ssylki (Po lichnym vospominaniiam i po pis'mam),' *Katorga i ssylka* (1928).

[29] Bykova, 'Istoriia Aleksandrovskago tsentrala', p. 68.

August 1909 Aleksandrovsk katorga prison housed 2,140 prisoners, while it had places for 1,005 prisoners. There were 1,460 prisoners in the main prison, 73 in the hospital, 280 in the external barracks, and another 327 out working in the mines and railroads. The severe overcrowding in the prison meant that is was more difficult for the prison administration to maintain order, as even the solitary cells housed two, three, or even more prisoners.

The Captain of the Main Prison Administration in 1909, Stepan Stepanovich Khrulev, made a tour of katorga prisons around Irkutsk and Zabaikal regions in September and October 1909.[30] His description of Aleksandrovsk prison in some respects confirms the positive impressions of the place relayed by George Kennan when he visited the prison in 1885.[31] The prison was situated in Aleksandrovsk village, about forty-six miles from Irkutsk, and six miles from the river Angar. The area was hilly and not suitable for arable farming, and was surrounded by woodland, which provided the prison with timber for fuel and building materials. The prison resembled a small town; its workshops manufactured the prisons' shoes, clothes, and underwear, and its gardens supplemented the prison diet with potatoes, cabbage, and greens. A two-storey brick building faced the street, and housed thirty-seven general and twenty-one solitary cells. The cells were meant to hold 1,005 prisoners, but the actual numbers were often significantly higher. Situated within the prison grounds were a library, a church, a school, a maternity unit, a chapel, and bathhouses for the staff and for the prisoners. The prison orphanage cared for around one hundred children. There were church services on every holiday day, and a prisoners' choir. The hospital was less than a mile away from the main prison, and separate buildings housed the kitchen, the bathhouse, and the laundry. The prison had its own farm and market gardens, all of which were worked by prisoners. The farm raised cattle and chickens, and produced milk. The fields were split into seven-acre plots, growing rye, oats, corn, cabbage, potatoes, beetroot, and carrots. Part of this produce was used to feed the prisoners, and the rest was marketed and produced an income for the prison.[32]

There were two main prisons within the complex, the katorga prison and the transfer prison, as well as barrack places for some 300 prisoners who were permitted to work outside the prison. The prisoners that lived and worked outside the prison, and the so-called 'free command', were able to take on paid work. They usually worked without an overseer, and they were not locked in until final night check. They worked on house-building, barrel-making, coalmines, and land clearing for the railway. Very few of the political prisoners were allowed to work outside the prison, because they were regarded as an escape risk.[33] There was a military garrison

[30] S. S. Khrulev, *Katorga v Sibiri: Izvlechenie iz otcheta nachal'nika glavnago tiuremnago upravlenie S.S. Khruleva o sluzhebnoi poezdke, v 1909 godu, v Irkutskoi gub. i Zabaikalskuiu obl.* (St. Petersburg, 1910), pp. 5–6.
[31] Kennan, *Siberia and the exile system*, volume 2, p. 344. See also Henry Lansdell, *Through Siberia* (Boston, 1882), chapter 21.
[32] Bykova, 'Istoriia Aleksandrovskago tsentrala', p. 50.
[33] Khrulev, *Katorga v Sibiri: Izvlechenie iz otcheta nachal'nika glavnago tiuremnago upravlenie S.S. Khruleva o sluzhebnoi poezdke, v 1909 godu, v Irkutskoi gub. i Zabaikalskuiu obl*, pp. 14–15.

in Aleksandrovsk village, with 630 soldiers and six officers. The garrison was housed in an overcrowded and ill-equipped barracks within the prison. The captain of the garrison had to make frequent requests for repair, cleaning, and heating of the garrison's buildings.[34]

Aleksandrovsk transfer prison was a large two-story wooden building. Its formal use was reduced after the restriction of exile in 1900, and by 1909 it housed katorga prisoners who were allocated out of prison status, and also those categorized as decrepit or in poor health, because of insufficient places in the central katorga prison, and also those transferred from Irkutsk town prison because of overcrowding. It also housed a small number of transfer prisoners and exiles, waiting to be sent on the foot stages to Irkutsk province and the Yakutsk region. In 1909, it housed 1,110 people, including 774 exile-katorga prisoners, 201 of whom should have been in prison, and 35 in other categories, including four women. Prisoners were separated by category into nine barracks. There was no church serving the prison, and the kitchen, bathhouse, and laundry were all dilapidated. The regime was much the same as in the katorga prison. There was no cold-water tap, so water had to be carried there in barrels from the pond, which involved a great deal of work. Those people who were exiled administratively, rather than by court order, were held in the transfer prison. Lydia Dan spent time in Aleksandrovsk transfer prison on her way to Siberian exile in 1904. Interviewed many years later, she remembered this time almost fondly:

> I don't have any bad memories of the place. The regime was so easy that you could escape... (There were) about seventy to eighty in the men's section, and fifteen or twenty women. It was not exactly comfortable, but we were young and didn't pay much attention to that. Of course, everyone wanted very much to escape from this communal life into his own little corner... since there was nothing to do, people talked about their lives and thus became acquainted with one another and with party work. This was all very informative.[35]

Dan's memoir provides a slightly conflicting picture of her experience. She emphasized that she networked and built relationships in prison, whilst at the same time admitting that all the inmates sought to withdraw from the collective and to protect their private space. The sixty years that had elapsed from her time in Aleksandrovsk to her recollections here must surely have filtered and coloured her recollections, and encouraged her to prioritize certain aspects of her memories over others.

Conditions in Aleksandrovsk were not static between 1905 and 1917, but shifted constantly. These changes in conditions were predicated partly on the size of the prison population, partly on national shifts in policy and mood, partly on changes within the prison administration, and partly on the microclimate created by the inmates at any time. A number of memoirists stress this mutability of

[34] *Katorga v Sibiri: Izvlechenie iz otcheta nachal'nika glavnago tiuremnago upravlenie S.S. Khruleva o sluzhebnoi poezdke, v 1909 godu, v Irkutskoi gub. i Zabaikalskuiu obl*, p. 13.
[35] Leopold J. Haimson (ed.) *The making of three Russian revolutionaries* (Cambridge, 1987), p. 161. These recollections were drawn from reminiscences recorded on tape between 1960 and 1965.

conditions.[36] The regime in Aleksandrovsk before 1907 was regarded as more liberal than in other katorga prisons. The prison's first two governors, Aleksandr Petrovich Sipiagin (1874–1901) and E.E. Liatoskovich (1901–1906) were renowned as liberal and enlightened prison governors. Sipiagin's regime represented the dreams of Russia's prison reformers to move away from punishment-based penitentiaries, and towards prison as a corrective institution. Shackles, punishment cells, and corporal punishment were phased out, while work programmes, a prisoners' theatre, orchestra, and school were introduced. Liatoskovich was himself an exile, and had been sent to Siberia after his participation in the 1863 Polish rising. He sought to lighten the fate of prisoners. Cells were open during the day, and prisoners were free to stroll around, wear their own clothes, and were unshackled. The shifts towards a more punitive regime after 1906 partly reflected the personalities of subsequent prison governors, but also reflected the change in national mood as a result of the 1905 revolution, and the massively increased proportion of prisoners with political convictions. Until 1906, the prisoners were predominated by those with criminal rather than political sentences, whereas in the subsequent period up to a third of prisoners were convicted on political offences.[37]

The hardening of the prison regime in Aleksandrovsk from 1907 onwards coincided with the appointment of Faddei Vladimirovich Savitskii as governor. Savitskii's attempts to put the regime 'in order' reflected a more punitive tone from central administration. Aleksandr Mikhailovich Maksimovskii was appointed captain of the Main Prison Administration in 1906. He published a circular on 16 December 1906 that katorga prisoners of all ranks must be shackled, and that to avoid disorder and escapes, cells should be locked at all times, and that time in the yard for walking must be restricted to one cell at a time.[38] Memoirists in other Siberian prisons commented on this shift towards more punitive prison management at the end of 1906.[39] A further circular on 20 July 1907 demanded total equality of treatment between criminal and political prisoners.[40] Maksimovskii's time in the role was brief. His attempts to make the penal regime more stringent for political prisoners made him a target of the Socialist Revolutionary Party's terrorist

---

[36] See for example Stanchinskii, who stresses the importance of prison microclimates, and especially the prisoners held there, in determining the climate of specific prisons. A.P. Stanchinskii, 'V Algachakh,' *Katorga i ssylka*, no. 3 (1922). See also Kramarov's description of the shift in Nerchinsk's regime from pre 1906 (prison heaven) to post-1909 (prison hell). (G. Kramarov, 'Nerchinskaia katorga. Doklad, prochitanii na zasedanii Istoricheskoi sektsii Doma Pechati v Moskve 8 Oktiabria 1921 goda. (1907–1910gg),' *Katorga i ssylka* (1922)). Another Nerchinsk inmate, Prokolii Dimidovich Klimushkin, who served ten years in Zerentui between 1907 and 1917, recalled that the regime in Gornyi Zerentui was severe and atrocious before 1914, but that it became significantly softer and more humane after 1914. (P. Klimushkin, 'K amnestii 1917 g,' *Katorga i ssylka* (1921).)
[37] Bykova, 'Istoriia Aleksandrovskago tsentrala', pp. 51–4.
[38] 'Istoriia Aleksandrovskago tsentrala', p. 104.
[39] See for example Kramarov's description of Nerchinsk. (Kramarov, 'Nerchinskaia katorga. Doklad, prochitanii na zasedanii Istoricheskoi sektsii Doma Pechati v Moskve 8 Oktiabria 1921 goda. (1907–1910gg).')
[40] Bykova, 'Istoriia Aleksandrovskago tsentrala', p. 106.

wing, and he was killed by a twenty-one-year-old music student, Evstoliia Pavlovna Rogozinnikova, on 15 October 1907. Rogozinnikova was executed by court martial the following day.[41]

Savitskii seems to have maintained a relatively liberal regime in Aleksandrovsk until the second half of 1907, but he introduced a range of more punitive measures after this, no doubt connected to Stolypin's stringent measures to crack down on the revolutionary movement. The punishment cells and solitary confinement were used more frequently, even for relatively minor infractions like impoliteness towards prison staff. Despite these revisions, the regime under Savitskii did not meet the more stringent requirements made by central circulars. Up until 1908, political and criminal prisoners were housed separately, and all katorga prisoners were unshackled. After this, though, prisoners were fitted with shackles, and the cells were locked, with only fifteen to twenty minutes per day out to walk around the yard.

P. Minaev was a political prisoner who arrived in Aleksandrovsk in December 1907 from Butyrka, the Moscow transit prison. Minaev described a distinct shift in the prison regime from 1907 to 1908. He recounted that initially the political prisoners were housed separately from the criminal prisoners, and that they enjoyed a high degree of freedom—the cells were open from morning until evening register, and they could stroll in the yards outside in the day, and attended lectures and literacy schools. Those with spare money could buy little pies (*pirozhki*) fried in a special pan in the yard. The administration was polite, and all questions of internal order were resolved through an elder who was elected by the political collective. Minaev's experience dated the shift to a harsher regime to a specific incident in March 1908. The residents of cell number 1 were told to carry water for bathing to the cell holding protected prisoners, the 'prison refuse and hangmen', who were separated from the other prisoners for their own safety. The prisoners refused, and were threatened with flogging from the prison administration as a result.[42] The political prisoners faced a series of repressive measures in the prison after this incident according to Minaev.

Savitskii died in 1910, and was replaced by E.S. Snezhkov. Snezhkov had a reputation for severity based on his governorship of Khar'kiv prison, and he further tightened the regime in Aleksandrovsk. Gran's report on Aleksandrovsk in 1913 noted that the regime in Aleksandrovsk was 'proper', with criminal and political prisoners shackled and treated the same, and that the regime was overall an improvement (i.e. harsher) than the conditions that existed in 1906.[43] Despite this reputation for harshness, Snezhkov's management of the prison sought to avoid excessive conflict with the political prisoners. N.K. Nikitin replaced Snezhkov in mid-1915. Nikitin's attempts to shift towards a harsher regime were thwarted by

[41] Margaret Maxwell, *Narodniki women: Russian women who sacrificed themselves for the dream of freedom* (New York, 1990), p. 151; James H. Billington, *Fire in the minds of men: origins of the revolutionary faith* (New York, 1980), p. 495.

[42] P. Minaev, 'Kak my bezhali iz Aleksandrovsk tsentrale,' *Katorga i ssylka* (1923).

[43] Petr K. Gran, *Katorga v Sibiri. Izvlechenie iz otcheta o sluzhebnoi poezdke nachal'nika glav. tiurem. upravleniia P.K. Grana v Sibir v 1913 g* (St. Peterburg, 1913), pp. 9–10.

concerted resistance from the political prisoners, and he ended up adopting the more conciliatory tactics adopted by his predecessor.[44]

DAILY LIFE IN ALEKSANDROVSK

> It's an old truth that only in prison can you know a person in all his most intimate details. Prison is something that reveals a person to his very core—it shows him from all angles at every step. And he who is a coward deep down, his cowardice will be discovered, no matter how much he pretends and hides it. And he who is brave, who is courageous, who is noble—this will be revealed of him, for prison is a great scalpel . . . It shows a person as he really is, in all his depth, tearing off the most cunning of masks.
>
>   (Andrei Sobol', inmate of Aleksandrovsk)[45]

Andrei Sobol' pops up on the pages of this book here and there. His memoirs of prison and exile are lucid and evocative, and give us a visceral sense of the author's emotional state. Sobol' was just eighteen years old when he was sentenced to four years katorga in 1906, for participating in an illegal Jewish Socialist organization. He became well known as a writer in the early Soviet period.[46] Like all our memoirists, his writing was shaped and filtered by his experiences in the interim between the events he described and the time that he wrote. Sobol' escaped from exile to Paris in 1909. He returned to Russia illegally in 1914, and after the February revolution of 1917 he worked for the Provisional Government as a Military Commissar. Sobol' took an anti-Bolshevik position after the October revolution, and was imprisoned between 1920 and 1921. In 1923, he officially recognized the Soviet regime in an open letter to Pravda.[47] In the extract from his writing that this section opens with, his tortured description of 'tearing off of masks' resonates with the cultural and political discourse of the 1920s, which Sobol', as a former counter-revolutionary, had to participate in actively.[48]

Sobol' suggested that prison life exposed prisoners' true selves, and forced them to drop the usual civilian deceits and niceties. What do other accounts tell us about daily life in Aleksandrovsk? On arrival, prisoners were housed in a special cell until they had been looked over by a doctor. If all was well, they were transferred to the general cells after three days. The twenty-seven general cells were high ceilinged,

---

[44] Bykova, 'Istoriia Aleksandrovskago tsentrala', pp. 55–6.

[45] Andrei Sobol', 'Otryvki iz vospominanii,' *Katorga i ssylka*, no. 13 (6) (1924), p. 153. Sobol shot himself in 1926. See Vladimir Kazan, 'Sobol, Andrei,' *YIVO Encyclopaedia of Jews in Eastern Europe* (Yale University Press, 2010), http://www.yivoencyclopedia.org/article.aspx/Sobol_Andrei.

[46] Zsuzsa Hetényi, *In a maelstrom the history of Russian-Jewish prose (1860–1940)*, (Budapest; New York, 2008), pp. 196–200.

[47] Andrei Sobol', 'Otkritoe pis'mo,' *Pravda*, 23 September 1923.

[48] For discussions of this, see Igal Halfin, *Terror in my soul: Communist autobiographies on trial* (Cambridge, Mass., 2003); *Intimate Enemies: Demonizing the Bolshevik Opposition, 1918–1928* (Pittsburgh, 2007).

light, airy, and clean, and were meant to house around forty people in each cell.[49] The noise in these cells was absolutely deafening, a jumble of voices arguing, chatting, swearing, and singing. Tolstoy described the noise of such cells eloquently:

> While still in the yard Nekhliudov could hear the din of voices and the general commotion going on outside, as in a beehive when the bees are preparing to swarm; but when he came nearer and the door opened, the din grew louder and changed into distinct sounds of shouting, abuse and laughter.[50]

The prison captain noted that new arrivals were utterly stupefied within a day by the perpetual racket, and singing, and dancing, and card playing. There were roll calls in the cells first thing in the morning, at around 7 a.m., and last thing at night, around 9 p.m. After the roll call, and a breakfast of black bread and tea, those prisoners with work duties went out to begin their working day, and the remainder stayed in the cells and occupied themselves with reading, chatting, arguments, washing their clothes, and particularly for the criminal contingent, card playing, often for money. Krivorukov recalled that the criminals in one cell set up a workshop for counterfeiting money. This money was used in cards and games, but also trickled into general circulation through the guards and overseers.[51] One former Aleksandrovsk inmate, Fabrichnyi, recounted the noise that swelled from the general cells in 1906,

> Cells were open then from morning till evening register, and the imprisoned spent all their time in the yard, playing '*lapta*' and '*V gorodku*', and the criminals played 'Orla' at cards, and lotto, and one could time and again here the shouts 'Drum sticks- number eleven', 'Moscow lookout—number twenty-six', 'Bakers' dozen—number thirteen', and so on.[52]

Political memoirs often attributed noise and disorder specifically to the criminal prisoners. Krivorukov described oppressive noise and filth in the cells,

> The endless noise and arguments from card games and the seven storey swearing made for an infernal symphony that made one feel like it was nearly impossible to exist.[53]

Gambling was certainly an important feature of criminal prisoner subculture.[54] The attribution of noise and disorder exclusively to criminal prisoners was disingenuous. V. Ul'ianinskii described long and heated arguments in the cells among political prisoners,

---

[49] F. Savitskii, 'Alexandrovskskaia tsentralnaia katorzhnaia tiur'ma,' *Tiuremnyi vestnik*, no. 10 (1907), pp. 754–6.

[50] Tolstoy, *Resurrection*, p. 419.

[51] E. Krivorukov, 'Bor'ba s "Ivanami" v Aleksandrovskoi katorge (po lichnym vospominaniiam),' *Katorga i ssylka* (1928), p. 93.

[52] P. Fabrichnyi, 'Gramota i kniga na katorge,' *Katorga i ssylka* (1922), p. 194.

[53] Krivorukov, 'Bor'ba s "Ivanami" v Aleksandrovskoi katorge (po lichnym vospominaniiam)', p. 90. Seven-storey swearing refers to elaborate swearing which involved multiple layers of obscene insults, often involving the recipient's mother, in a single sentence.

[54] Gentes, '"Beat the devil!" Prison Society and Anarchy in Tsarist Siberia', pp. 210–17. For insights into later twentieth century criminal subcultures, see also Bronnikov, *Russian criminal tattoo police files*.

Arguments were a big part of our prison life. We had a lot of free time, 16–18 hours per day, and we were young and passionate. Heated arguments developed on many questions, sometimes not just going on for several whole days, but occupying several whole days.[55]

He suggested that these disputes provided intellectual stimulation, education, and focus for prisoners. They also no doubt produced a lot of noise, conflict, and disruption. Some prisoners found the din in the general cells so unbearable that they petitioned the doctor to be transferred to a solitary cell. Around twenty prisoners usually did this. In addition to these sensitive souls, the solitary cells held those prisoners deemed at risk of attack (*samosud*) from their fellow prisoners.[56] Finally, known active homosexuals were housed in isolation cells. There were a number of cases of syphilis contracted from homosexual activity. The prison captain reported primly that

> ... there were quite a few of these passive pederasts in the prison, who started all too clearly and openly to devote themselves to debauchery, and developed a profitable industry.[57]

The common cells had plank beds that pulled down around the walls, and a large table running down the centre of the room. The plank beds became severely overcrowded when the cells were over-filled with prisoners. Dmitrii Strakhov described the tragicomic arrangements in place to allow prisoners to sleep in a cell at more than 200 per cent capacity:

> There were 100 people in the barracks. There wasn't sufficient space for them on the plank beds. A special regime was required, fulfilled by all those with a place on the beds; all had to sleep on their sides. This regulation could not however overcome the laws of physics, and two heads could not occupy one place. That is why there were often cases when, sliding apart in their sleep, we stuck out below, under the planks, with one or two lying on the edges. There were always falls (from the bed) at night, and they were not always peaceful. Often, a wail from the one below rang out with the sound of the fall. The sleeper could not understand why he had just been crushed, and hit out at the nearest guilty party—his neighbour, lying on the edge of the plank. In the twinkling of an eye, the happy sleeper turned out to be under the planks, and those below asserted their right 'by regulation'. A new victim in his turn, however, sometimes looked to establish his right to sleep on this side. The whole barrack entered into movement. Everything was clarified, advised, discussed, and at last got tired of, and all again decorously made themselves comfortable...[58]

This vivid depiction of convicts' sleeping patterns offers us a rare insight into prisoners' intimate space—we get a sense of how they accommodated one another, and literally bumped into each other, in the cramped conditions of incarceration.

---

[55] V. Ul'ianinskii, 'Ucheba na katorge (Aleksandrovskaia tsentralnaia katorzhnaia tiur'ma) 1906–1917gg,' *Katorga i ssylka* (1929), p. 122.

[56] Savitskii, 'Alexandrovskskaia tsentralnaia katorzhnaia tiur'ma', p. 758.

[57] 'Alexandrovskskaia tsentralnaia katorzhnaia tiur'ma', p. 758.

[58] Strakhov, 'V Aleksandrovskoi peresylke', p. 186.

Strakhov's account inadvertently humanizes the prisoners he describes; we are able to imagine them as sleepy, as grumpy, as smelly, and as real.

There were flushing toilets in all the prison buildings. These flushed into a cast iron tank, which was then carried and tipped out into a pit in the courtyard. From there, the waste was carried to the prison farm and used as fertilizer. The 1909 inspection noted rather drily that the prison's sanitary arrangements were satisfactory, considering the primitive plumbing arrangements and overcrowding of the prison.[59] A large tub in the corner of the cell was used as a toilet when the cells were locked, and the foul smell emanating from it dominated the room at night.

The degree of freedom allowed to prisoners during the day varied according to the governor at the time, as we have already discussed. Before 1908, prisoners were largely unshackled, and cells were unlocked in the day, so that the prisoners had collective access to the prison yard, where they could stroll around and interact freely. Up until 1906, a market operated in the prison yard, with a couple of Armenian traders selling a wide range of products. The establishment of a prison shop in 1906 curtailed this free market. Criminal prisoners staffed the prison shop, and its wares were sold to prisoners and staff. Prices were lower than at the local markets, and a wide range of goods were available, although prisoners could only afford basic products including milk, butter, white bread, sausage, sugar, salted fish, cigarettes, pencils, and notebooks.[60]

After 1908, prisoners were allocated a short period of time to walk in the prison yard, and at other times the cells were locked. Petr Mikhailovich Nikiforov arrived in Aleksandrovsk in 1910. He was a sailor and Social Democrat activist and had been sentenced to a life term of katorga after his original death sentence was commuted. He recalled the importance of exercise time:

> The cells opened, and people with a joyful noise, with the rattle of shackles, freely spilled out into the corridor, so that in the course of fifteen minutes they could breathe their fresh air for the whole day. People didn't stroll, but ran, trying to move as much as they could in the short time allotted for walking. But already the shout of the overseer, 'exercise (*progulka*) is over!' and at once all liveliness ended, and lazy and reluctant grey figures trooped around the courtyard to their damp and smelly cells.[61]

Nikiforov's account keenly evoked the prisoners' yearning for fresh air and movement. The most fiercely fought and contentious issue for political prisoners was the privilege of being housed in cells that housed political prisoners exclusively. This concession was won in 1912, when specific cells were allocated exclusively to political prisoners. Political prisoners operated a semi-legal association, *Kollektiv* (The Collective), which sought to protect political prisoners, to improve their material conditions, and to provide a collective voice in negotiations with the

---

[59] Khrulev, *Katorga v Sibiri: Izvlechenie iz otcheta nachal'nika glavnago tiuremnago upravlenie S.S. Khruleva o sluzhebnoi poezdke, v 1909 godu, v Irkutskoi gub. i Zabaikalskuiu obl*, p. 38.

[60] Bykova, 'Istoriia Aleksandrovskago tsentrala', pp. 101–3.

[61] P.M. Nikiforov, *Murav'i revoliutsii* (Moscow, 1958), p. 93. Nikiforov is a rare survivor of this period: he worked with the Bolshevik state, and took on a range of administrative roles. He died in Moscow at the age of ninety-one in 1974.

prison administration. *Kollektiv* was organized at some point between 1906 and 1909 (different memoirists have varying recollections of this). There had been cell-based organizations of political prisoners before then, but these were usually regionally or occupationally based—'the Moscow commune', 'the Polish commune', and so on. *Kollektiv* was formed in response to the growing numbers of political prisoners, and the perception that these new political prisoners needed intellectual and practical support. The numbers changed constantly as members arrived and left Aleksandrovsk, but were around 200 to 300. *Kollektiv* was arranged by cell, with the political prisoners in each cell electing an elder, who was to keep order in the cell, and represent his constituents in *Kollektiv*. The running of *Kollektiv* was dominated by a small group of predominantly Socialist Revolutionary and Menshevik intelligentsia. The leadership often made compromises with the prison administration. For example, in return for promising that no escape attempts would be made, and that prison officials would be treated respectfully, they were allowed to perpetuate the privilege of segregation from criminal prisoners, and self-administration within the cells.[62]

In 1909, on the day of the Main Prison Administration's inspection, 52 per cent of the prisoners did not work at all. This lack of labour in a hard labour prison was characteristic of Russian katorga prisons at this time. This was because there were insufficient workshops and large town settlements near the prisons. Aleksandrovsk, unlike Nerchinsk, was not built around a mining complex, so had relatively few on-site labour opportunities. Some prisoners worked within the prison, in workshops and gardens, and in the prison itself, in the kitchens, filling lamps, and supervising solitary cells and corridors. There were places for around 300 men to work within the prison workshops. Prisoners were paid for this work. The largest workshop was the sewing shop. As well as meeting prison needs, the shops fulfilled orders from outside the prison, including for example the production of signal flags for the Zabaikal railway. Between 1908 and 1911, the number of sewing machines in the prison sewing shop increased from 70 to 170. The joiners' workshop made furniture and building materials both for the prison and for outside orders. An art workshop was set up, which employed exclusively political prisoners. This shop produced a range of works, including oil paintings, Easter eggs, engravings, book binding, and so on. Local shops and private individuals commissioned the works. The prisoners' work was included in an exhibition in Irkutsk on 16 September 1911.[63]

A varying proportion of the prisoners worked outside the prison, either in the free command, which had its own barracks outside the prison, on the prison farm, or further afield in local industries, mines, and especially road and rail construction projects. Those prisoners with long sentences, and also around 500 state criminals, were not sent off prison grounds because of the risk of escape. Use of prisoner labour intensified during the First World War, as prisoners were utilized on road and rail building, and urgent infrastructure projects associated with the war.[64]

---

[62] Bykova, 'Istoriia Aleksandrovskago tsentrala', pp. 133–40.
[63] 'Istoriia Aleksandrovskago tsentrala', pp. 111–15.
[64] *Otchet po glavnomu tiuremnomu upravleniiu za 1915g*, part 6, pp. 50–7.

The lack of work within the prison complex meant that many prisoners were idle for much of their time. This rather confounds our imaginings of hard labour regimes, and left the prisoners seeking out means to fill their time in incarceration.

READING AND EDUCATION IN PRISON

The prison library was an important and valued resource for many prisoners. More than two thirds of Aleksandrovsk's prisoners withdrew books from the library between 1914 and 1916.[65] Discussion of the prison library enables us to humanize the often-anonymous criminal prisoners. Political prisoners took the initiative in forming and building the library, but criminal prisoners made up the majority of its readers.[66] Levels of literacy were high in Aleksandrovsk, and many prisoners received basic education through the prison school. The priest ran the school in principle, but in practice it was staffed exclusively by prisoners. There were two classes every day, each with thirty-five to forty students.[67] We have detailed information available for levels of literacy among political prisoners, and figures that are more impressionistic for criminal prisoners. The majority of political prisoners were literate, though 37.5 per cent had only primary education. Those with higher education were rare after 1900. Of the criminals, 44 per cent were illiterate, and of those that were literate, 32 per cent were self-taught, and 20 percent had only primary education.[68] It is important to question what was meant by 'literate' in this context; to be literate was indicative of an ability to read, but not necessarily an ability to learn through reading.[69]

Twenty-five per cent of criminal prisoners learnt to read while in prison, including the older men who would have been unlikely to develop literacy in their civilian lives.[70] In 1914, of 504 criminal prisoners using the library, 188 of them (37 per cent) learnt to read while in prison.[71] There was not much else to do; prisoners were isolated, lacked fresh impressions and freedom, and were strongly motivated by the desire to read letters from home, and to write letters home. This picture of criminals as motivated learners with reasonable levels of literacy contrasts with Iakubovich's often cynical and judgement-laden descriptions of the learning and reading interests of the criminals with whom he was incarcerated. Iakubovich recorded his attempts to teach a handful of prisoners to read in the 1880s, and describes his few students as reluctant and very poor learners.[72] His descriptions of

---

[65] Fabrichnyi, 'Gramota i kniga na katorge', p. 190 (figure based on average numbers of prisoners and readers between 1914 and 1916).

[66] 'Gramota i kniga na katorge'.

[67] Ul'ianinskii, 'Ucheba na katorge (Aleksandrovskaia tsentralnaia katorzhnaia tiur'ma) 1906–1917gg', p. 120.

[68] Bykova, 'Istoriia Aleksandrovskago tsentrala', pp. 91–2.

[69] Ben Eklof, *Russian peasant schools: Officialdom, village culture, and popular pedagogy, 1861–1914* (Berkeley, 1983), p. 474.

[70] Fabrichnyi, 'Gramota i kniga na katorge', p. 142.

[71] 'Gramota i kniga na katorge', p. 193.

[72] Iakubovich, *In the world of the outcasts: notes of a former penal laborer*, pp. 87–91, 100–9.

the prisoners' responses to literary readings resonate better with the evidence that we have from Aleksandrovsk. Although Iakubovich made pejorative judgements about the prisoners' responses, he acknowledged that they were utterly absorbed by Pushkin, Shakespeare, Lermontov, and most of all Gogol: 'In our prison, Gogol's heroes became common names- the best measure of success.'[73]

The Irkutsk prison library was established in 1906, in response to petitions and requests from the prison's political prisoners. The library served as an organizational and political centre for political prisoners. When the regime toughened, the library operated as a communication hub for prisoners from different cells. Some illegal political works were smuggled into the library, and filed under different names. The prison administration conducted periodic searches for such material. In August 1912, for example, the library catalogue was checked, and fifty-two books were removed, including two volumes of Marx's *Das Kapital*, and one volume of Kautsky on the economic teachings of Marx.[74]

The library's collection was made up almost entirely of donations. The size of the prison library grew relatively rapidly after 1905, due mainly to the donations attracted by and on behalf of political prisoners. In 1906 there were 1,822 books, which were withdrawn 6,983 times. The library started to expand after 1908, when the political prisoners recognized that they could expect to be in prison for many years. They made requests, first to relatives and friends, and later direct to writers and publishers, for book and journal donations. One political prisoner who was a former newspaper worker wrote a short article 'books with pictures' to appeal for the donation of illustrated publications, which resulted in the donation of 'a significant number of illustrated publications'.[75] By 1909 the prison library had 3,553 volumes.[76] By 1917, the prison library held 8,275 books.[77] The prison library established in Shlissel'burg katorga prison near Petrograd had less than half that number.[78]

Prisoners were allowed to withdraw books from the library to read in their cells.[79] Books were issued twice a week, and each reader had their own ticket. Some readers sought answers to specific questions, and others asked for 'something about love' or 'something funny'. Sometimes more specific requests were made: 'Give me Schopenauer, and if you don't have that, give me Conan-Doyle'. The criminal readers sometimes mispronounced the titles of the books that they wanted; 'Give me Brothers Abalmazovich'. Spring and summer tended to see a lull in book

[73] *In the world of the outcasts: notes of a former penal laborer*, p. 141.

[74] Bykova, 'Istoriia Aleksandrovskago tsentrala', p. 148.

[75] Ul'ianinskii, 'Ucheba na katorge (Aleksandrovskaia tsentralnaia katorzhnaia tiur'ma) 1906–1917gg', p. 109.

[76] Khrulev, *Katorga v Sibiri: Izvlechenie iz otcheta nachal'nika glavnago tiuremnago upravlenie S.S. Khruleva o sluzhebnoi poezdke, v 1909 godu, v Irkutskoi gub. i Zabaikalskuiu obl*, p. 17. There is a picture of the library on p. 18.

[77] Fabrichnyi, 'Gramota i kniga na katorge', p. 193.

[78] Gernet, *Istoriia tsarskoi tiur'mi v piatikh tomakh*, volume 5, p. 218.

[79] F. Savitskii, 'Alexandrovskskaia tsentralnaia katorzhnaia tiur'ma,' *Tiuremnyi vestnik*, no. 1 (1908).

withdrawals as 'there was more dreaming than reading' in those seasons.[80] Lev Nikolaevich Tolstoy was predictably the most popular novelist, with three of his works topping the borrowing charts (*Resurrection, War and Peace*, and *Anna Karenina*). Every single criminal reader apparently borrowed Alexandre Dumas' work, and Dostoevsky's *Crime and Punishment* and *Brothers Karamazov* were borrowed frequently. There was a strong interest in books about women including *Zhenskoe nastroenie* (*Women's mood*) and *Dusha zhenshchina* (*The woman's soul*), and an again predictably lively demand for books with a 'hint of pornography'. The outbreak of the First World War saw a big increase in the use of maps, atlases, and geography books.[81]

What do these lists of books tell us about our often-silent criminal prisoners? On one hand, they tell us little. The reading selections are perhaps more literary than one might have expected, but are otherwise unexceptional. What they do allow us, though, is a sense that the criminal prisoners were not only the bestial creatures often described in political memoir. Though they swore, and fought, and played cards, and exhibited an indifference to personal hygiene, knowing that they valued literacy and reading allows us to see them differently.[82] We do not know what their attitudes were towards the war, but we do know from these borrowing patterns that they were not indifferent to it, and that they sought to place themselves spatially, and to map out the lines of the conflict.[83] They chose to read Tolstoy, and Dostoevsky, and Dumas, because they sought escape, solace in words, moments of dreaming and of being elsewhere. Their engagement with literature allowed them to be human, to strive and to dream and to regret.

Criminals' engagement with literature also challenges some preconceptions about how different social groups coped with the experience of confinement. Maria Spiridonova argued that the experience of prison was borne best by 'higher intelligentsia', for whom the time in prison blended night into day as they took the opportunity to study and read. It was harder for the worker, 'the less developed individual' (*malorazvitoi chelovek*) to sit in prison, because such inactivity distorted and disfigured their whole understanding of what life was. She commented that several former soldiers and workers in katorga were sent to work in the gold mines, and wrote happy letters from there, because the work gave them fresh air and made them feel valued.[84] Semion Kanatchikov, a Bolshevik worker who spent time in prison, reinforced Spiridonova's assessment of workers' responses to imprisonment:

> . . . it was the workers, people accustomed to physical labour, who fell victim to mental illness most of all. The experience of complete idleness and their unfamiliarity with intellectual activity had such a murderous effect on the workers' nervous systems . . .

---

[80] Fabrichnyi, 'Gramota i kniga na katorge', p. 195.

[81] 'Gramota i kniga na katorge', pp. 196–203.

[82] On popular reading habits, see Jeffrey Brooks, *When Russia learned to read: Literacy and popular literature, 1861–1917* (Princeton, N.J., 1985), esp. pp. 27–34, pp. 59–80.

[83] For evidence that ordinary rural people engaged with the wider world during the First World War, see Scott J. Seregny, 'Zemstvos, peasants, and citizenship: The Russian adult education movement and World War I,' *Slavic Review*, no. 2 (2000).

[84] M. Spiridonova, 'Iz zhizni na Nerchinskoi katorge', *Katorga i ssylka* 1(14) 1925, pp. 188–9.

Materially, we workers were generally better off in prison than we were in our regular lives, when we worked in factories.[85]

Ultimately, the generalizations posited by Spiridonova and Kanatchikov are unconvincing. There were numerous cases of mental illness among intelligentsia prisoners—some clearly coped with punishment very poorly. Equally, though levels of literacy were much lower among 'simple' people, long periods of imprisonment actually gave prisoners an opportunity to develop their literacy.

While we are forced to resort to inferences and assumptions when we discuss the internal lives of criminals, we have much more information about the inner lives of political prisoners. Some memoirists describe Aleksandrovsk as the 'Romanovskii university', where political prisoners honed their political and practical education. This representation of prison as a revolutionary school had a long and proud history. Vera Figner, for example, gave a detailed description of educational activities in Shlissel'burg in the 1890s.[86] In Aleksandrovsk, education programmes and activities were not static, but shifted according to the proclivities of particular inmates, and the attitudes of the administration. One memoirist, V. Ul'ianinskii, recalled three specific phases. Between 1906 and 1909, he described rather fervid activity. Political prisoners, highly enervated by the political struggle of 1905, focused their efforts on discussions of the revolution, of party politics, tactics, organization, and the agrarian question. 'Comrade T' was a focal point of activity. Comrade T was a 'Marxist SR' student from St Petersburg,

> He was everyone's encyclopaedia, there wasn't a question that he couldn't answer... In the long prison winter of 1906–7, he gave a range of speeches, lectures in which he addressed a range of questions...

The arrival of a number of revolutionary intelligentsia into the prison in the winter of 1907–1908 marked a period of intense revolutionary work. Meetings were organized where representatives from across the revolutionary spectrum laid out their party programmes. 'Comrade T' delivered a series of lectures on the 'theory and history of scientific socialism'. The political prisoners published illustrated journals and leaflets.[87] The hardened prison regime after 1908 severely constrained the association and movement of political prisoners. Education activities continued, but on a smaller scale, often grouped around particular cells. 1912–1917 marked the third phase of activities, when the 'post katorga generation' sought to develop practical skills that would help them live through exile, including building, cattle-keeping, cheesemaking, agrarian skills, work in the prison farm and in the gardens.[88]

[85] S.I. Kanatchikov, *A Radical Worker in Tsarist Russia—The autobiography of Semion Ivanovich Katatchikov*, ed. Reginald E. Zelnik (Stanford, 1986), pp. 126–7.

[86] Vera Figner, *Memoirs of a revolutionist* (DeKalb, 1991), pp. 230–3, pp. 242–8; Lynne A. Hartnett, *The defiant life of Vera Figner: surviving the Russian Revolution* (Bloomington & Indianapolis), p. 270.

[87] Bykova, 'Istoriia Aleksandrovskago tsentrala', pp. 151–2.

[88] Ul'ianinskii, 'Ucheba na katorge (Aleksandrovskaia tsentralnaia katorzhnaia tiur'ma) 1906–1917gg', pp. 111–15. Fabrichnyi also mentions that political prisoners mostly worked in prison workshops in this period. Fabrichnyi, 'Gramota i kniga na katorge', p. 195.

Many of the political prisoners were soldiers and sailors whose imprisonment represented their first significant political experience. Their exposure to revolutionary ideas and training was presented in political prisoners' memoirs as an important formative experience in honing the new generation of revolutionaries. Different political factions formed in the prison, and competed to win influence among the revolution's 'new recruits'. Those without a party political affiliation (*bezpartii*) made up the largest contingent within the political prisoners. A full range of political groupings was represented, from Bundists to Anarchists, Social Democrats to Socialist Revolutionaries. Socialist Revolutionary Party members were numerically predominant throughout the period.[89]

A number of memoirists recall the rather elaborate organization that developed among military political prisoners.[90] One of the leaders of this organization was Arkadii Anotonovich Krasovetskii. Krasovetskii was a junior officer (*podporuchik*) in the Imperial army, and a Socialist Revolutionary since 1905. He participated in underground revolutionary work among the military, and was arrested in December 1907, then sentenced to nine years of katorga in 1909. He was a prisoner at Aleksandrovsk between 1912 and 1916.[91] He described how a mini-general staff course was formed, and a school for Junior Officers (*praporshchiki*), where military tactics, strategy, and practice were studied, in a group of twelve to fifteen students. The group met in cell seven on the lower corridor of the second corpus, and bribed the guards with gifts and cigarette papers to overlook these activities.

The outbreak of the First World War heightened the activities of the group. They obtained daily reports about the war through newspapers received illicitly from Moscow and Petrograd, and they received telegrams by telephone from Irkutsk every day with reports of military action. This information gave them the basis for endless conversations, and heated arguments about strategic questions. They played war games with great intensity, which went on over days and even weeks. The group produced an underground journal about the war, which circulated among political prisoners. After three or four issues of the bulletin, the writers were asked to contribute regular articles to the Irkutsk newspaper *Sibir* on military questions. The group contributed regularly, under the pseudonym G Sh, sometimes 5 or 6 articles per week. These articles were apparently keenly read by military circles in Irkutsk, and fostered great speculation among Irkutsk general staff about the identity of the writer.[92]

---

[89] Bykova, 'Istoriia Aleksandrovskago tsentrala', table 4, p. 221; Party make up of political prisoners in Aleksandrovsk central, 1900–1917.

[90] Fabrichnyi, 'Gramota i kniga na katorge'; Ul'ianinskii, 'Ucheba na katorge (Aleksandrovskaia tsentralnaia katorzhnaia tiur'ma) 1906–1917gg'; Arkadii Antonovich Krakovetskii, 'Voennoe delo na katorge (Iz vospominanii ob Aleksandroskom tsentrale),' *Katorga i ssylka* (1922).

[91] Krakovetskii was subsequently a commissar for the Provisional Government, and fought against the Bolsheviks until 1919 in the civil war. He subsequently worked for the Soviet state, and was shot in 1937 for terrorism, then rehabilitated in 1957. (L.G. Protasov, *Liudi Uchreditel'nogo sobraniia: portret v inter'ere epokhi* (Moskva, 2008), p. 319.)

[92] Krakovetskii, 'Voennoe delo na katorge (Iz vospominanii ob Aleksandroskom tsentrale)', pp. 118–19.

The political prisoners' memoirs are prone to glorifying their own life and times, a kind of 'revolutionary heroes' lives', and this kind of aggrandizement is evident in the accounts of prison education too. Reading between the lines, though, we see that there was significant diversity and divergence within the political prisoners. They did not form a coherent group, but rather, multiple subgroups that formed on the basis of political affiliations, regional or ethnic identities, or occupation. Some political prisoners had low levels of 'consciousness', and may have even, as one historian suggested, been hard to distinguish from common criminals.[93] Others, like Krasovetskii, were professional revolutionaries who devoted their lives to 'the struggle'. Some may well have lived by well-developed and self-abnegating moral codes. Others no doubt transgressed such codes, and sought to ameliorate their own difficult daily lives.

POLITICALS AND CRIMINALS

Between 1907 and 1917, nearly 1,400 political prisoners went through Aleksandrovsk prison.[94] The cliché about prisoner experience is that criminals were without privileges, while political prisoners were accorded many privileges, and were not exposed to the hardships of travel to exile.[95] This cliché has a basis in fact. In the pre-1905 period, when the numbers of political prisoners were relatively small, and disproportionately from the upper classes, they were indeed sheltered from some of the privations of the road, by the privileges accorded to them as nobility, and in some cases by personal wealth or support from friends or party organizations. Petr Iakubovich summarized these advantages succinctly;

> Being a 'political criminal' I entered *katorga* in relative comfort—in the stations I had a room separate from the criminal party, I rode in a cart, etc. In a word, I was a dilettante convict at that time, only just beginning to familiarise myself with my new status . . . '[96]

After 1905, these privileges were eroded, because of the increase in number of political offenders, the change in their social background, and a deliberate hardening of the regime towards political prisoners. The separation of political from criminal prisoners eroded steadily in the last years of the Imperial regime. The sharp binaries between political and criminal prisoners that were described by political memoirists need to be challenged.[97] Such polarization served the political prisoners' agenda of exceptionalizing their members, but did not necessarily reflect the realities of daily life. There were significant grey areas between criminals and

---

[93] Geifman, *Thou Shalt Kill; Revolutionary terrorism in Russia, 1894–1917*, p. 7.

[94] Bykova, 'Istoriia Aleksandrovskago tsentrala', p. 72.

[95] See Adams, who suggests that political prisoners were whingers. Adams, *The Politics of Punishment. Prison Reform in Russia, 1863–1917*, p. 5.

[96] Iakubovich, *In the world of the outcasts: notes of a former penal laborer*, volume 1, p. 5.

[97] This need to reconsider the political–criminal binary in memoir accounts has also been recognized in recent scholarship on the Gulag, see Wilson T. Bell, 'Gulag historiography: An introduction,' *Gulag Studies*, no. 2–3 (2009–10), p. 9.

political prisoners, which were rarely acknowledged by political memoirists, who preferred to emphasize harmony among political prisoners.[98]

Large numbers of people convicted for political offences in the wake of the 1905 revolution had been participants in various mass protests that year, particularly in the countryside and among army and navy personnel. Around 4,000 sailors and 2,000 soldiers were arrested, including around 40 per cent of the Black Sea Fleet. They were to provide a significant component of katorga prisoners after 1905.[99] Many of the 200 new political prisoners that arrived in Aleksandrovsk in the course of 1906 had participated in armed risings against the autocracy. Kronstadt sailors, black sea sailors, and peasants from the western provinces were key groups.[100] One memoirist recalled that the sailors were a vocal and visible presence within the prison, and that they had a significant impact on prison culture. The sailors sang revolutionary songs very loudly at the start and the end of every day. This singing lifted the mood of the other political prisoners, but drove the administration to a fury, as they struggled to prevent these open manifestations of dissent.[101] Other sources attest to the musicality of the sailors. V.N. Gart'veld, who travelled around Siberian prisons in 1908 collecting prisoners' songs, recalled the marching songs of the sailors who had been punished for their part in the Potemkin mutiny. The sailors hummed with closed mouths as they marched, and their shackles rang with cold clanks:

> It was a picture that sent shivers down your spine. This march was not for those with weak nerves, and it made an overwhelming impression on me when I heard it in the gloomy halt at Tobolsk katorga prison. It is hard to believe, but one of the overseers of the march wept. One can call this katorga hymn 'the shackled march' (*podkandal'nyi marsh*).[102]

Many ostensibly 'political' prisoners did not hold strong political convictions, and were regarded with grave suspicion by the more seasoned revolutionaries that filled the elite echelons of the political prisoners' hierarchies. Though the political prisoners vaunted their moral code and their 'consciousness', in fact those convicted because of political activity were heterogeneous in their backgrounds, their value codes, their belief systems, and their responses to persecution by the state. Some of the 'new wave' of post 1905 political prisoners did not fit comfortably within the political moral code. Iosif A. Tsingovatov-Korol'kov, a Socialist Revolutionary who was exiled to Yeniseisk region in 1909, made a clear distinction between 'morally and politically healthy' exiles, and others.

---

[98] For example, M. Spiridonova, 'Iz zhizni na Nerchinskoi katorge,' *Katorga i ssylka*, no. 14 (1925); Kramarov, 'Nerchinskaia katorga. Doklad, prochitanii na zasedanii Istoricheskoi sektsii Doma Pechati v Moskve 8 Oktiabria 1921 goda (1907–1910gg)'.

[99] Gernet, *Istoriia tsarskoi tiur'mi v piatikh tomakh*, volume 5, p. 72, p. 145.

[100] Bykova, 'Istoriia Aleksandrovskago tsentrala', p. 75.

[101] A. Fridman, 'Vospominaniia o minuvshikh dniakh,' *Katorga i ssylka*, no. 2 (1931), p. 150.

[102] Gartevel'd, *Pesnni katorgi*, p. 6.

while (convicted) exile-settlers were generally hardened revolutionaries, administrative exiles were often not at all. 'Anarchist-individualists' as they were fashionably known, were regarded as little more than criminals.[103]

Such distinctions were drawn elsewhere. A.P. Stanchinskii, a political prisoner who spent time in Nerchinsk, commented that the consciousness and 'revolutionary steadfastness' of those prisoners with shorter terms was significantly lower than those with longer sentences, and that they were 'made up predominantly of Latvian farmers'.[104] N.S. Klestov, a Menshevik exiled to Eniseisk district, went further when he said in 1909 that

> Now such a rabble find themselves in prison and exile, that it is impossible to ascribe to them guilt in state crimes... Half of the political exiles are made up of hooligans, bandits and simple criminals.[105]

The crime for which a prisoner was convicted was not a definitive delineator between political and criminal prisoners. The political elites defined themselves partly by their crimes, and partly by their conduct in prison, their political identification, and their broader culture. This, along with the heterogeneity of the prisoners themselves, ensures that these categorizations should not be used uncritically.

Those convicted of criminal offences were also a varied bunch, though all had been found guilty of serious offences, including murder, aggravated robbery, forgery, and a smaller number for sexual crimes.[106] More than 70 per cent of the criminals had hard labour terms of between four and ten years. They came from every corner of the Russian Empire, though 41 per cent came from European Russia, 17 per cent from Ukraine, and 14.6 per cent from Siberia and the Russian Far East.[107] Most of the criminals were of peasant background, and a smaller proportion were unskilled workers, skilled workers, and craftsmen. There was also a contingent of *brodiagi* (nomads) and *vori* (professional thieves).[108] There is evidence of a strong criminal subculture, with distinctive hierarchies and codes. The 'Ivans' were the highest ranking criminals, who effectively ruled and directed criminal prison life.[109] A. Stanchinskii was a Menshevik who was exiled to eastern Siberia. He emphasized that prison subculture was well developed, and that criminals usually submitted willingly to the prison regime and discipline:

> Prison is its own world. It has stood for centuries. Its residents change, they come and go, but little by little a kodex forms for its residents, and severe punishments are

---

[103] Tsingovatov-Korol'kov, 'Organizatsiia vzaipomoshchi Eniseiskoi ssylki (Po lichnym vospominaniiam i po pis'mam)', p. 111.

[104] Stanchinskii, 'V Algachakh', p. 74.

[105] Cited in Vasilii Vasil'evich Kudriashov, 'Men'sheviki v Vostochnosibirskoi ssylke' (Kandidatskii nauka, Irkutsk State University 2004), p. 65.

[106] Bykova, 'Istoriia Aleksandrovskago tsentrala', p. 223, table 5a.

[107] 'Istoriia Aleksandrovskago tsentrala', p. 229, table 8a. Home regions of criminal prisoners in Aleksandrovsk central, 1900–1917.

[108] 'Istoriia Aleksandrovskago tsentrala', p. 234, table 10a.

[109] Gentes, '"Beat the devil!" Prison Society and Anarchy in Tsarist Siberia'.

incurred if the norms are transgressed. . . . the mass of prisoners were lower in their development than the semi-literate prison administration, and with rare exceptions, mainly in the form of sectarians, prisoners had no principled questions connected with prison life, and in general entirely submitted to the ethical norms that were worked out over many years of prison practice and coming from the prisoners' instinct for self preservation; 'try, where possible, to flatter the captain', 'honour the strongest in your midst', 'don't do anything that could worsen the conditions of the imprisoned', and so on . . . [110]

Stanchinskii sought to represent criminal prisoners as a faceless mass, whose moral code was repugnant to the principled and self-denying political prisoners. This demonstrates the ways in which the political prisoners sought to define themselves as a crisp binary to the criminal 'other' in their midst. It does not necessarily tell us much about criminal prisoners' lives and subcultures. There is some limited evidence for relationships developing between political and criminal prisoners. Faddei Vladimirovich Savitskii, the captain of Aleksandrovsk central from 1907 until his death in 1910, suggested that relationships changed between political and criminal prisoners after 1905, and that this undermined the submission that criminal prisoners had generally shown to authority. He argued that political prisoners 'infected' criminal convicts, and that this led to an effective collapse of the regime.

> We can see a big difference in the last two or three years in the prison population. Before then the prison was exclusively criminal, and to be a katorzhan was to be cattle. Katorzhane treated the captains with great respect, and there was firm discipline. Now, thanks to the permanent and close relations between criminals and politicals, who are hoping for a rapid fall of this regime, and their future dominion, and who don't consider themselves criminals, but 'prisoners of war'—the criminal arrestees learn little things from revolutionary teachings. These 'little things' come to one thing in short; 'everything is necessary to crush them.' (*Davit' ikh vsekh nado.*) Prisoners have an increasing sense of citizenship, carrying themselves freely and independently. They don't address prison guards with even the most basic politeness. Katorga as it was no longer exists; now it is just a simple prison. [111]

This excerpt suggests that criminal and political prisoners did not inhabit entirely separate spheres in transit and in prison. Savitskii's suggestion that the criminal prisoners had a developing sense of citizenship and of self brings the criminals closer to the ways in which political prisoners represented themselves. It is certainly the case that the physical separation of political and criminal prisoners was significantly and progressively eroded between 1905 and 1917. While some political prisoners were imprisoned separately from criminals in transit, and others were lodged in criminal barracks, when they were in transit in eastern Siberia political and criminal prisoners marched, ate, and slept side by side.

---

[110] A.P. Stanchinskii, 'Ocherki tiuremnoiu byta; "Politika" i ugolovnyi,' *Katorga i ssylka* (1922).
[111] Savitskii, 'Alexandrovskskaia tsentralnaia katorzhnaia tiur'ma'.

Many political memoirs recount hostility occasionally veering into open conflict between criminal and political prisoners.[112] The distinct culture of criminal prisoners is reminiscent of some Gulag accounts. The criminals were broadly categorized in two groups, the recidivists (*blatnyi*), and the newcomers to prison life, variously referred to as 'friars' or 'the mare' (*shpanku*). The higher-ranking criminals, or Ivans, were drawn from the first group. This relatively small group of criminals governed the other criminals, and tended to dominate unofficial prison culture.[113] The Ivans' hegemony was challenged after 1906 by the arrival of significant numbers of soldiers and sailors, sentenced for their part in mass risings in 1905. A former katorga prisoner, E. Krivorukov, argued that after 1909 the regime mixed political prisoners with criminals deliberately, and used the criminal leaders, or 'Ivans' to intimidate and terrorize the political prisoners.[114] The prisoners were split into cells according to those who were manacled, and those who were not. Hostility between the criminal and political prisoners in Krivorukov's cell culminated in pitched battles, which in both cases the political prisoners, a pretty tough bunch including a member of the notorious Latvian 'forest brotherhood', bested the criminals.[115]

Dmitrii Yakovlev, a political prisoner who travelled across Russia to Siberian exile in 1915, recalled that only fifteen of the 300 prisoners travelling together were political prisoners. They formed a small group, and watched as the Ivans held court, and recounted their lives of violence and crime to their admiring audience. Once Yakovlev reached Aleksandrovsk transfer prison, he was assigned a place in an enormous cell shared with around 200 other prisoners, criminal and political. Yakovlev described a filthy, noisy bedlam, with crowds around the water buckets.[116] An account from the Nerchinsk katorga complex in 1913 recounted that political prisoners were distributed around criminal cells as a form of punishment.[117]

Grigorii Kramarov's memoir provides a startling insight into criminal and political codes and self-administered justice (*samosud*) in the last years of Tsarism. Kramarov was an Internationalist Social Democrat, who was sentenced to four

[112] See for example Aleksandr Nikolaevich Cherkunov, 'Zhizn politicheskoi ssylki i tiur'mi po perekhvachennym pis'mam. Po materialam Irkutskago gubernskago zhendarmskago upravleniia do 1912 g,' *Katorga i ssylka* (1926); on the persecution of a political woman prisoner by criminal women prisoners. He suggests that the women criminals were if anything worse than the men in their persecution of political prisoners.

[113] Stanchinskii, 'Ocherki tiuremnoiu byta; "Politika" i ugolovnyi'; Bykova, 'Istoriia Aleksandrovskago tsentrala', pp. 80–1.

[114] We see the same pattern towards the end of this work on the Gulag: Steven Barnes, *Death and redemption: the Gulag and the shaping of Soviet society* (Princeton, N.J., 2011).

[115] Krivorukov, 'Bor'ba s "Ivanami" v Aleksandrovskoi katorge (po lichnym vospominaniiam)'. The 'Forest Brotherhood' referred to peasant bands that formed in Latvia during 1905. In 1906 there were 5,000 'forest brothers' carrying out partisan-style attacks on military units trying to restore order. See Daina Bieiere, *Istoriia Latvii XX vek* (Riga, 2005), p. 65.

[116] Dm Iakovlev, 'Ot katorgi k ssylke; okonchanie sroka katorgi,' in *Sibirskaia ssylka: Sbornik pervyi*, ed. N. F. Chuzhak (Moscow, 1927).

[117] S. Bagotskii, 'Krakovskii soiuz pomoshchi politicheskim zakliuchennym,' *Katorga i ssylka* (1924), p. 169.

years of katorga in 1907.[118] On his journey from katorga to his place of exile, Kramarov came across a criminal by the name of Prozhivnyi, who had killed a political prisoner in 1907, and had been sentenced by the 'prison court' of political prisoners to a punishment, but had escaped before it could be administered. Kramarov's account suggests that he was prepared to carry out a death sentence against Prozhivnyi on their journey. This provoked an open battle between the criminal and political prisoners. Prozhivnyi subsequently escaped.[119] Kramarov's account recounts clear codes and fierce hostilities between political and criminal prisoners in these last years of Tsarism.

As with anything, we cannot take these generalizations as a blueprint for all relationships between criminals and politicals. Though I have not come across such a positive reference elsewhere, Iadov recounted that the criminal prisoners he travelled with broke the shackles for the political prisoners, out of goodwill.[120] Dmitrii Strakhov's account of Aleksandrovsk transfer prison describes a highly stratified world even within the political wing, and general hostility to the criminal prisoners, but he also recounts one particular criminal, Vetrov, who would come and talk to the political prisoners about what to expect in Siberian exile.

> We didn't know what awaited us (in Siberia). We received most information about the geographical, ethnographic and other (aspects of Siberia) in conversations with a criminal vagrant (*brodiaga*) of unknown origin called Vetrov. He knew everything, had been everywhere, everywhere had been measured with his steps ... In his words, everywhere was fine in Siberia, it was possible to live everywhere, [and] it was possible to leave anywhere. He had lost fingers on the Buriat steppe, and there was no place he either did not know personally or through the tales of his fellow vagrants. These tales were always soothing.[121]

This account presents the criminal as the holder of knowledge, and therefore of power, within the political community. A.P. Stanchinksii, when describing his time in the punishment cells in Algacha, Nerchinsk katorga complex, also recalled the 'wisdom' and knowing of the old criminal prisoner who sat alongside him.

> I didn't always sit alone in the cell. An elder was sent to [sit with me], a criminal sent to the punishment cell for playing cards with too much openness and passion. He was a 'returner', worldly wise, having travelled all around Siberia and Russia, and staying in all her prisons. The old boy recounted how he had received a ten-year sentence of katorga, but when it came to winter he refused to work, because his sentence was ten summers (*let*) not ten years (*god*). He was sent to the punishment cell and weakened, had a week in hospital, then went to work. 'It was hard then, it is easier now.'[122]

---

[118] Grigorii Moiseevich Kramarov was his known name, but his real name was Moisei Itskovich Isakovich. He was born in 1887 in Odessa, and arrested in October 1906 for participation in demonstrations. He fought for the Bolsheviks on the eastern front during the Civil War, and subsequently worked in the Komintern.

[119] G. Kramarov, 'Neudavsheiesia ubiistvo na etape (Popytka ubit ugolovnago prozhivnago v 1910g pri sledovanie avtora iz Gornogo Zerentuia na poselenie),' *Katorga i ssylka* (1930).

[120] Iadov, 'Iz angarskikh perezhivanii'.   [121] Strakhov, 'V Aleksandrovskoi peresylke'.

[122] Stanchinskii, 'V Algachakh', p. 86. The criminal's distinction between 'summers' and 'years' is a nonsense in Russian, as 'summers' are used to signify years in this context.

One criminal at Aleksandrovsk, a certain Gubanov, shared a cell with the Menshevik M. Konstantinov, who edited the prison's illustrated journal between 1911 and 1912, *Tiuremnaia mysl'* (*Prison throughts*). Gubanov became close with the political prisoners in the cell, based on their common interests in the journal. Gubanov wrote stories 'not at all badly', several of which were published in the journal. Konstantinov recalled that many of the readers 'guffawed with laughter at these stories, satirically mocking the wait of the katorga prisoners for the manifesto celebrating 300 years of the Romanov dynasty and their resultant disappointment'.[123] These accounts emphasize that the distinctions between criminal and political prisoners may well have been significantly more elastic than many political memoirists' accounts suggest.[124]

WOMEN IN AND OUT OF PRISON

Women have so far been largely absent from these accounts of life in Aleksandrovsk. Women lived in and around Aleksandrovsk, both as prisoners and as voluntary followers. Women prisoners and women followers will be discussed together here because the ways in which they were described and treated was closely comparable. Though the women prisoners were confined to the prison, and the women followers were not, their lived conditions and societal expectations were closely intertwined. Women followers and their children were lodged in prison-type barracks. They were subject to oversight, and had access to prison-based healthcare. Like the women prisoners, they were subject to both pity and censure, and were briskly judged by commentators for their moral failings.

Women made up a tiny minority of prisoners in Siberia's prisons. Of the 190,000 people in prison on 1 January 1913, not even 1 per cent (12,408) were women.[125] Women were responsible for just over 6 per cent of crimes committed in Russia between 1911 and 1913, and made up around 4.5 per cent of katorga prisoners in those years.[126] Women were much more heavily represented in the ranks of political prisoners, at around 10 per cent of politicals.[127] As with the men, there are no first-hand ego-documents from female criminal prisoners, but a number of such accounts from female political prisoners. Significant numbers of women followed their husbands into exile, though these numbers reduced after 1908, when the state decreed that it would not transport followers to Siberia at state expense. On 30 October 1907 there were eighty katorga wives in Aleksandrovsk's

[123] Bykova, 'Istoriia Aleksandrovskago tsentrala', p. 152.
[124] On the importance, and difficulties of 'knowing' the world of prisons and exile, see Sarah J. Young, 'Knowing Russia's Convicts: The Other in narratives of imprisonment and exile of the late Imperial era,' *Europe-Asia Studies*, no. 9 (2013).
[125] *Otchet po glavnomu tiuremnomu upravleniiu za 1913g*, p. 23.
[126] Sharon A. Kowalsky, *Deviant women: female crime and criminology in revolutionary Russia, 1880–1930* (DeKalb, Ill., 2009), p. 88; *Otchet po glavnomu tiuremnomu upravleniiu za 1912g* (Petrograd, 1913).
[127] Nikitina, 'Ssylka 1905–1010 godov', p. 16, suggests that of around 12,830 political exiles in 1910, around 1,300 were women.

family barrack, accompanied by 169 children, including seventy-seven boys and ninety-two girls.[128] In September 1909, thirty women lived there, with sixty-one children. A further sixty-one families lived in accommodation in the village. The prison inspector reported in 1914 that the number of families had reduced every year after the curtailing of state support in 1908. By 1914, only fifteen families lived in Aleksandrovsk. Of these, four lived in a special barracks for voluntary followers, where they had free lodgings.[129]

The distinctions between portrayals of criminal and political prisoners that we have already discussed were even more sharply drawn when looking at representations of women prisoners. Contemporaries often depicted women political prisoners in soft pastel tones, as martyrs to revolutionary Russia. More than that, they were portrayed as chaste, humble, self-effacing, simply dressed, and selfless. Gleb Uspenskii, a Populist writer, idealized Vera Figner, a woman who served a lengthy sentence for her revolutionary terrorist activities. The revolutionary women epitomized the notion of the ideal woman as a sexless creature, 'a new type of female body, shaped along the lines of an ascetic, martyred and inescapably Christ-like figure'.[130] The clothing and general appearance of the women politicals drew consciously on the ascetic ideals established by their Nihilistic predecessors in the 1860s, who eschewed the expectations of high society, and donned deliberately plain and unadorned clothing.[131] Vera Zasulich, a Nihilist made famous by her attempted assassination of General Trepov in 1878, wore clothes that were not just simple, but were a self-conscious statement of abnegation:

> Vera wore a shapeless grey outfit that might be described as a good sized piece of linen in the centre of which had been cut a hole for her head and on the sides two holes for her arms. This piece of linen was held in with a narrow belt, but its edges hung down on all sides, fluttering in the wind. On her head was something—not a hat, but more like a *pirog* (pie)—made out of cheap grey material. On her feet were flat, clumsy-looking boots that she later explained to me had been made for her according to her own design. Her linen body covering, of course, had no pockets, so in place of a handkerchief she simply picked up the edge of one of the hanging corners of the material.[132]

While not all political women went to these extremes of simple dress, all aspired to a simple and ascetic life. The roll call of the women's prison in the Nerchinsk katorga complex, Maltsev, offered a who's who of women in the revolutionary movement.

[128] Khrulev, *Katorga v Sibiri: Izvlechenie iz otcheta nachal'nika glavnago tiuremnago upravlenie S.S. Khruleva o sluzhebnoi poezdke, v 1909 godu, v Irkutskoi gub. i Zabaikalskuiu obl.*

[129] *Polozhenie tiuremnoi chasti i ssylki v Irkutskoi gubernii po dannym dokladov tiuremnago inspektora, 1911–1913gg*, p. 21.

[130] Henrietta Mondry, 'With short cropped hair: Gleb Uspensky's struggle against biological gender determinism,' *Russian Review*, no. 3 (2004), p. 483.

[131] For a lovely discussion of this phenomenon, see Victoria Thorstensson, 'The Dialog with Nihilism in Russian Polemical Novels of the 1860s–1870s' (PhD dissertation, University of Wisconsin-Madison, 2013), chapter 2.

[132] P.M. Plekhanova, 'Stranitsa iz vospominanii o V.I. Zasulich,' in *Gruppa 'Osvobozhdenie truda': Iz arkhivov G.V. Plekhanova, V.I. Zasulich i L.G. Deich*, ed. L. G. Deich (Moscow-Leningrad, 1926), p. 85.

Female revolutionary luminaries including Mariia Spiridonova, Irina Kakhovskaia, Anastasia Bitsenko, Mariya Shkol'nik, Aleksandra Izmailovich, and Vera Kaplan were housed here between 1906 and 1917. There are a number of accounts describing the women's life there. All emphasized the women's communal lifestyle, their devotion to self-improvement through education, their modesty and self-control, and their refusal to compromise with the authorities.[133] One historian described the treatment of women terrorists as representing 'a romantic cult'.[134] There is no question that these women's memoirs, and the recollections of them by male political prisoners, drew self-consciously on Chernyshevsky's Vera Pavlovna, and on the precedents set by the likes of Vera Figner and Ekaterina Breshkovskaia in their own milieu.[135] This representation placed them in sharp contrast with the depictions of criminal women. Shameless sensuality, foul language, indifference to dirt, and poor morals were all repeated features of criminal women, but the overwhelming reference point was their uncontrolled sexuality, as this account of political prisoners' lives exemplifies:

> The criminal woman (*professionalka*) is the personification of total licentiousness and vice in ninety-nine out of one hundred cases. The total internal world of these women takes the form of dreams only about carnal desires, and in so far as male criminals have other interests in prison (cards, endless plans about future robberies and murders and so on) in so far as the woman recollects sensory delights and follows a path of satisfying their carnal instincts.[136]

Voluntary followers and women prisoners were systematically sexually exploited, and engaged in paid sex work in order to ameliorate their situations.[137] Commentators dwelled on this in lurid detail and in so doing, exposed their own proclivities in representing women as either victims or whores. Lower class women were routinely represented as licentious, and possessed of a wild sexuality that needed to be kept in tight check. Olga Semyonova Tian-Shanskaia described village

---

[133] See Anastasia Bitsenko, 'V Mal'tsevskoi zhenskoi Katorzhnoi tiur'me 1907–1910 k kharakteristiki nastroenii,' *Katorga i ssylka*, no. 7 (1923); *Na zhenskoi katorge: Sbornik statei*, ed. Vera Figner (Moskva, 1930); Spiridonova, 'Iz zhizni na Nerchinskoi katorge'; 'Iz zhizni na Nerchinskoi katorge,' *Katorga i ssylka*, no. 15 (1925); 'Iz zhizni na Nerchinskoi katorge,' *Katorga i ssylka*, no. 16 (1925); E. Kakhovskaia, 'Iz vospominanii o zhenskoi tiur'me,' *Katorga i ssylka*, no. 9 (1926). For a critical analysis of Spiridonova's self-representations, see Sally Boniece, 'The Spiridonova case, 1906: Terror, myth and martyrdom,' *Kritika*, no. 3 (2003), and for an excellent treatment of female terrorists, see 'The Shesterka of 1905–06: Terrorist Heroines of Revolutionary Russia,' *Jahrbucher fur Geschichte Osteuropas*, no. 2 (2010).

[134] Amy Knight, 'Female terrorists in the Russian Socialist Revolutionary Party,' *Russian Review*, no. 2 (1979), p. 140, fn. 3.

[135] Figner, *Memoirs of a revolutionist*; Breshko-Breshkovskaia, *Hidden Springs of the Russian Revolution*; Nikolay Gavrilovich Chernyshevsky and Michael R. Katz, *What is to be done?* (Ithaca, 1989). Vera Pavlovna was the heroine of Chernyshevsky's enormously influential novel. In interview, the Menshevik Lydia Dan recalled that Vera Figner was one of the most influential figures in her youth. (Haimson, *The making of three Russian revolutionaries*, p. 56.)

[136] Cherkunov, 'Zhizn politicheskoi ssylki i tiur'mi po perekhvachennym pis'mam', pp. 183–4.

[137] Andrew Gentes discusses the abuse of women in an earlier period. Andrew A. Gentes, '"Licentious girls" and frontier domesticators: women and Siberian exile from the late 16th to the early 19th centuries,' *Sibirica: Journal of Siberian Studies*, no. 1 (2003), p. 20.

women's sexual mores in her late 1890s ethnographic study, presenting all women as willing to sell their sexual services for small gifts, and morally without a compass.[138] The Imperial system of regulated prostitution sought to control urban lower class women's sexuality. Lower-class urban women whose behaviour attracted attention from local residents as unduly promiscuous were reported to the municipal authorities with proposals that they be forcibly registered as prostitutes.[139] Out of control female sexuality absolutely dominated the ways in which female criminals were represented. This was the case for lower class and criminal women not just in Russia, but in other cultural contexts too.[140]

A letter sent from Irkutsk prison in 1912 epitomizes the ways in which criminal and political women inhabited different ends of the female spectrum from whore to Madonna. The writer, MF, a political prisoner, was imprisoned in Aleksandrovsk along with her two-year-old daughter, and recounted two events, both of which emphasized the wild licentiousness and immorality of women criminals. MF secured a place in the prison hospital as an assistant. Two male prisoners were sent, with an overseer, to repair the hospital boiler. When the hospital overseer went to lunch, the male prisoners 'began to "repair" (have sex with) the infected women on the venereal ward, [despite] understanding what ailed these women. The overseer stood on guard while the men "treated" these prisoners, then himself went "to heal" [the infected women] while the prisoners stood on guard.' MF upbraided the women for infecting the men, with the result that one of the criminal women beat MF until she lost consciousness, and only stopped hitting her because 'it will be a long term, if we kill her'. MF also recounted an incident where the criminal women sneaked a couple of male prisoners into their cell, and openly fornicated. She recounted that the women bribed the overseers to 'encounter' male prisoners in the toilet, in the bathhouse, and even in the yard.[141]

The sexual adventures of the criminal women were anathema to these political women, who sought to represent themselves as chaste and honourable in every sense of the word. The criminal women are characterized as shamelessly base and venal. This portrayal features in many accounts of criminal women, and serves to

[138] Olga Semyonova Tian-Shanskaia and David L. Ransel, *Village life in late tsarist Russia* (Bloomington, 1993), pp. 53–61.
[139] Barbara A. Engel, *Between the fields and the city: Women, work and family in Russia 1861–1914* (Cambridge, 1994), pp. 166–73.
[140] There is a substantial literature discussing the ways in which female sexuality and criminality were linked. In the Russian context, see for example Barbara Alpern Engel, 'Peasant Morality and Pre-Marital Relations in Late 19th Century Russia,' *Journal of Social History*, no. 4 (1990); Barbara A. Engel, 'St. Petersburg prostitutes in the late nineteenth century—A personal and social profile,' *Russian Review*, no. 1 (1989); Kowalsky, *Deviant women: female crime and criminology in revolutionary Russia, 1880–1930*. In the British context, see Annie Cossins, *Female criminality: infanticide, moral panics and the female body* (Basingstoke, 2015), for a study of how sexed bodies underpin the ways in which criminality was framed and understood. Also Ann-Louise Shapiro, *Breaking the codes: female criminality in fin-de-siecle Paris* (Stanford, Calif., 1996) for the construction of female criminality in turn-of-the-century Paris. For connections between 'female' crimes and sexuality in German context, see Dorothy C. Price, *Representing Berlin: sexuality and the city in Imperial and Weimar Germany* (Aldershot, Hants, England; Burlington, VT, 2003), pp. 82–7.
[141] Aleksandr Nikolaevich Cherkunov, 'Zhizn politicheskoi ssylki I tiur'mi po perekhvachennym pis'mam', pp. 183–4.

debase and dehumanize them. Even Lev Tolstoy, who reliably provides a humane other voice, ultimately presented the female criminal world as vile and corrupting. This is epitomized by the transformation wrought in Katya Maslova, his main female protagonist in *Resurrection*, when she is transferred from the company of the criminal women to the political prisoners. The political women, clean, modest, humble, and highly moral, enabled Maslova to leave the depravities of her former life as a prostitute behind her, and to find the best in herself.[142] Contemporary observers were more repelled by what was perceived as untrammelled female sexuality than by any other feature of prison life. It is very difficult to find accounts of female criminals that go beyond these stereotypical and insensitive boundaries.

The state made some provisions for the women and children that followed their men into Siberian exile. A 'family barrack' of two wooden buildings was built in Aleksandrovsk for the most needy families that had followed men to Aleksandrovsk. It had places for forty people, and there were provisions for a children's hospital and a nursery. The conditions of this family barrack were grim according to both prison inspectors and outside observers. One large building was divided into eight separate rooms, with a Russian stove in each for cooking. There were separate quarters for an overseer and for the sick. Light, fuel, and water all came from the prison. The material condition of followers' families was extremely bad in Aleksandrovsk, mainly because of a lack of work. Those women with children and living in the state building received means of 1 rouble 50 kopeks per month. While Aleksandrovsk's governor Faddei Savitskii recognized the practical difficulties faced by these women, he did not spare his moral condemnation of the women themselves, whom he regarded as lazy and unhygienic.

> ... Cells are always overcrowded. There are many children in the barracks. Keeping the cells clean is virtually impossible, because the common man is the enemy of cleanliness; to defend cleanliness in the prison, for example, he has to be kept under the lash. It is rubbish infested and dirty in the family barracks. The air is heavy and stifling. It is hard to breathe for an unaccustomed person, because children's shit festers in all the secluded nooks and crannies. With regards to the maintenance of cleanliness, the overseers have constant disorder and argument with the women. If a woman is sick or in the last stages of pregnancy, and cannot wash the floor, then, to be sure, her friend will not set to with the necessary labour for her. The walls in the barrack are not plastered, and in their chinks there is a mass of parasites. The population of Aleksandrovsk village is small and poor. Work and employment can only be found there in the summer. In the winter it is impossible to find anywhere even for a crust of bread. The katorga wives, not having permanent work, live in terrible need. The situation for many of them, in particular those burdened with little children, is desperate. Singly, these women sometimes leave for work in Irkutsk town or in Usol'sk village, in the match factory, or they earn a living by depravity.[143]

---

[142] Tolstoy, *Resurrection*, pp. 399–401.
[143] F. Savitskii, *Otdel neoffitsialnyi. Aleksandrovskaia tsentral'naia katorzhnaia tiur'ma (ocherki)*, (1906), p. 86.

Savitskii's emphasis on dirt, disorder, and a lack of moral fibre is characteristic of the ways in which criminal women were represented. Alongside these pejorative judgements, though, Savitskii introduces a note of sympathy and pity—the women's struggles to find work and their entry into prostitution are tackled with a rare note of empathy. The captain of the Main Prison Administration, Stepan Stepanovich Khrulev, questioned the women's capacity to care for their children in his evaluation of followers:

> Katorga wives, with a handful of exceptions, are idle and are not working. Several of them in the barracks leave their little children to the mercy of fate, with whole days sitting outside the prison windows, contemplating the devil's face of their husband through the iron bars.[144]

In Nerchinsk *katorga* prison, families accompanying prisoners that did not have private means were housed in buildings alongside the prison's outside barracks. In 1907 the Main Prison Administration's report noted that the families, who were overwhelmingly women and children, were extremely impoverished, and the majority of women 'under the influence of their needs, engaged in prostitution'.[145] Another official report in 1908 again stated that prisoners' families in both Nerchinsk and Aleksandrovsk lived in great need, because of the lack of paid employment for them in the region.[146]

The followers who became ill were treated at state expense, on the same basis as prisoners. Funds were raised for the establishment of a maternity unit (*rodil'nyi priiut*), built in the prison grounds, together with the prison chemists and out-patients' department. Between 1905 and 1913, there were forty-eight children born in Aleksandrovsk, and only two maternal deaths.[147] The hospital, maternity room, and children's orphanage were still operating by 1914. These provisions were paid for by an annual subsidy taken from the general capital for exiles. The women followers faced many of the same conditions as women prisoners, and were represented in similarly narrow ways. Their personal hygiene, sexual licentiousness, and capacity to care for their children were all frowned on by official observers, but these pejorative attitudes were leavened with a sympathy for their fate which was generally entirely missing from accounts of criminal women.

CHILDREN

Children appear on the peripheries of the stories about travel to exile. They are born in prison hospitals, carried by parents and kindly strangers, neglected by feckless

---

[144] Khrulev, *Katorga v Sibiri: Izvlechenie iz otcheta nachal'nika glavnago tiuremnago upravlenie S.S. Khruleva o sluzhebnoi poezdke, v 1909 godu, v Irkutskoi gub. i Zabaikalskuiu obl.*

[145] *Tiuremnyi Vestnik* no. 8–9, 1909, p. 859, 'Excerpt from the report of the Captain of the Main Prison Administration for 1907'.

[146] *Otchet po glavnomu tiuremnomu upravleniiu za 1908g*, p. 31.

[147] *Polozhenie tiuremnoi chasti i ssylki v Irkutskoi gubernii po dannym dokladov tiuremnago inspektora, 1911–1913gg*, p. 21.

mothers, abused and sometimes corrupted by the horror all around them. The sons and daughters of prisoners lived in the shadows of the prison, whether within or without the walls. They served as moments of purity and hope in an environment of vileness, though their lives were usually permeated by the dissipation, dislocation, and despair all around them.[148] There is fractured evidence of the human anxieties and concerns of prisoners about the fate of their children. The list of complaints and requests of prisoners to the elder advisor (*starshii sovetnik*) in Yakutsk included a number of enquiries about prisoners' children. The prisoner Sdyshev asked if there was any possibility that his children could be sent to Irkutsk, and that he could be sent to Aleksandrovsk prison near Irkutsk, or alternatively that his children be sent to Samodurovka village, Manzurskyi volost, to live with their relatives. The elder was clearly sensitive to this request, and his handwritten notes alongside this query asked 'what is Sdyshev imprisoned for? How was he convicted? How many children does he have? Where are they located? How old are they?'[149]

Zhavetian Faizulin wrote from his Yakutsk prison cell to the governor in 1909, asking that he be released for a few days in order to help his family prepare their land for sowing as 'the family has no-one to work the land and no means to pay for help. I humbly request that you free me for a short time for the sowing of the fields, in order that my family has a crust of bread for this year'. His request was turned down.[150]

The state sought to ameliorate the pains of prisoners' children, and provided guidelines on feeding prisoners' children and the establishment of orphanages for prisoners' children.[151] Near Aleksandrovsk prison, just over a mile from the house for prisoners' families, a school was established, which had ninety boys and thirty-three girls attending in 1909. The two teachers received means from the Ministry of Popular Enlightenment. The teacher reported that in the winter many children could not attend because they did not have warm clothes and shoes. The extremely undesirable conditions of these families led the committee of the katorga prison to take some measures to improve matters.

The establishment of schools by exiles was forbidden by a decree of 1906. Despite this, formal and informal schools were established, even in the most unlikely places. Aleksei Kirillov Kuznetsov, an exile settler who had been convicted for state crimes, was fined two roubles in December 1909 for opening a school in the Khatyn-Iadrinsk almshouse, in Yakutsk region.[152] In Nerchinsk, a free school for children was established by some of the political prisoners. Vladimir

---

[148] For an attempt at a demographic study of exile children in nineteenth-century Siberia, see Gentes, 'Towards a demography of children in the Tsarist Siberian Exile System'.

[149] NARS f. 12, op. 2, d. 5135, p. 58, p. 61, excerpts from the report of Yakutsk regional administration's elder advisor, 10 May 1910.

[150] NARS f. 12, op. 2, d. 5135, p. 48, letter to Yakutsk Governor from prisoner Zhavetian Faizulin, 23 April 1909.

[151] GAIO, f. 25, op. 6, d. 3104, pp. 10–12, letter from Irkutsk Prison inspector to Chancery of Irkutsk Military Governor, 9 January 1908; *Tiuremnyi vestnik* 1906, issue 2, p. 121, circular regarding the feeding of prisoners' children.

[152] NARS f. 12, op. 2, d. 4693, p. 182, Decree from the first Yakutsk region police inspector (*ispravnik*), 11 December 1909.

Abramovich Pleskov, a Menshevik and one of the teachers at this school, recalled that the school provided him with some of his happiest recollections of katorga. The school served the orphanage that had been established for katorga prisoners' children, but also came to attract children from around the region,

> Two hundred children of different ages went through our hands, and subsequently spread through different towns of Siberia; there were prison children, local and regional cossacks, peasants and merchants. They came to us from the darkest corners of the region, from 130 to 230 miles away, and from the villages around Zerentui.

The school was housed in a single room, with three teachers taking simultaneous classes, and a terrific racket all around. One of the teachers was the former Social Democrat deputy of the State Duma, Vasilii Matvei Serov.[153] The classroom was well equipped with books and illustrated journals, sent by sympathizers in the capitals. Pleskov recalls the strangeness that political prisoners were given complete freedom and authority to teach as they chose.

> ... there were even no inspections and in general no oversight. We were free to sow in the children's souls—sometimes tormented and deformed by the conditions of the prison life that surrounded them—the seeds of love, poetry and truth ... these were the best years of katorga; we had time to feel ourselves human, because we did living, human business.[154]

Pleskov's reflections encapsulate the complexity of emotions evinced by punished children—they were simultaneously the personification of carceral life's corrupting forces, and harbingers of life and hope.

THE FINAL STAGES

The final stages of the exiles' journey, from Aleksandrovsk on to their named places of exile, in the more distant parts of Irkutsk province, and some to Yakutsk region, were often the longest journeys of all. The means of exile transfer to Yakutsk region changed from the late nineteenth to the early twentieth century. From the end of the 1890s up until 1905, exiles were moved predominantly by barge up the Lena, and with the use of the winter pathways. From 1906 until 1917, winter routes were used less, with the summer route and river barges used instead. This was because it cost the authorities three times as much to transport prisoners using the winter

---

[153] Vasilii Matvei Serov (1878–1918) was an old Bolshevik, and member of the second State Duma. He was one of the group of five deputies that were arrested, and sentenced to five years of katorga followed by exile in eastern Siberia, for their alleged activities in fomenting revolution. He stayed in eastern Siberia after the February revolution, and fought for the Bolsheviks in the Civil War. He was killed in Chita by White forces in 1918.

[154] V. Pleskov, 'Na Nerchinskoi katorge (iz lichnykh vospominanii),' *Katorga i ssylka* (1921). Vladimir Abramovich Pleskov (1882–1938) was a Jewish Social Democrat who was born in the Don region. He was a victim of Stalin's terror, arrested and executed in 1938. (Petr A. Zaionchkovskii (ed.) *Istoriia dorevoliutsionnoi Rossii v dnevnikhakh i vospominaniiakh; Tom 5, ch. 2; Dopolneniia k t.1–5 (ch. 1), XV v.—1917g.* [Moscow, 1989], p. 153.)

routes.[155] Prisoner groups were moved along the rivers on passenger steamships, in the third-class section, and in exceptional cases on separate barges. This means of transport, alongside other passengers and without special security measures, was regarded by the Main Prison Authority as extremely difficult and inconvenient, and was only used to avoid difficult transfers on foot.

Many memoirists described their journey up the Lena in soft focus, as a period of relative peace and tranquility.[156] Memoirists of the period tend to dwell on the pleasant aspects of barge journeys—the rest, the views, fresh air. This is in marked contrast to Breshkovskaia's account of filth, squalor, and food shortages in 1878.[157] This change in depictions may have represented an improvement in conditions in the thirty years between these accounts, or it may have been more about the expectations of the prisoners themselves, who may not have seen poor conditions of this kind as worthy of comment. Lydia Dan, describing her journey from Aleksandrovsk to Olekminsk in July 1904, presents this position well:

> We travelled on a barge, a large flat-bottomed boat that floated downstream ... there were both criminals and politicals on board, and in general the conditions were not too bad. Perhaps they were bad, but since we all understood that we were going to be relatively at liberty, we were fairly patient and put up with the minor inconveniences ... If I were to tell all the details, people now would say that we had a bad time, but I don't remember it as hard and no one else did. It was pleasant, because we were headed for freedom. We were all young and we figured that a new life was beginning for us now.[158]

The state's attempts to reduce foot stages had very limited impact on the journeys of those exiled to Yakutsk and the northern parts of Irkutsk. From Aleksandrovsk transfer prison, journeys onwards into exile were usually a combination of foot stages, barges, and occasionally railways. The northernmost districts of Irkutsk province were used extensively for the settlement of political exiles in the post-1905 period, and these were the most remote parts of the province. Kirensk district, for example, bordered Yakutsk province, and was nearly 800 miles from the transfer prison. The lengthiest and most harrowing journeys were reserved for those who had Yakutsk region named as their place of settlement, more than 1,800 miles from Irkutsk. This route was broken into four sections, or tracts: 180 miles from Irkutsk to Verkholensk, 479 miles from Verkholensk to Kirensk, 738 miles from Kirensk to Olekminsk, and 435 miles from Olekminsk to Yakutsk.[159]

Security in transit tended to weaken the further one travelled from European Russia, and from the major prisons, regardless of the prisoner's status. While European Russia could boast a relatively well-developed network of gendarmes, and the major prisons and tracts employed military convoys, these melted away for prisoners directed to more remote locations. A letter from the Irkutsk governor

[155] Kazarian, *Iakutiia v sisteme politicheskoi ssylki Rossii 1826–1917 gg*, p. 249.
[156] See for example Dobrokhotin-Baikov, 'V Yakutskoi ssylke (zapiski rabochego)', pp. 181–4.
[157] Breshko-Breshkovskaia, *Hidden Springs of the Russian Revolution*, pp. 181–7.
[158] Haimson, *The making of three Russian revolutionaries*, pp. 165, 166.
[159] Kazarian, *Iakutiia v sisteme politicheskoi ssylki Rossii 1826–1917 gg*, p. 233.

general to the governor of Yakutsk in August 1902 clarified the problems inherent in transfer of exiles from Irkutsk to Yakutsk. He concluded that it would be desirable to reduce the numbers of exiles to northern parts of Irkutsk and Yakutsk, or even better to stop it all together, but certainly to organize proper military commands for the transfer of prisoners. In 1902, exiles were moved either by barge, with a military convoy, or on foot with a convoy drawn from the local population. This second method was considered unsatisfactory, mainly because of the ease of escape. There were no transfer prisons between Irkutsk and Yakutsk. The use of local peasants as convoy officers was of particular concern:

> Unarmed peasants, poorly understanding their duties and all the time shying away from work, themselves frightened of the convoy, and regarding their duties of observation altogether jauntily, worrying only about the quickest possible handover of the prisoners, even if there are only half as many of them as there were at the start. A significant part of the Lena local population have themselves been tried or been in exile... in such conditions, naturally, those prisoners who don't escape are only those who don't want to escape.[160]

Despite the urgency and directness of this letter, conditions did not change much, mainly because of limited resources. In 1910, a letter to Yakutsk's governor from the regional court specifically requested that a special military convoy be found to escort a party of prisoners;

> In view of the serious crimes of the prisoners—Egor and Anna Meluk, for premeditated murder, Varmalov for embezzlement, forgery and deliberate harm, and Sered, guilty of robbery and murder, I consider, for my part, that it is too risky to send these prisoners with a convoy of local Cossacks, from whom prisoners may easily escape thanks to the Cossacks' inadequate oversight of the journey, and this is particularly the case for Sered, sentenced for vagabondage and then guilty of being a runaway-katorga... [161]

This note indicates that supervision over exiles on their journey to places of settlement continued to be inadequate in our period, despite official concerns about escape. The irregular routes taken by exiles to more remote locations, alongside low or non-existent levels of supervision, meant that escapes were possible, though they happened relatively infrequently. The number of escapes increased in the 1904–1908 period. The Main Prison Administration explained this by the influx of 'more dangerous' (i.e. political) prisoners. The number of escapes was greatest from the foot stages, and from the stage buildings. Only ninety-five prisoners escaped in 1908, and seventy-six in 1909, and the vast majority of them were recaptured. Escapes in transit continued to reduce in number through 1909. The number of escapes was small, and occurred predominantly from foot stages. Of the 1,571,497 transfers of prisoners undertaken by the Main Prison Administration in 1909, twenty-three prisoners escaped from foot stages in twenty-two incidents in 1909, while thirty-eight prisoners escaped in

---

[160] NARS, f. 12, op. 2, d. 1260, pp. 120–4, letter from the Chancery of Irkutsk Governor General to the Governor of Yakutsk, 1 August 1902.
[161] NARS, F. 12, op. 2, d. 4693, p. 240, letter from Yakutsk Governor to regional court, 1910.

twenty-three incidents from stage buildings.[162] The Main Prison Administration provided a frank assessment explaining escape rates. The convoys were insufficient to provide adequate security, and the stage buildings were unfit for purpose, being ramshackle, wooden, and unlit. There were no toilets of even the most rudimentary kind, so prisoners had to go outside to relieve themselves. Most escapes took place when crossing wooded areas, or in the evenings in empty places near provincial towns. The situation was worsened by the fact that the convoy was often of a 'rather low moral level', and often spent days in ceaseless conversation with prisoners, sympathizing with them and as a result weakening their supervision over prisoners.[163] These points resonated with the concerns raised by Irkutsk's governor general in 1902. A number of our memoirists point out that after a term in prison, prisoners were actually looking forward to exile (something that they almost all quickly came to rue) as a place of 'freedom'. While escape from the convoy was possible, hard cash, planning, and good connections were necessary to successfully survive in the often-remote locations of transfer, and to actually return to European Russia, or even flee to Europe.

Memoirists describe their long slow journey up the Lena, with convicts being dropped off along the way in dribs and drabs at small settlements that were to be their place of residence. Vladimir Zenzinov recalls that 'For three weeks we drifted smoothly down the Lena, a distance of about 2000 miles.'[164] A. Dobrokhotin-Baikov described his journey from Aleksandrovsk central to his place of exile in Yakutsk. They completed about a third of the foot stage walking, and the other two thirds they were transported in 'poor Buriat two-wheeled carts'. At Kachuga, they were transferred onto the river Lena, and were able to rest on the barges, lying or sitting on the roof of the little wooden barge, warmed by the autumnal but still hot sun and admiring the beautiful Lena views. Exiles disembarked in small groups along the way. When the barge reached Ust-Kute the prisoners were transferred to an enormous barge, and then to a steamer that travelled to their final destination. By this time it was September, and the frosts started. Sometimes snow fell. The Lena was beginning to freeze. They began to feel colder and colder as they approached Yakutsk. They had summer clothes on, and suffered severely from the cold. When the exile party finally arrived, the steamer pulled up at its autumn stop, over four miles from town. Dobrokhotin-Baikov recalled his trepidation as he disembarked: 'As I walked to the town in the freezing snow, I thought, "I am sure that ruin awaits me in this emptiness".'[165]

Prison administration regulations stated that special stage buildings were to be built every fifteen to twenty miles for overnight stops. The stage buildings were usually wooden huts, and were maintained either by the local community or by the state, dependent on whether the tract was internal, or for exile. The stage buildings, even according to reports of the Main Prison Administration, were not fit for

[162] *Otchet po glavnomu tiuremnomu upravleniiu za 1909g*, p. 131.
[163] *Otchet po glavnomu tiuremnomu upravleniiu za 1908g*, p. 134.
[164] Zenzinov, *The road to oblivion*, p. 6.
[165] Dobrokhotin-Baikov, 'V Yakutskoi ssylke (zapiski rabochego)', p. 184.

purpose. In 1910 the stage buildings were described as 'in general . . . dilapidated, stuffy, poorly equipped and conducive to escape'.[166] They had changed little since Iakubovich had described them in the 1880s.[167] Irkutsk's governor general himself acknowledged that conditions for prisoners on foot stages were extremely miserable: for the whole 2,000 miles from Irkutsk to Yakutsk, apart from the first point outside Irkutsk, there were no stage buildings. Prisoners had to stay in small, dilapidated, and dirty township or village prisons, or even more frequently, because of the lack of such prisons, in the homes of residents, or in the open, or in tents.[168] Because of the lack of stage buildings, movement of prisoners was only possible in the warmer times of year. Money for food for these disordered transfers did not always get there in good time, and there was often a severe shortage of the clothes necessary for the severe northern cold.[169]

Vladimir Berenshtam, a lawyer who travelled to Siberia to witness conditions in exile for himself, and wrote forcible denunciations of the exile system, highlighted that the regime hardened its position against exiles in the post-1905 period, and argued that the measures taken were actually illegal.[170] Berenshtam described the stage buildings in Irkutsk and Yakutsk regions. In Irkutsk province the stages were surrounded by high wooden palisades, and had barred windows. In Yakutsk region the so-called 'village stages' stood in open ground, without a surrounding palisade. The stage building was a dark, wooden cell without windows, with cracks between the logs that one could pass a hand through. When, stopping at one of these points, he asked the guide in wonder, 'Is this really a stage?' the man sullenly answered, 'Yes, god help us, terrible bug infested places!'[171] Berenshtam's outrage about the conditions endured by exiles was not fully reflected in the memoir accounts. A number of exiles describe their journeys through eastern Siberia with nostalgia and even enthusiasm. Vladimir Zenzinov described his pleasure in setting off on his journey to exile eloquently:

> Tingling with joy, I started on my great journey. I was leaving behind eighteen months of imprisonment, of walls, bars and crowded captivity. Suddenly it had all fallen away. Free spaces, limitless snowfields, movement, an endless change of scenic effects, and overhead the open skies! I breathed deeply. I drank in the surroundings tirelessly. I was aglow with the pleasure of life and unrestraint, almost forgetting that I was going against my will, under guard and watch. The illusion of freedom was complete.[172]

Iadov, travelling from katorga to exile on the Angara in 1912, recalled his stop in a stage hut in Irkutsk province after a march of around nineteen miles. The prisoners were all allotted tasks, splitting wood and boiling potatoes. They slept on straw on the ground, and the guard was quartered with them.

---

[166] *Otchet po glavnomu tiuremnomu upravleniiu za 1908g*, p. 131.
[167] Iakubovich, *In the world of the outcasts: notes of a former penal laborer*, volume 1, pp. 15–21.
[168] NARS, f. 12, op. 2, d. 1260, pp. 120–4.   [169] NARS, f. 12, op. 2, d. 2160, pp. 120–4.
[170] Vladimir Berenshtam, 'Yakutskaia oblast' i ssylka,' in *Za pravo! Soderzhanie sbornika* (St Petersburg, 1906).
[171] 'Yakutskaia oblast' i ssylka', p. 208.   [172] Zenzinov, *The road to oblivion*, p. 24.

When the guard went out, one of the criminals offered to free us of our chains. After tea and potatoes we all fell to sleep like the dead—the fresh air, big transfer and mass of new impressions fatigued us.[173]

His description is actually quite homely, and reflects his overall positive recollections of his journey to a long-awaited freedom of sorts in Siberia.

Yakutsk town was a short stop for many exiles on their journeys further north. While the journey to Yakutsk town from Irkutsk was long and arduous, it could be overshadowed by many of the journeys exiles made to their final named destinations in among the most sparsely populated and remote parts of the Russian Empire. The four postal tracts in Yakutsk region give us a sense of the distances covered; the path from Yakutsk to Viliuisk stretched for 470 miles, from Yakutsk to Ust-Maia was 222 miles, from Yakutsk to Verkhoiansk was 596 miles, and the journey from Yakutsk to Sredne-Kolymsk was 1,534 miles.[174] Exiles and their convoys had to travel by sledge, on horseback, by reindeer, or with dogs in Yakutsk region, because of lack of roads, high rocks, hills, swamps, and impassable forest.[175] The difficulties of these journeys were compounded for those travelling with dependents. Yankel Sokolov was exiled to Viliuisk in 1903. As he arrived in Yakutsk with the first exile party of the year, he was expected to make the journey that summer. Viliuisk was 335 miles northwest of Yakutsk town. Sokolov's wife and two small children accompanied him, and he petitioned that their journey be postponed until a sleigh track was established in the late autumn, as his family could not bear the arduous journey on horseback. This petition was granted, and Sokolov and his family were given leave to stay in Yakutsk until the sledge path opened.[176]

Dobrokhotin-Baikov was sent to Viliuisk in 1912. He travelled with another exile, a factory worker called Sitnikov. The winter was already starting. They were given the clothes and things that they needed, and were sent to Viliuisk in a sledge with a Cossack and a Yakut as guards and guides. They stopped in Yakut *iurts* along the way. They travelled in a special long sledge drawn by reindeer. Sometimes they had to be freed from snowdrifts. Dobrokhotin-Baikov was unimpressed with the little settlement of Viliuisk: 'And so we came to Viliuisk. Yakutsk was a deaf hole, but this was a taiga slum.'[177] After a year in the region, he was recalled to Yakutsk by the Governor, Kraft, and travelled back:

The journey to Yakutsk was very nice. The weather was pleasant, the mosquitoes and gnats didn't bother us—they had been killed by the night frosts. I rode on horseback for ten days, with short stops in nearby settlements (*naslegi*), where the horses were changed. There was no road in the taiga—just tracks existed, that is why Yakuts went with us, taking us to named points. There were lots of wild fowl in the taiga, and on the lakes. Suffice to say that the guide provided us with plenty to eat . . . [178]

[173] Iadov, 'Iz angarskikh perezhivanii'.
[174] Kazarian, *Iakutiia v sisteme politicheskoi ssylki Rossii 1826–1917 gg*, p. 235, table 6.
[175] Berenshtam, 'Yakutskaia oblast'' i ssylka', p. 198.
[176] NARS, f. 12, op. 2, d. 1972, pp. 45, 48. Letter from Sokolov, undated, and response from the advisor of the second section of Yakutsk regional administration, 1 August 1903.
[177] Dobrokhotin-Baikov, 'V Yakutskoi ssylke (zapiski rabochego)'.
[178] 'V Yakutskoi ssylke (zapiski rabochego)'.

A number of other memoirists write almost nostalgically about aspects of the foot stages. Irina Kakhovskaia described her journey from Sretensk on towards the Nerchinsk katorga complex in dream-like hues:

> ... [on] the first days of our journey we actually rested our souls and our bodies after twenty-two days of wagon travel. We set off at dawn, the last stars shone in the sky, and the sun peeped up from the east. The steppe came alive before our eyes; the dew dried quickly. And by midday, we had covered more than half our distance, we halted somewhere by a lake. We rested on the grass, and sometimes bathed ... we drank tea, treated ourselves with berries [we had] collected on the road, had a little nap,—and refreshed, again set off on the road. Everything literally returned to life as a result of the air, the light, the space that we had been denied for many months and which we would be denied for many years, and for some, forever.[179]

Iadov's memoirs were similarly cheerful in describing his journey through the frozen north, and evoked adventure travel writing rather than carceral experience:

> We went ahead cheerfully and joyfully; going forward, who knew where... Everything went smoothly to Bratskyi ostrog,[180] with the exception of this, that our hands, feet, noses, ears, cheeks, were all frozen ... We got up early in the morning, cut through the taiga, and walked till the evening went towards the appointed place, where we spent the night.[181]

Another political exile, Grigorii Kramarov, finished his katorga term at Nerchink (Gornyi Zerentui) in 1910. He travelled to his place of exile in eastern Siberia, and recalled that

> They went along cheerfully, thinking about the possibilities of a return to new life. The weather helped the mood—bright sun; a golden Zabaikal autumn with a light wind and a smell of green. On both sides were pine trees.[182]

Two of these memoirists had completed hard labour terms, and were looking forward to the relative freedom that they imagined in Siberian exile, which may well have coloured their mood, and their accounts of transit. Kakhovskaia was on her way to start her katorga sentence, but she too used the beauty of the Siberian landscape and the tranquility of that relatively brief stage as a foil for the horrors that subsequently befell her party.

An important factor in how transit was experienced was the health and status of the prisoners themselves. A significant minority of the prisoners were infirm or sick, or accompanied by dependents, including young children. While the journeys in the far north were arduous for the young single men that made up the bulk of exiles, they took on a new dimension of trauma for those who were struggling with their own illness, or who had to provide care for vulnerable children. A number of memoirists vividly describe their own illnesses, and the illnesses and deaths of their

---

[179] Kakhovskaia, 'Iz vospominanii o zhenskoi tiur'me', pp. 157–8.
[180] Bratskyi ostrog was a fortress on the Angar tract, in Nizhneudinsk district, Irkutsk province. It was east of Kansk, and 220 miles from the nearest town.
[181] Iadov, 'Iz angarskikh perezhivanii'.
[182] Kramarov, 'Neudavsheiesia ubiistvo na etape (Popytka ubit ugolovnago prozhivnago v 1910g pri sledovanie avtora iz Gornogo Zerentuia na poselenie)'.

travelling companions. Dmitrii Iakovlev was transferred from Turkestan to Yakutsk exile in August 1915. He stayed in Irkutsk transfer prison for more than a month, and a typhus epidemic started there, in the filthy and overcrowded cell shared by around 200 people. He was already feeling unwell when he was called for transit to his place of exile, but he was determined to travel, and get away from the transfer prison. They had to walk about sixteen miles to the first stop. After six miles, Iakovlev requested a place on the cart for the sick, but was refused because he had no official statement of illness. He collapsed and was carried by other political exiles to the stage point. He was subsequently transferred, along with four other sick men, a further eighty-two miles to Bayandaya. All the men had typhus. When he recovered sufficiently to travel, he was transported by sledge to his place of exile in Yakutsk region. He recalled that,

> To go by sledge from stage to stage was good, if you didn't consider the extreme cold . . . 300 or 400 versts [*198–365 miles*] from Bayandaya to Tutury went comparatively quickly—the Siberian horses went all out, not considering the bumps and bitterness.[183]

The authorities were aware of the implications of travel for the sick. In 1907, of a party of fifteen political exiles due to be transferred from Olekminsk to Yakutsk, ten were too sick to travel, and had to remain in Olekminsk.[184] In 1915, a circular was issued about withdrawing exile sentences to those in ill health.[185] The problem with this amelioration was that it did not take into account the toll taken on health by the journey itself.

Individual prisoners' experiences relied heavily on the temperament and inclinations of the convoy officers they were assigned to. Many memoirs include no references to rude or inappropriate behaviour from the convoy troops. There were some examples of rudeness, corruption, and violence from convoy soldiers who abused their position. Drozhzhin recalled that on his journey to work on the Amur railway, the convoy officer of the first stage was decent, but that the officer overseeing the second stage was insulting and provocative, and made the prisoners' lives miserable.[186] Berenshtam recounts a number of unattributed anecdotes from exiles about abuses on their journey. In one case, the convoy officer forced exiles to buy goods only from them at vastly inflated prices. One exile recounted that he had looked forward to exile after a term in katorga, but that his convoy officer, while not evil, had taken the various circulars to heart, and made the exiles' lives on the road very difficult. Almost the whole party fell ill, including small children travelling with the party. The journey was especially hard on the days when it was raining

[183] Iakovlev, 'Ot katorgi k ssylke; okonchanie sroka katorgi'.

[184] NARS, f. 12, op. 21, d. 119, p. 87, letter from Olekminsk regional administrator (*ispravnik*) the Yakutsk Governor, 29 March 1907.

[185] 'Tsirkuliarnnyia otnoshenie Glavnago Tiuremnago Upravleniia na imia Gubernatorov, Nachalnikov oblastei i Gradonachalnikov, ot 30 Oktiabria 1915 goda, za no. 41,- o sobliudenii osoboi osmotritel'nosti pri razreshenii voprosov o priznanii ssyl'nikh nespposobnymi, po sostoianiiu zdorov'ia, sledovat v ssylku,' *Tiuremnyi vestnik*, no. 11 (1915).

[186] F. Drozhzhin, 'Listki iz zabytoi tetradi (Vospominaniia ob Amurskoi kolesnoi doroge),' *Katorga i ssylka* (1921).

(they were travelling in autumn). Requests for the sick to see a doctor were refused, without any reason. When the exile telegraphed to Irkutsk in the name of the party, painting all the horrors of their situation, his telegram remained unanswered.[187]

Irina Kakhovskaia gives a terrifying account of what happened in her convoy on the way to Nerchinsk. The first part of the journey was very peaceful, but after a handful of prisoners escaped, things got very ugly. The entire convoy was held responsible for the attempted escape. They were all woken roughly in the night, and subjected to searches and abuse. At dawn, they were woken and the prisoners were beaten with gun butts as they marched through a swamp. The prisoners were badly hurt, coughing blood and collapsing. She recalls that they longed then for the security of prison. This was a neat inflection of her earlier sentiments about the tranquility and freedom of the journey.[188]

The political exile K. Korneev recounted the evils of the convoy officer assigned to them on their journey towards Zerentui. Officer Rytov was portrayed as a cartoon villain, complete with enormous frame, jet-black hair, and a mouth overflowing with teeth. He was drunk, and violent, and played cards with the criminal prisoners. In the end, he shot and wounded one of the political prisoners, and was arrested by gendarmes at the train's next stop, 'drunk and tattered, with a cut and bloodied lip'.[189] Another cartoon villain was to be found in the incident that occurred at Olekminsk, a stage post on the route north, on 11 June 1904. The convoy leader, a drunk named Sikorskii, tried to sexually assault R. Veinermann, a nineteen-year-old girl who had been arrested for her connections with Jewish Social Democrat organizations, and was on her way to exile. The convoy group included one hundred criminal and thirty political prisoners. The politicals included six religious sectarians and Tolstoyans, and a number of exiles from Kirensk who were being sent further north as punishment for their protests against the regime.[190] Sikorskii's behaviour was so outrageous that even the convoy soldiers acted against him. The affair ended in scandal when he was shot and killed by one of the political prisoners, a student called Mark Minskii, in the convoy. Minskii himself was wounded, and another exile, N.G. Shats, was killed.[191] Minskii, incidentally, was tried in 1905 for his crime, was defended by a young lawyer called Alexander Kerensky, and acquitted on the grounds of self-defence.[192] These accounts of brutality and callousness were presented as both extraordinary and outrageous. This indicates that such abuses were not the norm. While individual convoy officers may have behaved outrageously, prisoners had an expectation of decent and humane treatment, and the political prisoners complained bitterly if this was denied them.

---

[187] Berenshtam, 'Yakutskaia oblast' i ssylka', pp. 214–20.

[188] Kakhovskaia, 'Iz vospominanii o zhenskoi tiur'me', p. 160ff.

[189] K. Korneev, 'Iunter-Ofitser Rytov (Vospominaniia ob Irkutskoi peresylnoi tiur'me),' *Katorga i ssylka* (1925).

[190] Sysin, 'Ubiistvo konvoinogo ofitsera Sikorskogo', p. 192.

[191] Kazarian, *Iakutiia v sisteme politicheskoi ssylki Rossii 1826–1917 gg*, p. 257.

[192] Sysin, 'Ubiistvo konvoinogo ofitsera Sikorskogo'.

CONCLUSIONS

Travelling enormous distances in Siberia at the turn of the twentieth century necessitated a range of privations for any traveller. Prisoners were denied liberty and autonomy, and suffered acute material deprivation, which enhanced these privations. It was individual circumstances, however, that defined how these privations were perceived and experienced by individual exiles. Conditions on the road were nearly unendurable for those who were ill, or caring for children. Prisoners who encountered cruel or uncaring convoy officers had their privations increased or accentuated. The privations of transit were mitigated by prisoners' communities, which provided moral and material support, and reduced the sense of alienation and otherness that prisoners experienced. For those who were healthy in mind and body, and looking forward to the final stage of their penal arc, exile, travel could be represented positively, as a transition away from the horrors of transit prisons and hard labour.

Incarceration was an integral part of the exile experience. All eastern Siberian exiles spent time in Aleksandrovsk prison, either in transit to other destinations, or as katorga inmates. Aleksandrovsk's conditions and subcultures were mutable, and depended on the numbers of inmates, the character of the administration, and the unique interactions and interrelations that developed between inmates at any one time. In this period of confinement, exiles forged and developed their relationships with other exiles, and established complex hierarchies and networks of association. Much of the memoir material emphasized the conflicts and divisions between criminal and political inmates. This chapter has questioned these accounts, and found that while hierarchies and clans within inmates certainly existed and developed, they did not form solely round a straightforward binary of politicals and criminals. Our understanding of criminal subcultures and hierarchies is extremely hazy and incomplete. This is even more stark when we consider female criminal prisoners. Our understanding of criminals' experience of life in Aleksandrovsk is circumscribed by a glaring absence of first-hand sources, and by the pejorative tone that permeates secondary accounts.

Travel was an integral part of Russian exiles' penal experience, and more than that, it was an integral part of their punishment. Exiles experienced a penal arc, from imprisonment or hard labour, through travel, to their place of exile. Travel to exile was an important stage of this penal arc, both practically and symbolically. It was an integral stage of the individual exile's divorce from society, a moving from the known to the unknown. Alongside this symbolic and real divorce, other processes went on, which were important in defining exile identity. The relationships that were forged during travel, towards other exiles, and to convoy officers, were formative in the construction of a distinct carceral identity for exiles, and in the development of the alienation and hostility towards the state that was already forged in the first stage of exile experience, imprisonment.

3

Life in Exile
Communities of the Punished

> An unbearable, painful, deadly loneliness would suddenly seize my soul as if in a pair of pincers, and everything would drop out of my hands. A sensation of utter isolation from the world so dear to me would pierce my brain like a needle, causing me almost physical suffering ... The thought of the thousands of miles and many long months of travel separating me from the world in which I had lived heretofore would breed thoughts of death ... I wanted to cry out so that the whole world could hear. I wanted to raise my head and howl even as the dogs here howl when they too, perhaps, are seized with a cosmic loneliness. At such moments I would take up the axe and start to chop wood, in order to drown the attack of despondency in physical fatigue and coarse labour.
>
> (Vladimir Zenzinov, describing his feelings in
> Russkoye Ustye, Verkhoiansk region, Yakutsk)[1]

Zenzinov's poignant account emphasized that loneliness and isolation from his customary life was at the heart of his carceral experience. Other former exiles' memoirs also prioritized isolation as the greatest pain of exile. Archival records and memoirists repeatedly refer to strong networks of support that developed among political exiles, in order to help them survive the difficulties of daily life in exile, morally and physically. The associations that exiles developed in transit to exile, and in prison, as we discussed in chapter 2, were maintained and expanded once exiles reached their destinations.

This chapter will explore the lived experience of exiles in their places of settlement, with an emphasis on interpersonal relationships, and the social and economic networks that developed and evolved to support exiles. One of the book's themes is how the Tsarist state delineated punishment, and the extent to which punishment was in any way rational. By evaluating the domestic experience of exiles and their families we expose how the treatment and categorization of the punished leached into the treatment and experience of innocent spouses and children. The section included here on exiles' communities, covering self-help activities and political activities, deals exclusively with political exiles. The other parts, though, on children, intimate relationships, relationships with the local community, and relationships with the state, draws on material from both criminal and political exiles.

---

[1] Zenzinov, *The road to oblivion*, p. 80.

The Soviet historiography emphasized the cultural, social, and political benefits that political exiles brought to Siberia, but regional authorities and local populations at the time highlighted the negative impacts of exile on their communities and economy.[2] Whilst this partly reflects the Soviet historiography's silence about criminal exiles, which were undoubtedly a more unambiguously baneful influence on regional life, it also reflects that the negative aspects of political exile on Siberian life have been sanitized in the literature on this topic. The material available on exiles' communities is skewed heavily towards political exiles, and information about criminal exiles is often sparse. This is a reflection of, on the one hand, the state's desire to 'know' the political exiles, and the voluminous memoir writing of the political exiles themselves, both at the time, and in the early Soviet period, and on the other hand the almost total absence of first-hand material from criminals themselves.[3] The regional administration spent significant time and energy collecting information about political exiles living in their jurisdictions. They generated an extraordinary amount of paperwork—there were reports on the numbers of letters sent and received, for example, snippets of what was in parcels, and explanations as to why specific letters were censored.[4] State observations allow us some insights on the marital status and family relationships of political exiles.[5] They also, however, give us some indications of state attitudes towards political exiles. The level of interest in the exiles' intimate sphere, their spouses and family relations, shows us that the state sought to know political exiles. This desire to know corresponded with a desire to control.[6]

EXILE DESTINATIONS

The state sought to isolate and exclude exiles from the broader social and political life of Russia, and to punish individuals for their social and political transgressions. The state's tertiary objective, of settlement, had slipped in significance by the early twentieth century, as increasing numbers of free settlers 'colonized' Siberia. While the objective of punishment was met by the social dislocation and material conditions

[2] For an example of the prevailing positive Soviet historiography, see N. N. Shcherbakov, *Vliianiie ssyl'nykh proletarskikh revoliutsionerov na kul'turnuiu zhizn' Sibiri (1907–1917)* (Irkutsk, 1984).

[3] For a discussion of the challenges of 'knowing' criminals, see Gentes, '"Beat the devil!" Prison Society and Anarchy in Tsarist Siberia', p. 206.

[4] For example, GAIO, f. 600, op. l, d. 385, writings about the observation of political exile settlers' correspondence for 1910 (373 pp); GAIO f. 600,op. 1,d. 471; Writings about the exile settlers of Kirensk district, working out the text of an appeal for the elaboration of questions linked with the situation of exile settlers in the region, December 1910–10 May 1911 (149 pp).

[5] See for example, NARS f. 15, op. 21, d. 67, Information about the conduct, form of life, and family of politicals for 1903 (65 pp), pp. 12–19, 23–34, 39–44, 49–65. NARS f. 12, op. 2, d. 5135; Requests of those imprisoned in Yakutsk prison about the end of their terms, requests for material help for their families, pp. 13–14, 21, 28, 33, 71, 124; NARS f. 15, op. 22, d. 128; File about the conduct, form of life, occupation, and provisional departures from the region of exiles in 1910.

[6] On state attempts to survey and 'know' their population, see Peter Holquist, '"Information Is the Alpha and Omega of Our Work": Bolshevik Surveillance in Its Pan-European Context,' *The Journal of Modern History*, no. 3 (1997).

of exile, meeting the objectives of isolation and exclusion were much more difficult. Eastern Siberia seemed to provide some answers to the quandary of isolation and exclusion. It was sparsely populated, and on the outer reaches of the empire. Moving unwanted elements of the population there removed them from European Russia, but did not 'vanish' them. Instead, it transferred the burden of their care and management onto a weak and distant part of the Imperial administration.

Exiles were designated a specific location to settle in by the regional governor. For the first six months, they were only free to move within the confines of the district, and with police permission. After six months, they were allowed to move around the province with permission from the police. The settlers were unevenly distributed around Siberia. There was no apparent system to send exiles to free land. Most exiles were sent to Tobolsk in western Siberia, and the smallest numbers to Yakutsk. The distribution of exiles within the named province or region was rather arbitrary. Exiles could apply for permission to move away from their named place of residence subject to good conduct. Very many exiles were granted this permission to move more widely around the region, which was usually necessary if they were to find work. There were quotas imposed on the numbers of exiles permitted to settle in urban areas, and this restricted most legal exilic movement to rural areas.

The aims of isolation and exclusion became increasingly difficult to meet in the early twentieth century, for three reasons. First, as the Trans-Siberian railway spread its tendrils across eastern Siberia, the region became more developed, more populous, and better connected to the rest of the empire. This meant that it was increasingly difficult to place exiles in locations that were remote from urban communities and from routes with escape prospects. Second, the numbers of exiles sent meant that it was increasingly difficult to isolate exiles from one another. Though the region was geographically vast, there were relatively limited locations that were suitable for exile settlement. Finally, the system of police observation over exiles was unable to cope with the large numbers of political exiles sent to eastern Siberia in the early twentieth century. This enabled large numbers of escapes. In principle, there was to have been one police observer for every five political exiles. In practice, this ratio was flagrantly breached. In Eniseisk province in 1916, for example, there were 103 police observers for 1,442 political exiles.[7]

What factors influenced choice of sites? Those exiles with eastern Siberia named as their place of exile were convicted of the most serious crimes, or administratively sentenced on grounds of political unreliability. The state sought to isolate the political exiles in particular from the rest of the Siberian population by placing them in remote locations. The state was anxious to keep political prisoners away from areas with density of working population, from fear of political contamination, and they imposed quotas for the numbers of exiles allowed to live in urban areas. The government had some grounds for fearing an influx of political exiles into urban and industrial areas. Exiles played a leading role in eastern Siberia's lively Social

[7] Kudriashov, 'Men'sheviki v Vostochnosibirskoi ssylke', p. 62.

Democrat organization, which was concentrated around the Lena region, the site of major industrial action in 1912. There were around 190 political exiles working in the Lena goldfields.[8] Two thirds of the 1912 strike leaders were political exiles.[9] The college advisor, Sofronov, made a special recommendation in 1913 on the siting of exiles to Irkutsk's Military Governor, Leonid Mikhailovich Kniazev,

> ... the dangerous and recidivists [should be sent] to more distant and less comfortable locations, and settling those less dangerous in more comfortable areas, and taking all measures to keep the serious exile elements away from the railway and water ways.[10]

The Ministry of Internal Affairs specifically asked Kniazev to report on political exiles' influence on the local labour movement.[11] They also sought to prevent escape of exiles by naming places of settlement that were remote from any transport links and means for fleeing. At the same time, the authorities generally avoided locations that were extraordinarily remote or inhospitable, because this would inhibit the exiles' ability to survive. Only a handful of the most 'dangerous' political exiles were settled in extraordinarily remote locations in the region, like Zenzinov in Verkhoiansk.

Neither the Siberian native population nor the regional authorities welcomed the empire's unloved. A report from the college advisor Sofronov to Irkutsk's military governor in December 1912 on the state of exile in the region found that both administrative and criminal exile was totally disorganized and harmful for the region. Sofronov found that:

> If the organisation of administrative exile is far from perfect, then exile by court sentence as an institution is entirely lacking in any sort of organisation, and if the first, with the carrying out of necessary reforms, will fulfil its aims, the second seems to be purposeless and more than this its results in the end are actually dangerous. History states that criminal exile was intended to take the criminal away from his old midst and place him in new conditions of labour and colonisation, in fact it only corrupted the weakest part of the native Siberian population. If the sending of criminals, the majority of whom are peasants, by their nature unspoilt, produces such results, then what can we anticipate from the political exiles, the main contingent of which come from the intelligentsia and the factory proletariat who have lost all human form? Falling from their natural world (*popav k stranu natural'nago khoziastva*), unaccustomed to usual 'intelligentsia' work, and not called for in any other occupation, apart from work in workshops, this 'proletariat' thinks above all about escape, and if that is not successful, become inveterate drunkards, and gradually removed from moral relations, they become real scourges for the local population...[12]

[8] 'Men'sheviki v Vostochnosibirskoi ssylke', pp. 117–18.

[9] M. Melancon, *The Lena goldfields massacre and the crisis of the late Tsarist state* (College Station; Texas A & M University Press, 2006), p. 83.

[10] GAIO, f. 25, op. 6, d. 5385, pp. 35–40. Report from college advisor Sofronov to Leonid Mikhailovich Kniazev, regarding state of exile in the region, received in Irkutsk December 1912, p. 40.

[11] GAIO, f. 25, op. 6, d. 5385, p. 397ff. Report from Irkutsk military governor to the Ministry of Internal Affairs, January 1913.

[12] GAIO, f. 25, op. 6, d. 5385, pp. 35–40. Report from college advisor Sofronov, to Mniazev, regarding state of exile in the region, 5 December 1912.

Sofronov emphasized that the system failed the state, as it was insufficiently organized and controlled, and that it failed Siberia, as it introduced dangerous and unstable individuals into the region without adequate supervision. This narrative fed into the debates nurtured by the Siberian regionalists from the end of the nineteenth century. It demonstrated that the state seemed unable to meaningfully reform the nature of Siberian exile, and that the problems it raised for local Siberian communities and for the state actually escalated after 1905. While eastern Siberia's remoteness made it seem to be the ideal 'isolation space' for exiles, in fact, as Yakutsk's governor emphatically stated in his report to the Irkutsk police in 1914, its isolation precluded it from being a suitable place for exile:

> Looking over two years of regional life, I ask myself why Yakutsk has been chosen as a place of exile, if the basis for this decision lies solely on its distance from other regions, but regional conditions and particularities have not been taken into account. The situation is such that exiles have nowhere to live in the region, they cannot find any means for their existence, and it is impossible to maintain paper or real observation over them. More than 92% of the population are *inorodtsy*, with wandering and nomadic forms of life, or in transition to settled life, continue in nomadic ways. They cannot support exiles, so the burden falls exclusively on the Russian village population, which makes up less than 2,500 households in the region, with 9,550 souls, men and women. This insignificant handful of Russian peasants physically cannot accommodate all exiles, the numbers of which exceed not only the number of households, but also the whole Russian village population. The exiles cannot find any kind of work in the villages, and there is only work in the towns, the only significant one of which is Yakutsk, for a few dozen people.[13]

Both the regional authorities and the settled community resented exile settlers. The prison section of Irkutsk provincial administration warned in 11 October 1911 that Irkutsk province, and especially Kirensk district, was 'completely full' with exiles.[14] The Yakutsk governor wrote many letters of complaint to the Irkutsk military governor about the negative impact exiles had on the region, and petitioned for a reduction in exile numbers for the region. He pointed out that the region was 'completely full', and that while weak local economic development meant that there was no work for exiles, the flip side was that local residents were menaced by exiles and often forced to give them money.[15]

The numbers of exiles settled in Irkutsk and Yakutsk increased steadily in the early twentieth century. The increase of exile numbers had significant ramifications for the region. In principle, exiles made up 12 to 13 per cent of Irkutsk province's population, though in practice more than 43 per cent (31,043) of exiles had run

---

[13] NARS f. 12, op. 21, d. 168, pp. 14–34; letter to the captain of Irkutsk police (*gendarme*) administration, from Yakutsk governor, 12 July 1914.

[14] GAIO, f. 25, op. 6, d. 3104, p. 68, letter to Irkutsk military governor from the first prison section of Irkutsk province, 11 October 1911.

[15] GAIO, f. 25, op. 6, d. 3104, pp. 59–61, letter from Yakutsk governor to Irkutsk military governor, 3 August 1911.

away or were absent without explanation.[16] Most were probably in the province, but away from their named settlement, moving around the region in search of work. In Yakutsk province in 1911, there were in principle 4,733 exiles, of which 20 per cent were no longer there, because of escape, death, completion of term, or return to katorga. This left around 4,000 exiles. Of these, only 480, or around 10 per cent, were political exiles.[17] Yakutsk's indigenous residents were overwhelmingly Yakuts (around 92 per cent), who were categorized as *inorodtsy*. Though exiles made up less than 2 per cent of Yakutiia's population, they formed a sizeable proportion of the region's ethnically Russian population. Yakutsk's governor, Ivan Ivanovich Kraft, consistently described exile numbers as high by comparing them with the numbers of Russian residents in the region.[18] He compared the number of exiles with the number of Russian peasants in the three most populous areas of the region, Yakutsk, Olekminsk, and Viliuisk, where there were altogether 4,811 Russian peasants.[19] Responsibility for exiles lay primarily on those who were ethnically Russians. Exiles were not usually placed in *inorodtsy* settlements, because the *inorodtsy* lived in *iurts*, which lacked stoves and any kind of basic privacy, both of which were regarded as indispensable for Europeans.[20] In addition to the incompatibility of *inorodtsy* ways of life with European Russian expectations, attempts to settle exiles with *inorodtsy* communities in the past had ended badly:

> . . . Several years ago the regional administration made an attempt to settle exiles in *inorodtsy* communities, but soon abandoned this attempt. There was not even temporary shelter available with *inorodtsy* families, so exiles were established in the administrative buildings of the area, and there demanded that they be provided with food and vodka, and their conduct inspired panic among the *inorodtsy*. The business finished with this, that the *inorodtsy* gathered several hundred roubles and gave it to the exiles, who disappeared without a trace. The only exiles that stayed on with the *inorodtsy* were the criminal exile 'goldsmiths', who hoped to open a money factory in these backwaters, and also those political settlers, so called 'conscious' types, [who carried out] subversive propaganda among *inorodtsy*.[21]

Given the unproductive and insalubrious nature of most exiles, the *inorodtsy* communities' unsuitability in hosting them must have been something of a blessing for the *inorodtsy* themselves. In Yakutsk region, accommodation was a difficult issue for the state when placing exiles in their often-remote places of settlement. The

[16] GAIO f. 25, op. 6, d. 5385, pp. 397–401, Report from Irkutsk military governor to the Ministry of Internal Affairs, 30 January 1913. On escapes, see *Polozhenie tiuremnoi chasti i ssylki v Irkutskoi gubernii po dannym dokladov tiuremnago inspektora, 1911–1913gg*, p. 85.

[17] Pavel L. Kazarian, *Iakutskaia politicheskaia ssylka (istorichesko-iuridicheskoe issledovanie)* (Iakutsk, 1999), p. 108.

[18] A.A. Kalashnikov and A.A. Pavlov (eds.) *Istoriia Yakutii v otchetakh Yakutskikh gubernatorov* (Yakutsk, 2007), pp. 85–8.

[19] GAIO, f. 25, op. 6, d. 3104, pp. 59–61, letter from Yakutsk governor to Irkutsk military governor, 3 August 1911.

[20] NARS f. 15, op. 21, d. 74, p. 179; letter from the provincial assessor to Yakutsk region police chief.

[21] NARS f. 12, op. 21, d. 168, pp. 14–34; letter to the captain of Irkutsk gendarme administration, from Yakutsk governor, 12 July 1914.

state clearly recognized a duty of care in providing suitable accommodation. A series of letters from the Yakutsk region police officer (*ispravnik*) to the provincial assessor (*zemskii zasedatel*) in 1904 indicate that this duty was taken seriously. He wanted to clarify that the three political exiles sent to Namskii settlement (*ulus*) on 11 March 1904 had appropriate accommodation, 'and if these accommodations had a Russian stove and are suitable for Europeans to live in, that is, if Europeans can live in these accommodations without extraordinary hardships'.[22] This wording was used repeatedly in other letters that tried to establish the same question. The letters also expose the burden exiles represented to local communities, and the difficulty of finding suitable accommodation. Political exiles were lodged in Russian villages and in the settlements of religious schismatics, mostly *skoptsy* and Old Believers.[23] The elder of Tilliminskii settlement (*naslega*), Ivan Filipov Pavlov, reported that the three political exiles lodged in his house did not want to stay in one house together, but demanded that they each be given a house, and that they should not be too far from one another. Pavlov pointed out that such accommodation was simply not available in one village, but the three men refused to be split up, leaving Pavlov, as he put it, 'in a difficult situation, and I don't know how to satisfy their request'.[24]

In the post-1905 period, when relatively large numbers of political exiles were sent to eastern Siberia, the most suitable locations in Yakutsk and especially Irkutsk regions were relatively densely populated by political exiles. The more populated southern districts of Irkutsk, which were closer to the railway or to transport routes, were used for settling women exiles, exile families, the sick and the elderly, and for those whose conduct in exile has been excellent over a very long period. The distribution of political exiles round the districts was such as to allow significant density of exile population. In 1913 there were 177 in Nizhneudinsk; 257 in Balaganskyi; 415 in Verkholensk, and 1,113 in Kirensk.[25] Though these numbers are relatively small, political exiles often lived close to one another, so small but significant communities were able to develop. Sofronov's report to Irkutsk's military governor in 1912 emphasized both the total lack of planning and control over exile settlement, and its deleterious outcomes for state goals:

> Administrative exile in the regions is absolutely not organised. There is no special organ for exile in the regions; exile business is done by anyone, but no-one in particular. This means that there is a total indifference to exile, and an unsystematic distribution of exiles around the province, no information about their total numbers, or their means of existence, no observation over them and no struggle with propaganda or unity of exiles

---

[22] NARS f. 15, op. 21, d. 74, p. 127, letter from Yakutsk regional police officer to the provincial assessor of the fourth section of Yakutsk region, 14 April 1904.

[23] For more on accommodation, see NARS f. 15, op. 21, d. 74; File about the places of settlement and conditions of life for political exiles and Dukhobors, 1903–1905 (211 pp).

[24] NARS f. 15, op. 21, d. 74, p. 210, letter to Yakutsk provincial assessor from the elder of the first Tilliminskii settlement (*naslega*), Ivan Filipov Pavlov, 8 March (no year).

[25] GAIO f. 25, op. 6, d. 5385, pp. 397–401, Report from Irkutsk military governor to Ministry of Internal Affairs, 30 January 1913.

in durable colonies and parties of different sorts. Exile is not organised in structure and together with this observation over exiles is totally disorganised.[26]

The numbers of political exiles settled in specific regions actively facilitated the creation of political exile communities, to Sofronov's dismay. These communities were an explicit failure for state policy, which sought to neutralize political dissidents through isolation and exclusion. There was rigidity in terms of where an exile was settled, and their movement and permission to work once there, but in practice the state was unable to prevent the establishment of political exile communities. In Irkutsk province, for example, those exiled for state crimes clustered in small settlements around the province's remote townships and districts.

What was it like to live in eastern Siberian exile? Much of the answer to that question was of course contingent on where exactly you were sent. This chapter incorporates some sketches of some of the key exile destinations to give a sense of the places that we discuss. Nizhneudinsk district was home to 177 political exiles by 1913.[27] It was in the western part of Irkutsk province, and between 156 and 200 miles from the railway. Most of the population lived in the mid-western part of the region, in particular around the Moscow postal tract, and along the banks of the Oka river and the Angara river, where the climate was somewhat milder. Only around 10 per cent of the land in the region was enclosed and owned. The population mainly made a living from farming and carting. There were around 59,000 residents in the region, the vast majority of whom were Russian peasants. In 1896 there were 8,225 exile-settlers in the region. Of the whole population in 1896, there were less than 2,000 people classified as literate. Fewer than 500 children in the whole region attended formal school, although there were 'home schools' in almost every significant village, where small groups of children received some basic education. Four doctors, six medical assistants, and two midwives served the whole region in 1896.

The region's capital, Nizhneudinsk, had around 6,000 residents in 1896. It had a small hospital and a college, and three churches. There was very little trade and industry, with the only craft workshops run by settlers. Most residents made a living through farming, but the poor quality of the soil meant that they only produced enough for their own needs. There was no cattle rearing, very little market gardening, and some residents took seasonal work in the Lena goldfields, or carting goods around the district.[28] Mikhail Feinberg was exiled to Tulun village, in Tulunovskyi township, Nizhneudinsk district, in 1912. His letter to Leonid Mikhailovich Kniazev, Irkutsk's military governor, requesting permission to move

[26] GAIO f. 25, op. 6, d. 5385, pp. 35–40; Report from college advisor Sofronov to Irkutsk Military Governor, Kniazev, 5 December 1912.

[27] GAIO f. 25, op. 6, d. 5385, pp. 397–401; Report from Irkutsk Military Governor to Ministry of Internal Affairs, 30 January 1913.

[28] F. A. Brokgauz and E. A. Efron, *Entsiklopedicheskii slovar Brokgauza i Efrona, volume XXI* (St Petersburg, 1897), p. 46ff.

gives us a vivid sense of the challenges facing exiles in living in these sparsely populated, underdeveloped places:

> I was exiled in 1912 by Irkutsk prison inspection to Tulun, where I live at the current time. Conditions of life are extremely hard at the moment: there are no industrial and a very few trading establishments, and there are a significant number of exiles looking for work, and labour is without value, so this excludes the possibility of finding permanent work. That is why I have been unable to find any work in Tulun, even though I am highly recommended by the regional administration and residents here. My situation is even worse, as I have a wife and three children in European Russia who are reliant on the goodwill of my parents, and even with their help are subject to distressing deprivations. I cannot bring my family with me, as I myself am sometimes short of money . . . my two older sons study at Derbentskyi College in Tulun . . . but even there I cannot get work.
>
> These difficult circumstances may change for the better, since thanks to my older sister, who is wife of the staff-captain, I have been offered permanent work in the stores of a trading firm Vtorova in Verkhneudinsk town . . . I therefore ask for permission to transfer to this town. (Signature)[29]

The governor subsequently granted Feinberg's request. This letter utilizes the usual conventions of late Imperial petitions, and may exaggerate the supplicant's neediness.[30] This letter's level of detail rings true, however, and exposes the stark realities of exile life in Nizhneudinsk, which were categorized by isolation, poverty, and lack of work.

MATERIAL CONDITIONS IN EXILE

There were significant variations in the material conditions experienced by exiles. The most significant factor was probably the wealth of the individual exile. For the tiny minority that had private means, the challenges of Siberian living could be cushioned. It is from this tiny minority that the best-known memoirs emanated. Vladimir Zenzinov provides an extreme example of the difference that substantial private means could make to one's experience. In preparation for his four-year exile in remote Russkoye Ustye, Zenzinov purchased an enormous trousseau of necessaries:

> I made up a list of necessary articles, including canned goods, groats, ten pounds of tea, 36 pounds of sugar, and a medicine chest. Through my friends I obtained from Moscow a photographic camera, alcohol thermometers, and a pocket aneroid barometer to determine altitude . . . I carried in my luggage a splendid Winchester rifle, a two barrelled Sauer shotgun, a small calibre French gun, and even a revolver . . . Of course, I had not neglected to take a large supply of powder and gunshot . . . My whole library comprised between twenty and thirty volumes . . . [31]

---

[29] GAIO, f. 25, op. 6, d. 5385, p. 299 (Positive response from governor on p. 306).

[30] Siegelbaum and Moch, *Broad is my native land*, p. 27, for useful discussion of repertoires in letters to authority.

[31] Zenzinov, *The road to oblivion*, pp. 11–13.

Zenzinov also secured false identity papers to facilitate escape, and a quantity of alcohol to curry favour with local people. His memoirs never once referred to financial considerations. His wealthy family supported him generously.[32] Other prominent revolutionaries also enjoyed substantial private means. Lydia Dan and Boris Savinkov had a cushioned experience in their exile to remote Olekminsk in 1904. They read a lot and took up photography to pass the time.[33] Ekaterina Breshkovskaia, who was exiled to Kirensk district from 1907 till 1917, was materially comfortable thanks to generous donations from 'the women of Westover school' (in Middlebury, Connecticut), who sent her $50 per month.[34]

The vast majority of exiles, however, lacked private means, and they were exposed to the day-to-day difficulties of Siberian life. Criminal exiles were altogether unrepresented in memoir material, but were almost without exception severely impoverished. The financial status of political exiles after 1905 was in general also very poor. Most political exiles after 1905 were working-class towns-people. The vast majority of them were without independent means. Even estab-lishing the financial condition of exiles does not, however, provide a definitive answer to their experiences of exile. To give an example, those exiles who had lived and worked as peasants might have been better equipped to build a life of sorts for themselves in eastern Siberia. A number of sources note that those with experience of agricultural work were able to get work as hired labourers, or even to take on a plot of land of their own. Such work was not viable for those without experience of manual farm labour. One of the challenges of this work is to speculate on how social background, economic condition, and individual temperaments may have affected individuals' perceptions of their material conditions.

There were some ambiguities about who was responsible for the care of exiles. Support from the state was only ever partial, and levels of support depended on the category of the exile, and to some extent on location. Administrative exiles were given sums of money towards their food and accommodation expenses by the state. The sums provided varied depending on the location and family situation of the exile; those who had children to support were given additional money.[35] In 1903, in the fourth section of Yakutsk region, there were twenty-five administrative exiles, and all received an allowance of twelve roubles per month from the state, except those with children, who received nineteen roubles sixteen kopeks. Those exiles with salaried work were not given state means, but this group was in a small minority.[36] Lydia Dan, administratively exiled to Olekminsk in 1904, recalled

---

[32] Zenzinov had substantial private wealth provided by his wealthy merchant family. See *Iz zhizni revoliutsionera* (Parizh, 1919).

[33] Haimson, *The making of three Russian revolutionaries*, p. 168.

[34] Ekaterina K. Breshko-Breshkovskaia and Alice Stone Blackwell, *The little grandmother of the Russian Revolution: reminiscences and letters of Catherine Breshkovsky* (Boston, 1917), p. 280, letter to George Lazareff, 22–5 May 1914, p. 294, letter to Miss Blackwell, 9–22 February 1916.

[35] E. Sh. Khaziakhmetov, 'Polozhenie politssyl'nikh Sibiri mezhdu revoliutsionami 1905 i fevralia 1917,' in *Ssyl'nye revoliutsioneri v Sibiri* (Irkutsk, 1974), p. 180.

[36] See sample in NARS f. 12, op. 12, d. 800, for 1904, for example. Most of the 66 exiles lived on state means, except the handful, all professionals like dentists and doctors, who had paid employment.

being given: '17 or 18 roubles a month, and that was a fair amount of money. You couldn't live on it, but it was basic.'[37]

Exile-settlers were not in principle eligible to any support from the state.[38] In practice, though, the exceptionally difficult conditions of life in Yakutsk region meant that the administration did provide some support to political exiles. In February 1907, Viliuisk regional police administration asked that the allowance for political exiles be increased to fifteen roubles per month, and that those with families should be allocated thirty roubles per month.[39] Other concessions were made to political exiles in Yakutsk region. In 1904, political exiles were given permission to buy grain from state stores at a reduced cost. In the letters dealing with this issue, the Yakutsk governor acknowledged the difficult conditions for these exiles.[40] As is often the case, however, the records were silent on any measures to support criminal exiles. Criminal exiles were not offered special consideration by the state, even though their difficulties in day-to-day life were equivalent to the trials faced by political exiles.

The provision of financial support to exiles from the state indicates a certain duty of care, and suggests that the state recognized an obligation to care for exiles. This could have some strange repercussions. One political exile, a peasant called Pavel Gribov (also known as Solov'ev), was sent to Verkhoiansk region in September 1907, but he ran away from Yakutsk on 25 November. After his recapture on 29 January 1908, he requested backdated state payments for the period when he had run away. Yakutsk regional administration wrote to the police administration on 16 February 1908 to clarify that means were only to be given to those under police observation who have not run away.[41]

It is difficult to attribute meaning to the sums of money provided by the state without an understanding of costs of living. These costs of living were locally specific, and could differ significantly according to local conditions. They also changed over time; the cost of living increased steadily between 1905 and 1914, but then increased rapidly because of wartime inflation and shortages of basic goods. Necessities were often much more expensive in more remote places. This is evident in the sliding scale that the state used to allocate daily allowance to prisoners in transit—the daily allowance in Yakutsk region ranged from fifteen kopeks per day in Yakutsk town to thirty-two kopeks per day in Verkhoiansk town.[42]

A group of exiles in Verkholensk conducted a survey to establish how much money political exiles felt that they needed every month, and how many of them received the amount of money they needed to meet their minimum needs.

---

[37] Haimson, *The making of three Russian revolutionaries*, p. 166.

[38] V. Vilenskii-Sibiriakov, 'Poslednee pokolenie Iakutskoi ssylki (1912–1917gg)', *Katorga i ssylka* (1923).

[39] NARS, f. 12, op. 21, d. 119, p. 44, request from Viliuisk regional police administration to Yakutsk regional administration, February 1907.

[40] NARS f. 15, op. 8, d. 157; File about the giving of means to political exiles, 1904–1905, 24pp.

[41] NARS f. 15, op. 20, d. 84, p. 29, from Yakutsk regional administration to Yakutsk regional police administration, 16 February 1908.

[42] Kazarian, *Iakutiia v sisteme politicheskoi ssylki Rossii 1826–1917 gg*, p. 246, table 7.

Verkholensk lay in the north of Irkutsk province. More than a sixth of the region's area lay under water, with Lake Baikal dominating the scenery. The Lena River stretched across Verkholensk for more than 200 miles. It was navigable for around six months, between April and October. Verkholensk was comparable to Portugal in area, but had a population of around 60,000, with significant groups of Buriat and Tungus peoples. The land was high and hilly, with many springs and swampy areas, and the climate was harsh, with long, cold winters and a very short growing season. The population's main occupation was farming, but despite the sparse population, average landholdings were extremely small, around five acres per person, because so little land was suitable for cultivation. The soil was relatively fertile, but grain was not grown because of the early frost. Some of the Buriat people reared cattle, but fishing and fur trapping comprised the bulk of other occupations, and there was very little industrial development. The region's capital, Verkholensk, was 180 miles north-east of Irkutsk. It was in a picturesque location on the banks of the river Lena, but had only 1,043 residents in 1889, almost all of whom made their living through farming. Poor peasant dwellings straggled around the town for two miles. There were no factories, workshops, or craftsmen's enterprises in the town, and it held no market or bazaar. The total lack of urban infrastructure and trade enterprises, combined with harsh climate and difficult growing conditions, made Verkholensk a challenging place to settle for any exile, but especially for those with an urban background. One anonymous political exile's letter recalled of Verkholensk:

> I don't want to hope, that it will come to me to live a long time here, I don't want to feel myself at home, I don't want to feel myself properly a part of this cursed place. (Znamensk, Verkholensk district, Irkustk province)[43]

How much money did one need to live in Verkholensk? Two hundred and four exiles responded to the survey about conditions of life in the district, and their responses varied significantly, according, as the surveyors pointed out, to the needs of each individual. Thirty-eight per cent named ten to fifteen roubles as the necessary monthly sum, and 27 per cent named fifteen to twenty roubles per month. More tellingly, 112 individuals, or 54 per cent, answered that they did not receive the bare minimum that they needed to meet their most basic daily needs. Most lived thanks to help from relatives or 'comrades'. It was nearly impossible to find permanent work. Sixty-eight per cent of the individuals surveyed did not have a permanent source of means for existence. A quarter of survey respondents rented their own flat, but the majority shared a room. The main part of the exiles' budget was spent in buying bread. European Russians regarded bread as a necessary daily staple, but it was hard to come by in eastern Siberia, where the early frosts and harsh climate mostly precluded its local production. This meant that grain and flour had to be imported from grain growing areas, which made it expensive and sparse. Only half of the exiles that completed the

---

[43] Cherkunov, 'Zhizn politicheskoi ssylki i tiur'mi po perekhvachennym pis'mam', p. 173.

Verkholensk survey ate a hot meal every day.[44] A survey on the cost of living in Irkutsk province in 1914 came to similar conclusions, which were that it was possible to live on fifteen to twenty roubles per month, and satisfy basic needs.[45] These surveys give us an insight into the variance of living conditions for exiles depending on their individual circumstances, and indicate that overall exiles lived rather poorly.

BROADER COMMUNITY AMONG EXILES

Political exiles forged networks of practical support and friendship across eastern Siberia. These networks were developed in the prisons and staging posts, and on the road, on the way to exile. Exile communities provided a number of important functions for exiles. At a most basic level, they guarded against the isolation that represented one of the greatest pains of exile punishment. Contact with other exiles, even if brief, provided opportunities to speak their native language, to share news, to offer and receive advice, and to enjoy the companionship of others. In those communities that evolved or developed, the community could also act as a safety net for exiles by providing subsidized canteens. Finally, community could provide a forum for workers' cooperatives, thus helping exiles find paid work and so improve their material situation. Nikolai Alekseev Skripnik (also known as Skripnin) lived in Viliuisk town, 285 miles from Yakutsk town. He was an administrative exile. The police searched his flat on 26 July 1911, and found a leaflet that gives some idea of the scope and ambition of exile organization in the town. It also gives a useful overview of the types of activities that exile communities aspired to. The leaflet outlined 'regulations of the organisation for mutual aid of political exile-settlers'. The aims of the organization's mutual aid were to give loans and grants, to provide medical and occupational assistance, and popular education, and to establish a canteen and help in finding cheap accommodation. The organization established a mutual aid fund, and organized lectures, readings, courses, and a library. The fund was financed by monthly deductions from wages of members and from voluntary deductions, and donations. The organization was only open to political exiles, and was regarded as illegal by the regional police authorities.[46]

Dmitrii Iakovlev, a political exile who served a term of katorga, recalled his time in exile between 1915 and 1917 very vividly. When he first arrived in Tuturskii colony, his place of exile, a village near Verkholensk in Irkutsk province, not far from the river Lena, he was astonished by the lack of formality and apparent freedom of exile when he first arrived:

> We arrived at the township [administration]. [It was] a large wooden building. I went inside. The driver gave over papers. I was asked my name, how old, what state

---

[44] Ia Ianson, 'Iz zhizni Verkholenskoi ssylki 1914g,' *Katorga i ssylka*, no. 4 (1922).
[45] RGASPI, f. 459, op. 1, d. 25, p. 224; Form sent by Krakov Union for the assistance of political prisoners and exiles, and completed by exiles in Paishet village, Nizhneudinsk district.
[46] NARS 15, 23, 51, p. 33. Document dated 26 July 1911.

possessions I had, and so on. Finished. 'Go' they said to me. I don't understand where to go. 'Go—you are free.' I was dumbfounded, and stayed standing on the spot, not moving. Someone I had met when I arrived took me by the hand and led me out of the door.[47]

On the street outside, he met several acquaintances from Aleksandrovsk. There were around thirty exiles in the area, and most of the exiles were sent administratively, with a few exile-settlers, and a handful of former katorga prisoners. Iakovlev stated explicitly that all the exiles in his region were political, not criminal, and if criminals did turn up 'they soon went elsewhere'. He fondly recalled his warm welcome from other exiles in the village, with a cosy room, comradely chat, and a bubbling samovar. Iakovlev claimed that the exiles did not really argue, and that all attended lectures, regardless of differing political affiliations. The exiles clubbed together and formed a canteen, with one man delegated to buy salt, cabbage, flour, and potatoes, and to prepare simple meals. They each paid twenty kopeks for lunch. As well as providing food, the canteen formed something of a hub for the exiles in the colony. They were sent a good range of journals and newspapers from Moscow, Petersburg, and Kharkov, and these were kept at the canteen. The colony even published its own journal, *Elan*. Iakovlev suggests that despite the oversight of a guard, they were freer in their exile than in the rest of tsarist Russia.

> We were somehow entertained by winter. They made an ice rink where exiles and the local population gathered. Everyone went in the way that they were good at—on sleighs, or directly on lats. Spectacles were organised. Best of all were our own evenings, where the majority were exiles and a few from those well known to us in the local population. They read poems, tales, songs, and sometimes did folk dancing. . . . When the spring came, the exiles split up, some to hunt for paid work, others to look round the place.[48]

Was this account representative of political exiles' experiences? Some common themes certainly emerge. First, the denial of any involvement with criminals is characteristic of other accounts. Second, the importance of community and shared resources resonates with other memoirs. The impression of comradely harmony is, however, less universal. A number of accounts describe contestation and hostility among exiles.

Iadov was exiled to Angar in 1912 after a term of seven years' hard labour in Butyrka.[49] Angar was a tiny village more than 400 miles due north from Irkutsk. Iadov recalled that in his region, there were only four other political prisoners. The isolation of exiles here precluded the development of more advanced community networks, but despite this, human relations between exiles were very important. Of these, one man, Krig, was an important figure that supported the other exiles passing through.

[47] Iakovlev, 'Ot katorgi k ssylke; okonchanie sroka katorgi', p. 116.
[48] 'Ot katorgi k ssylke; okonchanie sroka katorgi', p. 116.
[49] Butyrka was the main transfer prison in Moscow. It established a katorga section in 1908.

Krig lived with his family, who had come with him from Ukraine, in absolute poverty. He had big influence over the peasants in his and neighbouring villages, and in a large area around. . . . without exception, all exiles, criminal and political, went to him in difficult times. Many received work from local peasants through his recommendations. Only thanks to Krig could one get credit at the local shop, and only with Krig's help could one organise an escape.[50]

The mention of criminal exiles here is very unusual, as they were not usually referred to in political memoirs. It hints that in fact, as one would expect, criminals formed an integral part of exile communities. Iadov's description of Krig's role evokes the importance of personal networks for exiles if they were to establish themselves tolerably in their new and often alien environment.

Dobrokhotin-Baikov was a Moscow worker arrested in 1911 for involvement in an 'autonomous revolutionary group', along with eleven other people, the majority of whom were typesetters and print workers. He was first settled in Viliuisk. He only stayed there for a week, however, as together with other exiles in the town, he participated in a protest organized by the exiles about their non-receipt of allowances for winter clothing. For this alleged 'disorderly conduct' he was sent, along with another political exile, to the distant Niubrinsk region.[51] The population in Niubrinsk was overwhelmingly non-Russian, and Dobrokhotin-Baikov missed Russian speech and culture terribly. He was utterly isolated by his inability to communicate in the Yakut language, and vividly described his feelings of utter loneliness. He encountered a Yakut who had worked in the mines and was acquainted with 'Russian culture', categorized by the Yakut as drunkenness and card playing. This man gave Baikov a Yakut–Russian dictionary. Baikov studied with vigour, and was able to master the basics of the Yakut language, which enabled him to communicate with the Yakut population that he lived with. After his first lonely winter, a few more political exiles were sent to within thirteen miles of him. He received journals and newspapers from them, as they had links with Russia's cultural centres. He regarded these meetings as like celebration days; he used the bathhouse, exchanged ideas and chatted with comrades, and shared their papers and journals, 'and received new energy and gladness . . . which carried me through the snowy emptiness and the dirty *iurts*. Newspapers were two or three months old and even older, but for us they were the first news and a source of joy.'[52]

Kirensk district was home to the largest population of political exiles in the region—by 1913, 1,113 political exiles had Kirensk named as their place of settlement.[53] The story of communal living in Kirensk provides an insight into the intensity and importance of community relationships in exile. Kirensk district was in the north-east, bordering the Yakutsk region, and was the largest of all Irkutsk's districts, at 56,000 square miles, an area bigger than Greece. There were

[50] Iadov, 'Iz angarskikh perezhivanii', p. 173.
[51] Dobrokhotin-Baikov, 'V Yakutskoi ssylke (zapiski rabochego)', pp. 181, 185.
[52] 'V Yakutskoi ssylke (zapiski rabochego)', p. 188.
[53] GAIO f. 25, op. 6, d. 5385, pp. 397–401; Report from Irkutsk military governor to Ministry of Internal Affairs, 30 January 1913.

around 54,000 people living in the district, including 1,200 in Kirensk town. Kirensk town was 680 miles north-east of Irkutsk, on the right bank of the river Lena. It incorporated 250 houses and limited services—schools, a hospital, a couple of churches, and shops. Because of the small population, there was little trade, though the town's traders supplied the Lena goldfields with hay, vegetables, and potato flour, and traded in furs that were sent on to Irkutsk. The Lena was closed by ice in Kirensk for 204 days of the year. When the river was navigable, residents sold foodstuffs along the banks to passing barges. The district was high and hilly, with much of the higher part of the district covered by conifers, larch, redwood, and cedar. The only industrial developments were a couple of salt factories. The land was mostly swampy or stony. The population was distributed mainly along the tracts of viable land for farming, along the length of the Ilim and Angara rivers, in the west and south-west. There was very little grazing land, no workshops or factories, and little craftwork apart from shoe making and tailoring. Most of the district's residents subsisted through hunting and fishing. Many of the town's residents took seasonal work in the Lena goldfields.[54]

The lack of opportunities to work, alongside an extremely isolated position, made Kirensk a particularly difficult exile destination. L. Simanovich was an exile sent to Preobrazhensk township, Kirensk district. He recalled that he was taken aback and delighted to see an old friend when he arrived, Efim Berel'man, whom he had known from Odessa. He was relieved to discover that he was to be part of a political community of exiles. After a tasty lunch of fatty meat, Simanovich asked Berel'man a range of questions about life in the district—whether it was possible to build, to find work, and so on. Berel'man replied:

> They don't live here, here they vegetate, run away, or die. Don't think about work here . . . there is no work anywhere, and that is why we are hungry. Some people manage to run away, and several committed suicide, but I am still sticking it out here. There are three more people here, but these 'little sons' receive good support from home, and that makes it possible for them to stay here; exiles die of hunger in the other villages of this township.[55]

The combination of a relatively dense community of exiles and challenging living conditions facilitated the formation of exiles' self-help groups in some areas. S. Korochkin described aspects of life in the Kirensk colony, which was made up of the village of Kirensk and three other villages. Korochkin recalled that in general, the difficult material conditions of life in exile promoted cooperative enterprise and collective feeling among exiles. Communes, artels, mutual aid societies, and canteens were established, but personal conflicts between members meant that they were usually short-lived. The vast majority of the exiles in the colony were impoverished, and the lack of paid work made it seem hard to plan for any

[54] F.A. Brokgauz and E.A. Efron, *Entsiklopedicheskii slovar Brokgauza i Efrona, volume XV* (St Petersburg, 1895), p. 114ff.
[55] L. Simanovich, 'Ocherki iz zhizni v ssylke (Kirenskoi uezd, Irkutsk gub),' *Katorga i ssylka*, no. 6 (1923), pp. 240–1.

improvements. The death by starvation of one of the exiles, a man called David Gerbovskii from Bochkarev, in February 1913, however, inspired a further collective effort to set up a canteen for political exiles in Kirensk. After some false starts, attributed in the early Soviet memoir that describes them to the evil machinations of various Socialist Revolutionaries on the organizing committee, the canteen was established. It was managed by the colony's mutual aid society. All exiles paid 1 per cent of their wages towards its maintenance. By summer 1913, it provided lunch for up to 200 people, and in winter for around one hundred people. The authorities were reportedly accepting of this enterprise, though there was official concern about their lack of control over these kinds of associations.[56]

As well as its role in providing subsidized food, the canteen came to be known by exiles all around Irkutsk province, and formed a hub for exile life in Kirensk, where political exiles could meet and share news. The Mutual Aid Society established in Kirensk was apparently a site of fierce hostility between Socialist Revolutionaries, Social Democrats, and a strong, variegated, and belligerent cohort of Anarchists. Despite these internal rivalries, the Mutual Aid Society 'protected our life', and organized celebrations for May Day and for New Year that drew almost all the exiles of the district together. In time, the exile colony came to offer services for Siberian residents. There was only one bakery in the town, so the canteen set up its own bakery, which supplied bread for all the north-bound steamer exports as well as for the local community, and subsequently a little shop was opened on the banks of the Lena, where the steamers stopped.[57]

While some memoirs paint glowing pictures of close cooperation in exile, others hint at high levels of conflict and tension among exiles. One of the largest unions of political exiles was formed in PriAngar in 1908. This group was involved in a broad range of activities, including cooperatives, libraries, legal help, and support for escapes.[58] The records of its last meeting in 1916, however, were dominated by reports that conflicts between members made any constructive work very difficult.[59] Little sense of community developed in the village of Paishet, Nizhneudinsk district, Irkutsk province. There were fourteen exiles in the village in 1914, with three out of the village to work in the district as woodcutters. Six were intelligentsia, two were unskilled workers, and six were skilled workers. Only four of them received any financial support, and most had been able to get some kind of work. They had not formed any kind of self-help organization because the colony was small, and because residents were highly mobile, and often left the village trying to find work, and finally because the colony was young—the first resident only arrived in January 1913.[60]

---

[56] S. Korochkin, 'Istoriia odnoi stolovki,' in *Sibirskaia ssylka: Sbornik pervyi*, ed. N.F. Chuzhak (Moscow, 1927).

[57] 'Istoriia odnoi stolovki'.

[58] Kudriashov, 'Men'sheviki v Vostochnosibirskoi ssylke', p. 69.

[59] K. Protopopov, 'Poslednii s'ezd ssyl'nykh Priangar'ia,' *Katorga i ssylka* (1930).

[60] RGASPI, f. 459, op.1, d. 25, p. 224, Form produced by the Krakov Union for the assistance of political prisoners and exiles, completed by exiles in Paishet, May–June 1914.

The voluminous literature on political exile has tended to focus on the political activities of the exile community in eastern Siberia.[61] There is evidence of a strong underground revolutionary movement in Siberia. This movement was largely organized by and around political exiles.[62] Political activism could draw individuals together and provide a basis for their interactions with native Siberians as well as with one another. Exiled Mensheviks and Socialist Revolutionaries were important figures in the cooperative movement in eastern Siberia that developed between 1910 and 1915.[63] They played a significant role in the establishment and development of eastern Siberia's periodic press. Many of the political exiles of the post-1907 period had experience in literary activities and publishing. Exiles strengthened the oppositionist tendencies in the Liberal press, as well as initiating new publications. They worked as correspondents, editors, and technical workers. The Menshevik V.S. Voitinskii, for example, was a permanent correspondent for the newspaper *Irkutskogo slova*. He started his correspondence with the paper while still serving his katorga sentence in Aleksandrovsk.[64]

An editorial collective in Irkutsk published the newpapers *Narodnaia Sibir* and *Otgoloski zhizni*, with the aim of organizing and steeling the working population of Siberia. The police department liquidated the collective in 1916. Luka Nikolaev was the initiator and key member of the group. He was a Socialist Revolutionary who had been active in the Volga region before his exile. Nikolaev was ordered to leave Irkutsk and go back to his place of settlement in Manzursk township but despite this order, Nikolaev returned to Irkutsk and took a job as secretary of the regional war industry committee, with the agreement of the president of the committee, Nikolai Lavrov, but without the permission of Irkutsk's military governor. He was described as a 'dangerous and a fanatical revolutionary activist'. He slept in different safe houses every night to avoid arrest, but was apprehended at his place of work on 17 February 1916.[65] His work for a formal state-sponsored organization for several months speaks volumes of the state's inability to control and oversee its punished population.

The presence of political exiles in small-town eastern Siberia enabled them to develop relationships and friendships with local residents. A 1906 police report reported how Nikolai Grigorevish Afanasev, a former teacher at a primary school, and a Yakutsk townsman, developed close acquaintances with

[61] See for example Pavel L. Kazarian, 'Rol politicheskikh ssyl'nikh v podgotovke trudiashchikhsia mass Iakutii k vospriiatiiu idei klassovoi bor'by,' in *Iakutskaia politicheskaia ssylka (XIX- nachalo XX v.) Sbornik nauchnikh trudov: Chast I*, ed. L.M. Goriushkin and V.N. Ivanov (Iakutsk, 1989); S.E. Nikitina, 'Politicheskaia ssylka i krest'ianstvo Yakutii (konest XIX- nachalo XX veke),' in *Iakutskaia politicheskaia ssylka (XIX- nachalo XX v.) Sbornik nauchnikh trudov*, ed. L.M. Goriushkin and V.N. Ivanov (Yakutsk, 1989).
[62] N.P. Kuruskanova, *Nelegal'nyi izdaniia Sibirskikh Eserov (1901-Fev 1917)* (Tomsk, 2004); Kudriashov, 'Men'sheviki v Vostochnosibirskoi ssylke', pp. 92–195.
[63] 'Men'sheviki v Vostochnosibirskoi ssylke', p. 158ff.
[64] 'Men'sheviki v Vostochnosibirskoi ssylke', pp. 185–9.
[65] GAIO, f. 600, op. 1, d. 1024, pp. 85–6, letter from Colonel Balabin to the Sixth Section of the Police Department, 24 February 1916.

political exiles, in whose circles he preferred to circulate.[66] He held an illegal meeting in his flat in 1907. He was searched, and a substantial reserve of illegal literature was found hidden around the oblast. Afanasev was arrested and imprisoned for six months, and subsequently put under permanent police observation.[67]

There were various reports of political exiles participating in revolutionary propaganda among the local community. Lydia Ezerskaia was a prominent figure in the Socialist Revolutionary Party. She was sentenced on 29 October 1905 to thirteen years in katorga for attempting to murder the governor of Mogilev province, N.M. Kleinberg. She served part of her sentence in Akatui, a section of Nerchinsk prison, along with revolutionary luminaries including Mariia Spiridonova and Aleksandra Izmailovich. She contracted a severe form of tuberculosis, and as a result was released from prison in 1909, to serve out her time in exile. She initially settled in Kabansk, in Zabaikal region.[68] She reportedly lived well in Kabansk, and attracted sympathy from the local intelligentsia. She gathered money to support other former katorga prisoners, and to facilitate their escapes. Ezerskaia was well known to exiles; one memoirist recollected that 'the Socialist Revolutionaries grouped around Lydia Ezerskaia, a very sensible woman.'[69] The authorities anticipated that she would 'no doubt carry out revolutionary propaganda'.[70] Ezerskaia was subsequently moved to Yakutsk region, where she died of bronchial asthma in 1915.

The biggest and best-known collective political action of exiles in Yakutsk was the so-called Romanov rising in February 1904, which was a protest against a series of measures passed by the administration in relation to political exile. The numbers of political exiles arriving in Yakutsk region increased dramatically in the early twentieth century—between 1870 and 1901 there were around sixteen political exiles sent to Yakutsk region every year. In 1902, there were forty-five; in 1903, 136; and in 1904, 206 political exiles arrived in Yakutsk.[71] While conditions in Yakutsk were always challenging, the regime had always been relatively accommodating towards political exiles. While criminal exiles that violated the terms of their exile by moving away from their place of settlement without consent were faced with deportation to Sakhalin, political exiles usually faced nothing more than a fine. This lenience towards political exiles was ended with the appointment of Count Kutaisov as governor general to Eastern Siberia in 1903. Kutaisov issued a circular in August 1903 stipulating stricter treatment for political exiles. In particular, exiles in transit from Irkutsk to Yakutsk were forbidden from meeting other political exiles, and halts along the way were to be stationed a minimum of three miles from

---

[66] NARS f. 12, op. 12, d. 802, p. 240, letter from Yakutsk head of police to Yakutsk governor, 7 June 1906.

[67] NARS f. 12, op. 21, d. 168, p. 33, letter from Yakutsk governor to the captain of Irkutsk police administration, 12 July 1914.

[68] X, 'Pamiati L.P. Ezerskoi,' *Lenskii krai*, 4 October 1915.

[69] Vilenskii-Sibiriakov, 'Poslednee pokolenie Iakutskoi ssylki (1912–1917gg)'.

[70] GAIO, f. 25, op. 6, d. 3104, p. 47; Letter from captain of the police administration in Zabaikal region, to director of the police department, 22 February 1911.

[71] Kazarian, *Iakutskaia politicheskaia ssylka (istorichesko-iuridicheskoe issledovanie)*, p. 98, table 4, 'Number of political exiles arriving in Yakutsk oblast'.

settlements.[72] Political exiles that violated the terms of their exile by leaving their place of settlement without permission were to be transferred to Yakutsk's most distant northern regions, Verkhoiansk and Kolyma. This hardening of political exiles' treatment coincided with a more punitive regime associated with the appointment of Viacheslav Von Plehve as Minister of the Interior in 1902.

Kutaisov's circular stimulated agitated meetings and discussions among the political exiles collected in Yakutsk town. More than forty political exiles armed themselves with revolvers and hunting pistols and barricaded themselves into the Romanov House on 18 February 1904 for eighteen days. Their numbers subsequently increased to fifty-eight—until the last days of the siege, the building was relatively porous, and exiles discreetly entered and left the building, despite the barricades. The protesters presented a written petition to the regional administration. They demanded that the transit costs for return from exile be borne by the state, the abolition of administrative measures for self-willed absences, the abolition of the circular prohibiting meeting with comrades on the journey, and a guarantee of personal inviolability for the individuals taking part in the protest. Yakutsk's governor was reasonably conciliatory, and met the protesters for talks, but was unable to diffuse the situation. Soldiers surrounded the house on 1 March, and shouted foul insults at the men and women barricaded inside.[73] On 4 March, the protestors shot and killed two soldiers. The soldiers immediately returned fire. Iurii Matlakhov was killed, and a certain Khatsevich was seriously wounded. The protesters refused to surrender, so the soldiers maintained a steady bombardment of the building. The protesters finally surrendered on 7 March. Of the fifty-six protesters committed to Yakutsk prison, seven were transferred straight to hospital. At the trial of the insurrectionists, held between 30 July and 6 August 1904, fifty-seven people were each sentenced to twelve years in katorga, though they were subsequently freed by the October 1905 amnesty.[74]

The Romanov rising became an emblematic event among political exiles at the time, and among Soviet historians later on.[75] A rash of 'incidents' broke out across eastern Siberia after the Romanov affair, as political exiles sought to show solidarity with their imprisoned comrades.[76] Outside the community of political exiles, however, there is little evidence that the *Romanovtsi* attracted broader popular

---

[72] V. Kolpenskii, *Yakutskaia ssylka i delo Romanovtsev* (St Petersburg, 1920), p. 9.

[73] *Yakutskaia ssylka i delo Romanovtsev*, p. 21.

[74] *Yakutskaia ssylka i delo Romanovtsev*, pp. 21–7.

[75] As well as a substantial literature generated by participants in the events, the Romanov rising also attracted a significant body of work from Soviet historians, seeking to emphasize the political role of the Bolshevik party in the region. *Yakutskaia ssylka i delo Romanovtsev*; M. Krotov, 'Romanovskii protest i proklamatsiiakh yakutskikh politicheskikh ssyl'nikh,' *Katorga i ssylka*, no. 5 (1924); P. Rozental, *'Romanovka'. Yakutskii protest 1904 goda. Iz vospominanii uchastnika* (Yakutsk, 1924); Grigorii Isaakovich Lur'e, 'Iz dnevnika "Romanovtsa",' *Katorga i ssylka*, no. 9 (1926); P.U. Petrov, *Iz istorii revoliutsionnoi deiatel'nosti ssyl'nykh bol'shevikov v Iakutii* (Yakutsk, 1952); I.S. Kliorina, *Meshcheriakov v Yakutii* (Yakutsk, 1963); G.P. Basharin, *Romanovskii vooruzhennyi protest* (Yakutsk, 1964); E.E. Alekseev, *Po puti pol'nago ukrepleniia vlasti samikh trudiashchikhsia* (Yakutsk, 1970); Kazarian, 'Rol politicheskikh ssyl'nikh v podgotovke trudiashchikhsia mass Iakutii k vospriiatiiu idei klassovoi bor'by'.

[76] Sysin, 'Ubiistvo konvoinogo ofitsera Sikorskogo'. See also Kolpenskii, *Yakutskaia ssylka i delo Romanovtsev*, p. 27ff.

support. V.N. Chepalov, a socialist who participated in revolutionary activity in Yakutsk, wrote in his diary that 'the population of Yakutsk relate to them (*Romanovtsi*) unsympathetically. The merchants offered their services—to burn their dwelling, and the students also [offered] to beat them . . .'[77] The *Romanovtsi* had issued a range of proclamations while the siege went on, including one to the soldiers of the Yakutsk command, with calls not to shoot the exiles. These pleas had absolutely no effect on soldiers, who fired thousands of bullets at the protestors. While the Romanov rising became important for the political exile community, there is no evidence that it attracted sympathy from the local population, or played a role in radicalizing the region.[78]

EXILES AND THE NATIVE SIBERIAN POPULATION

Administrators at the time distinguished the native Siberian population very crisply between the indigenous non-Russian groups, referred to as *inorodtsy* (aliens), and the ethnically Russian settler population. This discussion of exiles' engagement with the native Siberian population includes both indigenous and ethnically Russian populations. The existing literature is saturated with accounts of the positive impact political exiles had on Siberia, from the Decembrists onwards. Contemporary representations and accounts do not resonate with these evaluations, but rather, they present a picture of unremitting hostility from native Siberians towards the exile population. While the political exiles certainly represented an injection of conscious European Russians into eastern Siberia, they also put significant pressure on eastern Siberian resources and capabilities, and represented an injection of hostile, cultural imperialism. V. Nikolaev encapsulated this attitude well:

> Political exiles constituted virtually the only source of culture in the north. Among the semi-literate civil servants and priests, wallowing in the sludge of philistines, drunkenness and card games . . . political exiles were the bright light in that dark, unenlightened tsarism.[79]

Criminal (rather than political) exiles are mentioned very little in the historiography. Where they are mentioned, it is to draw the contrast between their unwholesome and burdensome influence on Siberian life and communities, and the altogether positive impact evinced by those exiled for their political activities. The burden of caring for criminals fell very heavily on the indigenous population, who themselves lived so poorly that they faced starvation in a poor season. The criminal settlers abused the indigenous population, and subjected them to robberies

---

[77] Vasilii Fedorov, *Yakutiia v epokhu voin i revoliutsii* (Moscow, 2002), pp. 148–9.
[78] *Yakutiia v epokhu voin i revoliutsii*, pp. 148–9.
[79] V. Nikolaev, 'Ssylka i kraevedenie; Yakutskii krai,' in *Sibirskaia ssylka: Sbornik pervyi*, ed. N.F. Chuzhak (Moscow, 1927), p. 89.

and attacks, as well as bringing a corrupting influence into local life, characterized by drunkenness, veneral disease, and gambling.[80]

Criminal exiles that were sent for settlement in Yakut villages were obliged to roam (*brodiazhnichat*) because they did not know the language and had no means for existence. Furthermore, with rare exceptions, they did not want to work, and relied on the community for fuel, food, clothes, and money. Despite a law forbidding decrepit, invalids, or the over-forty-fives from being sent to Yakutsk, in practice these injured souls were settled in the villages anyway, because there were insufficient places in almshouses. This meant that 'they received food from society and lived a long time'.[81] There were numerous examples of the harmful influence individual criminal exiles had. K. Popov, for example, who had been exiled to Yakutsk in 1885 after his katorga term for murder, terrorized the native population of Khatylinskii settlement (*nasleg*), demanding food and money and threatening residents. The police administration estimated that every exile settled in an *inorodtsy* village cost the village twenty roubles per month.[82]

While we have no memoir material from criminal exiles, political exiles wrote extensively about their experiences, often lionizing themselves and their political influences in the process. Both the memoirists and the historiography that arose from these memoirs presented the political exiles as the bringers of light to dark places. This intersects with the myth-making built up over a century that started with the Decembrists in Siberia.[83] More than that, though, this narrative of enlightenment more generally overlaid deep hostilities about the native populations of Siberia. It also resonates with the ways in which Russia's rural population as a whole was represented by elites.[84] Exiles' accounts are suffused with pejorative attitudes towards the native Siberian population, and towards the indigenous Siberian population in particular. This too chimes with other literature on treatments of Siberia's indigenous peoples.[85] The Menshevik V.D. Vilenskii Sibiriakov commented that 'one had to do something useful for the local population, and that is why Yakutsk flourished in the hands of our brother-exiles'.[86] We have extensive literature on the impact of political exiles on literary culture in Yakutia,[87] and lots of material on political interactions (and light-giving thereof) of political exiles with

[80] E.G. Makarov, *Ugolovnaia, religioznaia i politicheskaia ssylka v Yakutii vtoraia polovina XIX v* (Novosibirsk, 2005), p. 198.

[81] *Ugolovnaia, religioznaia i politicheskaia ssylka v Yakutii vtoraia polovina XIX v*, p. 192.

[82] *Ugolovnaia, religioznaia i politicheskaia ssylka v Yakutii vtoraia polovina XIX v*, p. 193.

[83] See for example, Ludmilla A. Trigos, *The Decembrist myth in Russian culture* (New York, 2009), pp. 1–93.

[84] See for example Diment and Slezkine, *Between heaven and hell: The myth of Siberia in Russian culture*; Cathy A. Frierson, *Peasant Icons: Representations of rural people in late nineteenth century Russia* (Oxford, 1993).

[85] See for example Slezkine, *Arctic mirrors: Russia and the small peoples of the North*, pp. 56–60, pp. 73–92.

[86] Vilenskii-Sibiriakov, 'Poslednee pokolenie Iakutskoi ssylki (1912–1917gg)'.

[87] M.G. Mikhailova, 'Politicheskaia ssylka i russkaia literatura v Iakutii,' in *Iakutskaia politicheskaia ssylka (XIX- nachalo XX v.) Sbornik nauchnikh trudov: Chast II*, ed. L.M. Goriushkin and V.N. Ivanov (Iakutsk, 1989); Makarov, *Ugolovnaia, religioznaia i politicheskaia ssylka v Yakutii vtoraia polovina XIX v*, pp. 187–90.

Yakutsk's peasantry, Russian and non-Russian.[88] The relentlessly negative tone of the exiles' recollections of indigenous Siberians, however, rather clouds these visions of positive relationships. Dobrokhotin-Baikov, for example, described the Yakut people as dirty, and 'at a very low level of development'.[89]

Vasilii Nikolaevich Sokolov, a leading Bolshevik who was arrested and exiled in 1907, offered a harsh and unflinching account of relationships between exiles and Siberians, and among exiles themselves, which is in many respects set apart from the often sentimental accounts of other exiles. His position was heavily influenced by his own position as a prominent Bolshevik publicist and editor—he was on Pravda's editorial college from 1924. He prioritized class struggle and Marxist dialectic in his analysis. Despite these caveats, Sokolov's analysis is substantiated by some other local sources. Sokolov argued that the social background and numbers of political exiles after 1905 was a strong determinant in their treatment by Siberians, and their experience. The romance of Siberia's warm welcome to pre-1905 political exiles is explained by Sokolov as an outcome of these early exiles' ability to provide cultural and practical assistance to the Siberian community without remuneration. This was to contrast harshly with the post-1905 generation, who needed paid work if they were to survive. The post-1905 political exiles were predominantly from urban working-class backgrounds, whereas the pre-1905 exiles were predominantly from privileged and intelligentsia backgrounds. While there were comparatively tiny numbers of political exiles before 1905, there were substantially more after 1905.

> The mass of new exiles arrived in Siberia not by wagon, but by train. And they were immediately distributed around the deaf (*glukhyi*) villages. They were rarely left in towns, and were sent to villages not singly, and usually not in small groups, but in large parties.[90]

Sokolov suggested that the romance of Siberia as a place that received political exiles kindly was crushed by the realities of large numbers of mostly single, working-age urban men arriving in the localities. A useful illustration of Sokolov's point can be found in the provision of medical care by the pre-1905 exiles, a significant proportion of whom had some sort of medical training. Medical support was extremely sparse across eastern Siberia. For many residents of the settlements of Yakutiia, political exiles with any kind of medical training (doctors, medical assistants, student medics, midwives) were the only medical assistance available to them at all. S.E. Mitskevich, a student of Lenin, was sent to Kolym region between 1899 and 1903. He organized support and personally oversaw the care and

---

[88] S.E. Nikitin, 'Politicheskaia ssylka i krest'ianstvo Yakutii (Konets XIX- nachalo XX v.),' in *Yakutskaia politicheskaia ssylka (XIX- nachalo XX v.) Sbornik nauchnikh trudov: Chast I*, ed. L.M. Goriushkin and V.N. Ivanov (Iakutsk, 1989); Makarov, *Ugolovnaia, religioznaia i politicheskaia ssylka v Yakutii vtoraia polovina XIX v*, pp. 207–34. Sections in this devoted to medical help, legal help, and educational activities of state criminals in the second half of the nineteenth century.

[89] Dobrokhotin-Baikov, 'V Yakutskoi ssylke (zapiski rabochego)'.

[90] V. N. Sokolov, 'Sibir i ssylka,' in *Sibirskaia ssylka: Sbornik pervyi*, ed. N.F. Chuzhak (Moscow, 1927), pp. 31–2.

treatment of the population during a measles epidemic in 1902. He studied the Yakut language in order to be able to communicate with the population better, and opened the first medicinal points in Nizhnekolymsk and Verkhnekolymsk, which continued to function until late in the twentieth century. He also busied himself with cultural-enlightenment activities.[91] The urban workers that dominated the post-1905 generation had neither the skills nor the resources to provide such welcome support to the population. Their need to earn money in a small and under-employed economy depressed the labour market.

Local Siberian communities exploited incoming political exiles ruthlessly. The prices of basic foodstuffs increased 300–400 per cent in the first three weeks of their arrival. Exiles were paid significantly less for work than locals doing the same tasks. Exiles who were able to secure credit paid much higher rates than locals. Sokolov argues that by 1910–12, very few were left in their original village communities, and most had dispersed and assimilated into district centres and to the mines for work.[92] Iadov's description of his party's arrival into Bolshoi Mamyrsk township substantiates aspects of Sokolov's representation, in particular the commodification of exiles:

> The peasants from the township questioned us, who we were, where from, for what, from where, they looked over our official papers. We all had something to sell, and started to haggle. I exactly remember the prices I received for my things—foot shackle—3 roubles, hand shackles 1 rouble 50 kopeks (these were things necessary to peasants for the hobbling of horses); 3 roubles for shoe covers and so on . . . [93]

He recalled that his sales were insignificant compared to those exiles who sold everything they had, and kept only a pair of underwear and puttees. Overall, though, many exiles' accounts are suffused with a romantic glow in their recollections of relationships with the local community. N.E. Teterin, a political exile in Kirensk district, epitomizes this nostalgia in his effusive account of relationships between political exiles and native Siberians. He commented on the absence of medical, legal, and educational support for local residents in the region, and suggested that the help provided by political exiles in these spheres induced great sympathy for them: 'Among men this feeling of sympathy was expressed in respect to exiles, as people both wise and educated, but from women it took on a tender, even loving character.'[94] Teterin presented exiles as an entirely positive influence on the region, bringing 'a bright ray of light into Tsarist darkness in the region'. These positive recollections were reinforced by other accounts:

> Speaking about the population surrounding us, it is necessary to say that their relationships with exiles were excellent. We did not feel any hostility, and they related to us with absolute trust. Local peasants gave them credit by for bread, milk and so on,

[91] S.E. Nikitin, 'Deiatel'nost politssyl'nykh medikov v Yakutii,' in *Osvoboditel'noe dvizhenie v Rossii i Yakutskaia politicheskaia ssylka. Chast 1*, ed. V.N. Ivanov and P.L. Kazarian (Yakutsk, 1990).
[92] Sokolov, 'Sibir i ssylka'.   [93] Iadov, 'Iz angarskikh perezhivanii', p. 171.
[94] N. Teterin, 'Politicheskaia ssylka i narodnoi poezii Kirenskago uezda,' *Katorga i ssylka*, no. 6 (1924).

and at local shops. Local peasants had surpluses of bread, meat and other products, but they needed money, and every penny had value, nothing was spent carelessly. In several places absolute hospitality was preserved.[95]

The stark differences between Sokolov's dry assessment and these more florid accounts can be accounted for partly by divergences in individual experience. The romanticism that Sokolov scornfully referred to at the start of his article also plays a role in rose-tinting exile recollections. When we turn to known responses of local communities to exiles, we find that Sokolov's account of hostility is better supported than Teterin's vision of dreamy admiration and respect. Local communities voiced antagonism towards exiles across the region. The Yakutsk regional police officer reported that the *skoptsy* communities had 'prejudiced, almost hostile relationships with exiles', and refused to make any repairs to their vacant buildings in order to make them useable for exile incomers. Two administrative exiles settled in the *skoptsy* village of Kil'demsk, Tsekhnovitser, and Roitman, strongly petitioned to be moved to an old believers' settlement, Pavlovts, because of the tense relations they endured with the *skoptsy*.[96] Overall, we can see that relationships between the native population and exiles were complex and contested. The pejorative attitudes of many exiles towards the native population must have tainted their ability to communicate and cooperate within local communities, while the financial and practical burden that exile settlers represented for Siberians surely inhibited the warmth of their welcome.

INTIMATE RELATIONSHIPS

The records show that exiles, men and women, experienced life in eastern Siberia as humans experience life everywhere, with romance, personal tragedies, failed love affairs, deceit, and children born and lost. These records are silent about some categories of intimacy. I have no references to same-sex relationships in exile, though there are some allusions to homosexuality in prison. The only mentions of prostitution referred to the women who practised it but not to their clients. Sources are very thin on the details of intimate relationships in general, since political exile memoirs rarely or never mentioned such matters, and the state had no interest in cataloguing such information. The state offered a degree of support to those who chose to follow prisoners into Siberian prisons and exile, and encouraged exiles to marry. Exiles could marry in their places of settlement, and those exiles whose spouses did not accompany them were allowed to ask permission to marry again.[97] Voluntary followers, both spouses and children (defined as those under the age of fourteen) were provided with necessary clothes and shoes, and an allowance for food.[98] A decree of 1908

[95] Iakovlev, 'Ot katorgi k ssylke; okonchanie sroka katorgi', p. 116.
[96] NARS f. 15, op. 21, d. 74, p. 207, letter from Yakutsk region police officer to Yakutsk governor, 23 September 1904.
[97] E.E. Kraft, *Zakony i pravila o ssyl'no-poselentsev i ikh semeistvakh* (Yakutsk, 1912), pp. 28–9.
[98] *Zakony i pravila o ssyl'no-poselentsev i ikh semeistvakh*, p. 32.

discouraged followers by denying support for travelling expenses. This change of policy reduced the numbers of exiles being accompanied by followers.[99]

State records enable us to get a sense of the proportion of exiles that were accompanied by spouses and children. Some were left by their wives or chose not to take their families into exile, and in a handful of cases their wives followed them voluntarily.[100] Samples from 1911 in Yakutsk confirm that the vast majority of political exiles under observation were young, single, urban men.[101] A group of exiles in Verkholensk district, Irkutsk province, took a detailed survey of exiles in the region between January and February of 1914. The survey estimated that between 270 and 280 political exiles lived in the seven townships surveyed, in colonies of around forty people. Two hundred and four individuals were included in the survey. Ninety per cent were men, and 90 per cent were under the age of 35. Sixty-five per cent were educated only to the lowest level; 45 per cent were workers; and 25 per cent were professionals. The majority of those surveyed were single (62 per cent), 25 per cent were married, and only eight were part of families with children. Most (74 per cent) had been imprisoned for joining an illegal society, and the majority were affiliated either with the Social Democrats or with the Socialist Revolutionaries.[102] This profile of exiles as mainly single men is substantiated by other examples. Of the 105 individuals listed as political exiles under police observation in Yakutsk region in 1903, only three were women, and only three exiles were accompanied by wives and children.[103] Of the sixty-six exiles listed in the regions of Verkhoiansk, Kolymsk, and Yakutsk town in 1904, fifty-one were single. There were nine women, two of whom were exiled with their husbands. There was only one child. Spouses accompanied eleven of the fifteen married people.[104]

One historian, Pavel Kazarian, argued that family life was one of the factors that allowed exiles to overcome their 'difficult morally oppressive conditions'.[105] This is a difficult case to assess. On the one hand, the warmth of intimate human relations and the joy of children may have brought comfort and a sense of purpose and identity to exiles. On the other hand, though, the stress of trying to provide for a family, and maintaining children's health in challenging material and climactic conditions, could just add further torment to the exiles' position. The acute poverty faced by exiles was made particularly intolerable if one had to support a spouse, or

---

[99] *Polozhenie tiuremnoi chasti i ssylki v Irkutskoi gubernii po dannym dokladov tiuremnago inspektora, 1911–1913gg* (Irkutsk, 1914), p. 21.

[100] For example, NARS f. 12, op. 21, d. 48, pp. 2–34; Record book detailing political exiles' circumstances, and their receipt of state means, 4 December 1902–10 June 1906.

[101] See for example NARS f. 15, op. 22, d. 136; File about conduct, activities and searches for exiles (789 pp).

[102] Ianson, 'Iz zhizni Verkholenskoi ssylki 1914g'.

[103] NARS f. 12, op. 21, d. 48, pp. 1–34; Record book detailing political exiles' circumstances, and their receipt of state means, 4 December 1902–10 June 1906.

[104] NARS f. 12, op. 12, d. 800, pp. 3–15.

[105] Pavel L. Kazarian, 'Semeinoe polozhenie politicheskikh ssyl'nikh Yakutii,' in *Osvoboditel'noe dvizhenie v Rossii i Yakutskaia politicheskaia ssylka. Chast 1*, ed. P.L. Kazarian and V.N. Ivanov (Yakutsk, 1990).

even worse young children. This question of poverty intersects acutely with the problems of finding work in eastern Siberia. The vast majority of exiles in eastern Siberia were unable to secure permanent work, which meant that they had to rely on private or state means for their daily existence. The four exile families living in Markhinsk village in Yakutsk in 1916 provides a little fabric to these notions of familial poverty. Markhinsk was a tiny and isolated settlement about 500 miles north-west of Yakutsk town. There were four family groups among the fifteen administrative exiles living in Markhinsk village in 1916. Sergei Shuzhkin lived in exile with his wife and three little children aged two, five, and seven. They had no property and no income, save the one rouble per day he earned working as a day labourer (*batrak*) on peasants' fields. Vladimir Korzhuk had his wife and baby daughter with him. He was a gold and silversmith by trade, but was unfit for peasant work as he had never done it, so had no work. The family relied on the allowance provided by the state, which as we heard elsewhere, was barely adequate to make ends meet. Tikhon Marmuzok lived with his wife and five small children, who were aged six months, five, six, eight, and ten. He was able to work, and had received fifty roubles for two months' work labouring on a house. Evfrosin Kamenkov had two young children with him, and no job, so the family had to subsist on their state allowance.[106] This stark information gives a hint of the daily struggles encountered by these individuals in providing for their children in this extraordinarily isolated location.

Some exiles forged relationships and marriages while in exile.[107] The odds were, however, against this, as there were significantly fewer women than men in the region. In the 1897 census, 53 per cent of Irkutsk province's population was male.[108] Kazarian suggests that marriages between exiles and Yakut women were 'relatively common'.[109] The state was very cagey about these relationships.[110] The state actively promoted marriage for criminal exiles, but sought marriages to an idealized type of Russian woman. Marriage was equated with settlement, and with agrarian success. Lanskoi declared in 1860 that 'marriage is the most important material and moral means of rehabilitating the katorzhniks.'[111] The gender imbalance was believed to be responsible for disorder in Siberia, and the 'right sort of woman' was believed to be a

---

[106] NARS f. 15, op. 18, d. 217, pp. 107–8, information on administrative exiles settled in Markhinsk village, Yakutsk region, for 1916.

[107] NARS f. 12, op. 2, d. 4693, p. 140, letter from Sered asking for confirmation that he is a bachelor so that he can enter into a marriage, 7 September 1909.

[108] Irkutsk province had the most unbalanced gender ratio in eastern Siberia. Zabaikal region had near parity, Yakutsk oblast had 51 per cent men, and Enieisk had 52 per cent men. (Statistics from http://www.demoscope.ru/weekly/ssp/rus_gub_97.php?reg=73 [29 October 2015]).

[109] Kazarian, 'Semeinoe polozhenie politicheskikh ssyl'nikh Yakutii'. There are examples in the archives of exiles asking for permission to marry while in exile—they had to have their marital status certified before they could enter into marriage, so such instances are recorded. See for example, Kox, 23 October 1902 (NARS f. 12, op. 2, d. 1945, p. 149); Sered, September 1908 (NARS f. 12, op. 2, d. 4693, p. 140).

[110] Schrader, 'Unruly felons and civilizing wives: Cultivating marriage in the Siberian exile system, 1822–1860,' p. 251.

[111] 'Unruly felons and civilizing wives: Cultivating marriage in the Siberian exile system, 1822–1860', p. 239.

tool, rather than an agent, for civilizing exiles. The authorities believed that marriage made exiles more stable and less likely to escape: 'Singletons, when it comes to escape, are a much less reliable element than the married.'[112]

A grant of fifty roubles was offered by the state towards the costs of establishing a household for exile settlers who got married, as an incentive for marriage.[113] Exiles and their prospective spouses were well aware of these provisions. Anna Terentina Bartinova was a former katorzhanka who had been settled in Viliuisk region. She wrote to the Yakutsk governor on 30 January 1910:

> I the below signed girl, having completed my term of katorga work, live in settlement in Antonovsk, and have special relations with the administrative-exile Stepanov Iva-novich Vakhtin, and wish to marry him, in view of this I request that you send me the sum of 50 roubles, as a settler entering into legal marriage, a sum given to settlers when they marry, for the first necessary expenses for the establishment of the household; further, I ask you about the assigning to me, as the wife of an administrative-exile, monthly means, for the term of exile of my husband; and also I ask that you clarify to me the following; can I, as a settler, after the completion of my husband's term of exile, settle in any named place of residence in Russia? (Written on her behalf because of her illiteracy.)[114]

This letter illustrates a canny awareness of the possible advantages of marriage, and fed into the discourses that developed between the authorities and the punished on questions of rights and delineations of punishment.

There are some examples of love found and lost that emerge from the archives. A former exile, Teterin, suggested that the handsome young men among the political exiles turned the heads of the local women in Kirensk district. While he emphasized the value local residents placed upon exiles' culture and education in general, he suggested that the local women particularly valued the political men's moral codes and values. Teterin recalled that political exiles

> did not get drunk, were not debauched, they did not swear foully, and they kept their clothes and dwellings clean and tidy, and in their free time they read books, helped one another in need, not just relatives, but those around them.

We can certainly question Teterin's romantic view of the political exiles; it is hard to imagine that they all maintained the high standards that he indicated here. Teterin's recollections of *chastushki* (songs) heard around the village do however ring true, and give us a rare glimpse of women's voices, and the romantic interest that these newcomers may have attracted:

> I stand before the window,
> I see myself,
> I love a political,
> I don't see my husband.

[112] GAIO f. 25, op. 6, d. 5385, p. 404, note from Eniseisk governor, 28 April 1911.
[113] Kraft, *Zakony i pravila o ssyl'no-poselentsev i ikh semeistvakh*, p. 31.
[114] NARS f. 12, op. 2, d. 4693, p. 252, letter to Yakutsk governor from Anna Terenteva Bartinova, unmarried girl (*devitsa*), 30 January 1910.

> I walk along the street,
> I trip over a stone,
> I love a political,
> I forget my husband.
>
> I love a political,
> He goes around smartly,
> In his black suit,
> I'll go out of my mind.
>
> Oh, oh, please god don't,
> Get to know a political,
> They are arrested, and sent away,
> It is hard to be parted.

Teterin suggested that the local women were enthralled by the politicals, particularly because of the contrast between them and the coarse local men. The local men themselves would no doubt have noted such unfavourable comparisons. A song sung by young men,

> Our girls have learned,
> To wear tight skirts,
> Our girls have learned,
> To go [have an affair] with the politicals.

We do not know how these songs were heard, or recorded, or how they were received. This is a common problem for any ethnographic material collected in this period; Teterin could have misheard or misrepresented these verses—they certainly served his own agenda of lionizing Siberia's exiles. Despite this note of doubt, the songs give us an elusive glimpse into the intimate sphere of interactions between exiles and native Siberians, and hints at the cultural and personal tensions that exiles could provoke among native Siberian communities.[115]

We have some other fragments of romantic life and misadventure in exile. Anna Nazarova Evstratova, a peasant from Kaluzha province, apparently found love in Siberia. She was sent to Eniseisk province for settlement by Kiev court for membership of an illegal political party. She married the former Justice of the Peace, Karl Petrov in 1913, and the couple was granted permission to live in Irkutsk in 1914.[116] Anna Galitskaia was a peasant from Minsk region, who was sentenced to six years in katorga followed by exile in 1906, when she was only nineteen. She gave birth to a son, Nikolai, while still serving her katorga sentence, on 7 May 1911. She successfully petitioned Irkutsk's military governor in January 1913 to settle her in Yakutsk region on completion of her katorga term, so that she could follow her lover Andreev, another exile settler. On arriving on 13 June 1913 at her place of exile, Galitskaia could not find Andreev. She subsequently found out that

[115] Teterin, 'Politicheskaia ssylka i narodnoi poezii Kirenskago uezda'.
[116] GAIO f. 600, op. 1, d. 802, p. 75, report from captain of Eniseisk prison inspection to the Captain of Irkutsk police administration, 20 January 1914.

Andreev was already married and that he refused to support her. 'Having in her arms a little child and remaining without any assistance and not having any means for life, Galitskaia sought to get out of this situation through transfer to Verkhne-udinsk district, where it's considered that she had the possibility of a better existence.' Her petition was granted.[117]

CHILDREN

A substantial number of children entered the exile system, though we lack precise figures on their numbers in the early twentieth century.[118] One statistic that gives an indicator of the number of children born to exile families comes from Yakutsk in 1917, when the Yakutsk governor petitioned the Provisional Government to provide financial support for criminal exiles and their families to be evacuated from Yakutsk. One list recorded 771 criminal exiles, accompanied by 521 family members.[119] The state sought to show compassion to children associated with exiles, and to ameliorate the impact of their carers' punishment; there were provisions providing for spouses and children, and protecting nursing mothers.[120] In practice, the funding and infrastructure in eastern Siberia was unable to provide adequately for exiles' children. The state's concern about children was, however, reflected in the language of exiles' petitions, which sought to draw on the language of pity in order to engage with the state.[121]

There is evidence that the state considered family status as a factor for lessening burdens of exile, and that exiles themselves utilized the language of pity and appealed to the state directly in relation to their family situation. These petitions enable us to draw out the narratives created by exiles themselves. Varvara Fedor-ovna Pliuchareva was the wife of the exile settler Aleksandr Denisov Pliucharev. She wrote to Ivan Ivanovich Kraft, the governor of Yakutsk, on 27 June 1909 to appeal for permission for her husband to live in Yakutsk town. She explained that they had been living in Olekminsk region for five years. Her husband was a joiner, and had been unable to find any paid work in his trade, and they had two daughters to support.[122] Gavril Sergeev Larionov, an exile-settler from Olekminsk region, was sent to Zhedaisk village on 12 June 1910, and was accompanied by his wife and

---

[117] GAIO f. 25, op. 6, d. 5385, pp. 208–14; Letter from Yakutsk governor to Irkutsk military governor, 29 February 1916.

[118] Andrew Gentes presents a preliminary demographic analysis of children in the exile system in the nineteenth century (Gentes, 'Towards a demography of children in the Tsarist Siberian Exile System').

[119] Kazarian, *Iakutiia v sisteme politicheskoi ssylki Rossii 1826–1917 gg*, p. 276.

[120] Kraft, *Zakony i pravila o ssyl'no-poselentsev i ikh semeistvakh*, pp. 32–6.

[121] For study of petitioning in other contexts, see Emily E. Pyle, 'Peasant strategies for obtaining State aid: A study of petitions during World War One,' *Russian History-Histoire Russe*, no. 1–2 (1997); Golfo Alexopolous, 'The Ritual Lament: A Narrative of Appeal in the 1920s and 1930s,' *Russian History*, no. 24 (1997).

[122] NARS f. 12, op. 2, d. 4693, p. 19, letter to Yakutsk governor from Varvara Fedorovna Pliucharev, 27 June 1909.

four young children. Larionov busied himself with fishing, hunting, and market gardening, but he had no means to sow land, and as a result of this, coupled with the year's harvest failure and rises in grain prices, he was in poverty and falling to destitution, despite his hard work and good conduct.[123] The nobleman and engineer Vladimir Alexandrov Voznesenskii, who was sentenced to exile in Yakutsk region for five years for state crimes on 26 April 1900, was given leave to remain in Yakutsk town by the Yakutsk governor 'because of his family situation'; he was accompanied by his wife and eighteen-month-old son.[124] These individual petitions give us a sense of the personal suffering and individual struggles that exile families underwent. The case of Voznesenskii indicates that in some cases at least, the authorities tried to ameliorate the lives of exile families.

Siberia's tiny civil society was energized and mobilized by the plight of exiles' children. Catriona Kelly, in her study of childhood in Russia, noted that it became 'fashionable' to be involved in children's issues in late Imperial polite society, and that children's charities attracted supporters from both radical and conservative elements in society.[125] The women's section of the Society of Prison Trustees in Irkutsk province devoted itself exclusively to the care of prisoners' children, and founded an orphanage for them in Irkutsk. Existing buildings were used, and it held between fifty and seventy children. In 1913, the average number of children in care was fifty-three, of whom thirty-six were girls and seventeen boys. The orphanage provided primary education and taught the children various trades, including shoemaking and bookbinding. There were ten employees in the orphanage, including one female teacher and two trade teachers. This emphasis on training for trades and manual work was a feature of late Imperial institutions for lower class children, and reflected societal desires to prepare children for a moral hard working life.[126] Means for the orphanage came from state contributions for feeding the children, and charitable donations, which reportedly dwindled in the few years leading up to 1913. The women's section was unable to provide for all the needy children in the region, so in 1912 Irkutsk prison formed a prison orphanage that took those children that had not been able to get a place in the women's section orphanage. The prison orphanage was housed in the prison itself, and housed, on average, fifteen children.[127]

Funds were raised for the establishment of a maternity unit (*rodil'nyi priiut*) for Irkutsk prisoners and exiles. It was built in the grounds of Aleksandrovsk prison, together with the prison chemist and outpatients' department. In the course of a year, there were twenty-eight births, of which twenty-four were exile-katorga

---

[123] NARS f. 12, op. 2, d. 5619, p. 35, Verification from Zhedaiskii village elder, Nokhtuisk township, Olekminsk region, regarding Gavril Sergeev Larionov, 18 January 1911.

[124] NARS f. 12, op. 10, d. 25, pp. 6–7, p. 12, form describing Vladimir Alexandrov Voznesenskii.

[125] Kelly, *Children's world: growing up in Russia, 1890–1991*, p. 164, p. 174. See also, Brenda Meehan, 'From contemplative practice to charitable activity: Russian women's religious communities and the development of charitable work, 1861–1917,' in *Lady Bountiful revisited: Women, philanthropy and power*, ed. Kathleen D. McCarthy (Brunswick NJ, 1990).

[126] Kelly, *Children's world: growing up in Russia, 1890–1991*, pp. 168, 179.

[127] *Polozhenie tiuremnoi chasti i ssylki v Irkutskoi gubernii po dannym dokladov tiuremnago inspektora, 1911–1913gg*, p. 98.

families. There were no deaths.[128] The hospital, maternity room, and children's orphanage were still operating in 1914. These provisions were paid for by an annual subsidy taken from the general capital for exiles. Exile children of school age went to school alongside the guards' children from both the Aleksandrovsk prisons.[129]

Yakutsk town orphanage for the children of exiles and arrestees was in principle financed by Yakutsk's prison committee, but in practice these means were not sufficient for the number of children requiring care.[130] The orphanage was equipped for ten children, but eighteen children were resident in October 1907. The president of the orphanage's council reported that the additional children had no beds, or clothes or crockery, as the institution's means were exhausted.[131] The budget allowed specific daily sums for the maintenance of each child, which was proscribed in much the same way as prison diets. The finances of the orphanage were apparently parlous, and relied heavily on charitable donations. The president of the orphanage's soviet wrote to the president of Yakutsk's charitable society in October 1907:

> all the material finances of the orphanage have been exhausted. Recently the orphanage was allocated 200 roubles by the Circle of Lovers of Music and Literature, but these means barely suffice for the improvement of food and the repair of clothes, for the establishment of a necessary inventory and for clothes for the ten new arrivals from exile-settler [families]. The orphanage has absolutely no means. Taking into consideration that the children from exile [families] that we have taken in are clients of the Yakutsk Charitable Society, that the orphanage, apart from shelter and food cannot give any more due to lack of means, humbly ask you to put to the Charitable Society if it cannot find means to come to the help of the orphanage, or assign for the use of the council of the orphanage the sum of 624 roubles.[132]

The prison committee assigned money to the orphanage fund.[133] There is evidence that Yakutsk's civil society were very warm towards this cause, and made lively efforts to support the orphanage. As well as direct donations of food and fabric, the orphanage's council successfully mobilized society in charitable efforts.[134] The orphanage's board was very active—its meetings were extremely well attended, with almost all twenty board members attending every meeting.[135] A lottery-raffle was organized regularly, and seems to have attracted support from businesses and

[128] Khrulev, *Katorga v Sibiri: Izvlechenie iz otcheta nachal'nika glavnago tiuremnago upravlenie S.S. Khruleva o sluzhebnoi poezdke, v 1909 godu, v Irkutskoi gub. i Zabaikalskuiu obl.*

[129] *Polozhenie tiuremnoi chasti i ssylki v Irkutskoi gubernii po dannym dokladov tiuremnago inspektora, 1911–1913gg.*

[130] NARS f. 15, op. 10, d. 2731, pp. 8–9, information about the situation of prison churches, schools, general lessons, and libraries for prisoners, Yakutsk prison, 1913.

[131] NARS f. 206, op. 1, d. 562, p. 1, Letter from president of soviet of orphanage for arrested children to the president of Yakutsk charitable society, October 1907.

[132] NARS f. 206, op. 1, d. 562, p. 1, Letter from president of council of orphanage for arrested children to the president of Yakutsk charitable society, October 1907.

[133] NARS f. 15, op. 8, d. 86, p. 1, Letter from Chancery of prison committee, Yakutsk, to the Yakutsk orphanage council, 17 January 1907.

[134] NARS f. 15, op. 8, d. 86, p. 4, Advance receipt for goods received by the president of the Yakutsk orphanage council, 7 February 1907.

[135] NARS f. 509, op. 1, d. 8, Journal of the Yakutsk orphanage council, for 1909.

individuals in Yakutsk. Accounts record the items donated, and the size of cash donations, which gives an insight into societal interest in this particular cause. K.A. Averenskii and Co., for example, a fancy goods store, donated goods to the value of thirty-six roubles, including a photo album, two bouquets of flowers, and a paper lampshade.[136] Captain Akutskii donated a silver wine glass, a silver salt pot, a teapot, a dessertspoon, an ashtray, and a brooch, to the value of twenty-six roubles.[137] The lists of donations to the annual lottery show that shops and individuals donated funds. In 1909, the lottery-raffle raised 1,010 roubles, and attracted goods to the value of 168 roubles 52 kopeks.[138] One Yakutsk resident sent a curious letter to the Yakutsk administration. He had heard that they needed a typewriter, and that he was able to donate his own machine, a 'Remmington special, on condition that 100 roubles be given to the orphanage, and a further 175 roubles be paid to the author'. There is no response on record, so we do not know if the government office took up this offer.[139]

The number of children in the orphanage fluctuated significantly, depending on the season; significant numbers of exile-settlers' children were expected in the winter months, when families found the challenges of daily life particularly over-whelming. In 1907, the numbers varied from eight children on 1st April, to twenty-one children in November. That children were placed in the orphanage by living parents is indicative of extreme levels of poverty, as the orphanage was clearly regarded as an absolute last resort. Children were placed in the orphanage by parents sometimes for a matter of weeks before being withdrawn again, which indicates that parents used the orphanage when they were no longer able to provide for their children, but then withdrew them again as soon as they were able. The prisoner Aleksandr Belenkov wrote from his prison cell in Yakutsk to Yakutsk prison committee, asking that his three children, as he put it, 'confined in the Yakutsk orphanage for arrestees' children, be released and given over to my wife Paraskova Belenkova'.[140]

Information on the children enrolled in the orphanage, and the conditions of their life there, are extremely patchy. Based on what we know of the operation of orphanages in the late Imperial period, the character of orphanages was usually ascetic, and moral education and training were highlighted over comfort and care. Although there were significant disparities between institutions, orphanages tended to be run primarily as corrective institutions. Societal assumptions about the genetic components of criminality may have made provisions for prisoners and exiles' children particularly severe. On the other hand, recent historical studies suggest that attitudes towards abandoned children shifted in the late Imperial

[136] NARS f. 15, op. 8, d. 87, p. 12, receipt from K.A. Averenskii and co., trading house.
[137] NARS, f.15, op. 8, d. 87, p. 13, list of goods donated for the lottery fund.
[138] NARS f. 509, op. 1, d. 8, p. 9, Journal of the Yakutsk orphanage council, meeting of 9 May 1909.
[139] NARS f. 12, op. 2, d. 2102, p. 214, letter to his honour Andrei Innokentevich Popov, 4 December 1903.
[140] NARS f. 15, op. 8, d. 86, p. 19, handwritten letter from Alexander Belenkov to Yakutsk prison committee, 7 February 1907.

period, away from an emphasis on the children as a social threat in need of discipline, and towards a sense that they were needy individuals who required care and family love.[141]

The children in Yakutsk's orphanage ranged in age from two to sixteen, and most were boys. Sibling groups often arrived together; in January 1907, there were 13 children enrolled in the orphanage. There were four Kazyrov siblings, ranging in age from three to fourteen. Their father was in prison.[142] There were the five Belenkov siblings, ranging in age from three to thirteen.[143] In October 1907, three Dublinskii children were enrolled, Fedor, age thirteen, Yazik, aged nine, and Raisa, aged eight, when their exile-settler father died.[144] Two Nikulina children who were in the orphanage in August 1907 had both parents in prison. Petr and Anna Dinisimov were the orphans of a father who had died in prison. Mikhail Tiulenev was the son of an exile-settler. Klavdiia and Aleksandra Dobroklenskaia, aged five and eight, were admitted to the orphanage at the end of July 1907. Their mother's letter to the Yakutsk governor elaborates on the conditions of their enrolment. Their father Nikolai Dobroklonskii, an exile-settler from Viliuisk region, was murdered in his home. His widow explained her situation:

> I was left to the mercy of the court with three small children; all my husband's property has been sold, because I needed money for the children. About two months ago I went to Sunmarsk village but I didn't receive any money. Now I am absolutely without means for existence and for the sustenance of my children. I ask that two of the children be taken into the orphanage; two girls aged 5 and 7, at the expense of the state.

The police chief confirmed on the back of her letter that she had absolutely no means, and was unable to work as she had to care for the children.[145] Such official responses to petitions were sometimes, but not always, recorded. In this case, the police chief's intervention clearly supported the petitioner's request.

Those members of Yakutsk society who took an active role in the orphanage were granted public and national recognition for their good works, with the awards of medals and special orders by the Yakutsk governor. Maria Nikolaevna Gribanovskaia was a doctor's widow, and managed the orphanage between 1897 and 1899, then again from 1908 until 1912. She was fifty-one in 1912, and was awarded a silver medal of Stanislavskii in that year. The description praising her conduct is rather chilling, and gives a Dickensian flavour to our imaginings of the orphanage:

> In relation to her duties as overseer of the orphanage, for all the time of her service the orphanage has been placed at the proper elevation, having the necessary authority to establish and defend sensible discipline, not shirking from measures of special severity,

[141] Kelly, *Children's world: growing up in Russia, 1890–1991*, pp. 157–92. A. Lindenmeyr, *Poverty is not a Vice: Charity, society and the State in Late Imperial Russia* (Princeton, 1996), pp. 222–3.
[142] NARS f. 15, op. 8, d. 86, p. 185, List of children in the orphanage for August 1907.
[143] NARS f. 15, op. 8, d. 86, p. 13, List of children in the orphanage, 1 January–1 February 1907.
[144] NARS f. 15, op. 8, d. 86, p. 212, List of children in the orphanage for October 1907.
[145] NARS f. 15, op. 8, d. 86, p. 145, Letter to Yakutsk governor from widow of Nikolai Dobroklonskii, 22 July 1907.

she has done and continued to do much in order that an appreciation of useful work be instilled into her charges, and she is diligent and accurate in the discharge of her duties.[146]

The Salmanoviches were less gloomy awardees; Josephine served as a trustee, and Vladislav was president of the Soviet. They were originally from Vilensk, and were nobles. Both had donated substantial sums for the improvement of the orphanage, and were active in its organization and management. Vladislav, who had already been granted multiple orders of Stanislav for his good works, was reported to have improved conditions in the orphanage, and increased the number of children that could be cared for. His wife Josephine was awarded a gold medal:

> Having been appointed trustee, she has set about her duties with intelligence and love, so that she can be described as one of the leading figures within the orphanage, for the last year she has been president of the Soviet of the orphanage. She gives more than 2,000 roubles per year to the orphanage, and gives a mass of energy and labour, which has improved not only the internal appearance of the orphanage, but its means so that the establishment's reach can be significantly broadened.[147]

The care provided for exile children provides an insight into both the material and spiritual conditions experienced by eastern Siberian exiles, and into the attitudes of eastern Siberia's nascent civic society in their attempts to provide care for the unfortunates' children. The fate of these children allows us to explore the implications of location, poverty, and isolation for exiles.

CONCLUSIONS

This chapter has questioned prevailing assumptions about the relationships between exiles and the community around them. Exiles, political and criminal, put pressure on the resources of strained eastern Siberian communities. The historiography is overwhelmingly dominated by discussions of the benefits that political exiles brought to eastern Siberia. The discourse of local governors and administrators, however, focused on the negative implications of exile in their region, as they struggled, and ultimately failed, to control and manage the exile population. Local governors sought to reduce and even end their region's use as places of exile, so their development of a narrative that emphasized the negative aspects of exile could be seen as a strategy for them to meet their goals. Their impressions of exile harmonized with the perspectives of the Siberian regionalists. This chapter's look at the impact of exile from a local perspective corroborates their views that exile was overall deleterious to the region.

---

[146] NARS, f. 206, op. 1, d. 610, pp. 7–8, List of prizes for charitable and generally healthy activities in the employment of the Ministry of Justice, January 1912.

[147] NARS, f. 206, op. 1, d. 610, pp. 47–8, List of prizes for charitable and generally healthy activities in the employment of the Ministry of Justice, 17 May 1912.

Political exile memoirs claimed that the exiles brought 'light to the darkness' of eastern Siberia. The political exiles' attitudes towards native Siberians, both ethnically Russian and especially *inorodtsy*, were profoundly pejorative. These derogatory attitudes are reminiscent of educated Russians' attitudes towards the rural population in the late Imperial period.[148] Attitudes towards eastern Siberia's *inorodtsy* population intersect with attitudes both in Russia and across the western empires towards so-called 'uncivilized' peoples. This cultural imperialism enabled incomers, whether they were exiles or colonizers, to reinforce their own sense of superiority, and to vindicate their subjugation of indigenous peoples.[149] In our case, the political exiles' cultural imperialism limited their ability to interact meaningfully with native Siberians. Alongside the challenges of communication and interaction, the material burden that exiles represented can only have further limited their capacity to contribute and engage with many local communities.

The state sought to 'know' their political exiles. This desire to know reflected a desire to control. In practice, though, the state had very weak supervisory networks, and failed to know and track its population effectively. The communities of political exiles that developed in remote locations around eastern Siberia are testament to the state's failure to control and govern exile. The primary objective of political exile was to isolate the offenders both from each other and from the rest of society. Exiles ultimately defied this isolation, and met their human needs to interact and to share lives. The state was less engaged by the project of supervising and overseeing criminal exiles. Criminal exiles are intriguing by their absence in our sources. They are systematically written out of the political exiles' self-penned narratives, and they receive only the most perfunctory treatment in the historiography. We find glimpses of their lives in this chapter, but ultimately their human networks and personal trajectories remain unknown.

The exile communities that developed allow us to explore the exiles' strategies to develop coping mechanisms in challenging emotional and environmental conditions. We see that communities sought to meet material needs, in shared housing, pooled resources and mutual financial support, and spiritual needs, through shared reading materials and social events. While comradely spirit was often the defining feature of exile memoirs, contestation and hostility between exiles emerges as a key theme. Exiles' shared persecution and shared material circumstances did not necessarily override differences and dispute among individuals and among political groupings. Squabbling and discord were as much a part of exile life as friendship and mutual support. Finally, we are able to glimpse into the exiles' intimate sphere, through their relationships with spouses, lovers, and children. These glimpses give us a unique insight into the human costs and challenges of daily life in exile.

---

[148] Frierson, *Peasant Icons: Representations of rural people in late nineteenth century Russia*, for a definitive discussion of this problem.

[149] For an exploration of this, see for example Edward W. Said, *Culture and imperialism* (New York, 1993).

4

'Taming the Wild Taiga'
Work and Escape in Siberian Exile

For many exiles, once out of prison they roam extensively around the districts, either looking for work, or because a nomadic existence suits them. They beg for charity, and if they cannot get that, they may resort to a range of crimes to get means for their subsistence.

(Letter to the Chancery of Irkutsk military governor, from Irkutsk prison inspector, January 1908)[1]

The defining features of daily life for most exiles were the search for work, the practice of work, and unemployment. To live, you had to somehow earn money for your living expenses. Eastern Siberia, however, offered very few opportunities for paid employment, even in its urban centres. The challenge of finding work was particularly acute for the post-1905 generation of political exiles, who were predominantly from urban, working-class backgrounds. Unemployment was commonplace, and was a state that ensured utter penury for exiles. Unemployment also ensured that exiles inflicted the maximum possible burden on the communities that they settled alongside. The negative impact of exiles on eastern Siberia was a constant refrain from the region's governors, and they explicitly connected this with the lack of work available in the region for exiles. Escape was in some respects a corollary to the search for work. While some escape narratives were shaped around dramatic exits from the region, many unauthorized absences were a side effect of exiles' mobility.

As we have seen in chapter 3 on communities, exiles constituted a significant burden on the region. This burden was intimately connected with the lack of paid employment available for exiles. Those with agricultural skills and experience struggled to establish viable homesteads because of limited land availability and harsh conditions. Those from urban backgrounds were blighted by unemployment, as their urban trades and skills could not find a place in eastern Siberia, which was characterized by little major industry, very underdeveloped towns, and a small urban population. Russia's central administrators, regional governors, prison reformers, and exiles themselves all stressed the importance of useful labour in exile.[2] This

---

[1] GAIO, f. 25, op. 6, d. 3104, p. 10, letter from Irkutsk Prison inspector to Chancery of Irkutsk military governor, 9 January 1908.

[2] For example, I.A. Malinovskii, *Ssylka v Sibir. Publichnaia lektsiia. Chitaniia v Tomske v Noiabre 1899 goda* (Tomsk, 1900)—this focused on the unhealthy impact of exiles on the region and their lack of facility for work; NARS, f. 12, op. 2, d. 4693, p. 254; letter from Yakutsk townsman Mitrofan

resonates with the discourse of penal policies in an international context, which sought to place useful work at the heart of both punishment and reform. Without work, exiles could never be settlers, only beggars and nomads. The state of the exile system attracted significant attention from reformers and activists within state bounds and outside. All were agreed on the woeful inadequacies of the system, whether taken from the perspective of efficient punishment, humane conditions, or effective settlement. Work highlights some of the central contradictions that beset state policy towards the use of Siberia. The government was ambiguous in its desire to settle Siberia for constructive economic development, and in its use of Siberia as a dumping ground for the punished. If the use of Siberia as a place of settlement as well as punishment was to be effective, then exiles had to work.

We have already heard in chapter 3 how the lived experience of exile was heavily determined by the extent of material support that exiles enjoyed. The dominance of well-known political exiles' accounts has left a distorted picture of daily life in exile. Many of the better-known political exiles recalled exile as a place for leisure, study, and reflection. Ekaterina Breshkovskaia sets the tone with her account of Barzugin, on the eastern shores of Lake Baikal in 1879. She became acquainted with young exiles in Barzugin who were clearly handsomely provided for financially. She commented waspishly that they whiled away their exile sentence going hunting, and the pursuit of 'wine, women and song'. They were popular with the inhabitants of Barzugin because 'they paid well for the least service and gladly shared anything they had'. She herself did not take any paid work, and never referred to financial need.[3] This model, of political exiles as wealthy people, who were handsomely supported from home or from comrades, is enduring. Vladimir Zenzinov, in his distant Yakutsk exile in 1911, whiled away his time with study, writing, expeditions, and natural history.[4] The vast majority of exiles, political and criminal, had no private means. The enforced leisure and study time recalled by Zenzinov, Dan, and others, did not epitomize the experiences of most exiles. Accounts from official sources and from exiles themselves reveal a desperate daily struggle to keep body and soul together, and to try and stay alive.

PATTERNS OF EMPLOYMENT

The working patterns of political exiles are described in observers' reports, Siberian official reports, and biographical data. The challenges of finding paid employment in eastern Siberia were common to criminal and political prisoners alike. The sources are unfortunately almost silent on the activities of criminal exiles, except

---

Serovatskii asking that his three children be taken into the town orphanage so that they could be 'workers not parasites', 22 March 1910. RGASPI, f. 459, op. 1, d. 40, p. 1; The London Committee for the Assistance of Political Prisoners, in its appeal of 5 April 1915, stressed the 'conditions of chronic unemployment' that exiles lived in.

[3] Breshko-Breshkovskaia, *Hidden Springs of the Russian Revolution*, pp. 211, 215.
[4] Zenzinov, *The road to oblivion*.

to emphasize their proclivity for crime and vagabondage. Those criminals who did find paid employment would have worked predominantly in unskilled labour, in mines, railways, agriculture, and labouring.

The members' list of the society for former political prisoners and exiles provides a quantitative indicator of patterns of work in eastern Siberian exile for political exiles.[5] The sample presented here draws on the biographical data presented for 299 members who were exiled to eastern Siberian locations including Irkutsk, Yakutsk, and the Zabaikal region, and who were affiliated with the Socialist Revolutionary party. Thirty-eight women are included in the sample. Records of employment in exile are larger than the records for employment at home, because some exiles listed multiple jobs, and these have all been entered here. This data is not comprehensive or conclusive; not all exiles subsequently joined the society, and the Socialist Revolutionaries who made up this selection may not represent the broader socio-economic pattern of exiles. Still, the detailed biographical information about these individuals enables us to get some sense of the occupational pathways taken by eastern Siberian exiles (see Figure 4.1).

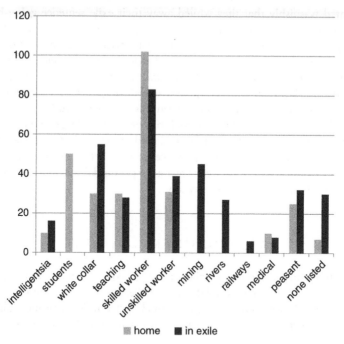

Figure 4.1. Occupations of 299 political exiles before arrest, and in exile in eastern Siberia, 1902–17

[5] M.M. Konstantinov and F.M. Tochilin (eds.) *Politicheskaia katorga i ssylka: Biograficheskii spravochnik chlenov obshchestva politkatorzhan i ssyl'no-poselentsev* (Moscow, 1934).

The data shows that manual labour of various kinds made up an absolute majority of exile jobs—62 per cent of exile jobs came within this category, while 56 per cent of exiles were in manual professions before arrest.[6] Around 29 per cent of exile jobs came from intellectual labour, while around 43 per cent of exiles were in intellectual work before arrest.[7] These statistics obfuscate key features of exile working life. First, while the biographical information listed various occupations undertaken by individuals in exile, this did not mean that these occupations were long-term or full-time. Many of those working in white-collar jobs and teaching were also employed in manual work at some time. The work history of I.N. Sergeev, a fitter from Tambov, exemplifies this occupational mobility. Sergeev was exiled to Irkutsk in 1907. He initially worked as an unskilled worker, a fitter, and a bookbinder. He was employed as an instructor in a cooperative in 1916, and in 1917 worked as a shop assistant and as a bookkeeper on the river Lena.

Teaching was often cited by exiles as providing employment, but of the twenty-eight individuals who listed teaching as their job, not one of them had a salaried post. State regulations were ambivalent on allowing political exiles to take employment as exiles. Many exiles did teach, but this was sometimes in contravention of local guidelines. Exiles' teaching work usually involved offering piecemeal lessons to local children, and was paid ad hoc. It was very unlikely to provide enough income to live on. N.N. Davydov, for example, a university student from Simbirsk, was arrested in 1906 and exiled to Irkutsk. He worked as a peasant, taught children to read and write, and was employed as a statistician in Irkutsk. R.M. Raukhman, a shoemaker from Dvinsk in Latvia, was arrested in 1907 and exiled to Irkutsk. In exile, he made shoes, worked as a peasant, worked in the mines, and from 1912 taught in the villages.[8]

Siberia's great rivers provided an important source of employment for exiles. The river Lena was eastern Siberia's most important waterway, and her only navigable thoroughfare to the north. All trade to the northern provinces, and all population movement, came along the Lena and its tributaries. Twenty-seven exiles, or 9 per cent of all exiles in the sample, worked on the rivers. The waterways were only navigable between May and September, when it was fully thawed; most river work took place in a very short season. For the rest of the year, exiles had to seek alternative employment. Exiles worked on the rivers as dockers and stokers, as sailors and river clerks. They built boats, and broke them down again. They fitted out steamers, and worked on the river rafts. S.I. Neumeichev, a teacher from Voronezh exiled to the region in 1907, worked on the steamers of the Lena first as a sailor, and then as a clerk, up until 1917.[9] One political exile described how, in the winter,

[6] Two hundred and thirty two of the 369 exile jobs listed fell under the category of manual labour (skilled and unskilled work, mines, rivers, railways, peasant); 176 of the 299 pre-arrest jobs listed fell under this category.
[7] Of the 369 jobs listed, 107 fell under the category of intellectual labour (white-collar work, intelligentsia professions, teaching, and medical work); 130 of the 299 pre-arrest jobs listed fell under this category.
[8] Konstantinov, *Politicheskaia katorga i ssylka*.
[9] Konstantinov, *Politicheskaia katorga i ssylka*.

he dreamed of the work opportunities that would be available in the summer, which would provide some income, and which provided the pleasure of physical labour, 'carrying bags at the port, loading and unloading barges with comrades'.[10] The density of exile employment on the river incidentally provides some explanation for the high rate of escape from eastern Siberia; friendly faces on the only transport out of the region were a great asset to would-be absconders. An official report on escapes from Yakutsk province in 1913 noted, '[Political exiles] almost always [escaped] with the assistance of the steamer company, especially the steamer of A.M. Gromov. Most of the employees of this company, with the exception of simple workers, are political exiles and people associated with them.'[11]

Many exiles worked in the mining industry at some time. Fifteen per cent of the sample's 299 political exiles worked in the mines as their chief occupation, and for some it was their sole occupation. Eastern Siberia rested on a great wealth of mineral resources. There was a range of mining enterprises in the region, producing salt, coal, tungsten, nonferrous metals, and gold and semi-precious stones.[12] A number of accounts commented that many exiles resorted to travelling around the region from one mining area to the next to secure paid employment. A party of exiles arriving in Yakutsk in September 1908, for example, lost no time in making requests for special permission to move away from their place of settlement, and to try their luck finding work in the goldmines in the mountainous regions of Olekminsk and Vitimsk.[13] M.S. Mirnyi, a white-collar worker who was exiled to Irkutsk in 1906, travelled around the region as a miner, working first in the salt-works at Ust-Kute, then in 1913–15 in Vitimsk mining region, and finally the Lena mines between 1915 and 1917.[14] Numerous reports attest to the highly injurious conditions in mines, which contributed to a rapid deterioration of workers' health.[15] Ivan Ivanovich Kraft, the governor of Yakutsk, commented that:

> Those who go into the gold mines are quickly turned from workers into invalids by the difficult working conditions and extremely adverse sanitary conditions. This is the reason that such a high proportion of exiles require charity and care. These places strain them to death.[16]

Petr Iakubovich, a hard labour convict, wrote a detailed account of his experiences working in the mines of Akatui, one of the Nerchinsk katorga prisons, in 1891. We can use this to gain some sense of conditions for miners more generally. Iakubovich's recollections of mining (for lead-silver ore) dwelled on the cold,

[10] Cherkunov, 'Zhizn politicheskoi ssylki i tiur'mi po perekhvachennym pis'mam', p. 174.

[11] NARS 12, 21, 168, letter to Irkutsk police from Yakutsk governor, 12 July 1914, pp. 15–16.

[12] N.L. Zhukovskaia, *Istoriko-kul'turnyi atlas Buriatii* (Moscow, 2001), p. 210; V.N. Ivanov, *Istoriko-kul'turnyi atlas Yakutiia*, ed. V.N. Ivanov (Moscow, 2007), p. 47.

[13] NARS, f. 15, op. 18, d. 191, pp. 153–4; Note from Yakutsk police administration to Yakutsk region administration, 16 September 1908.

[14] Konstantinov, *Politicheskaia katorga i ssylka*.

[15] Sokolov, 'Sibir i ssylka', p. 43, commented that mine workers suffered from scurvy and illnesses from eating worm-ridden meat.

[16] GAIO, f. 25, op. 6, d. 3136, p. 11. Report from Governor Kraft to Irkutsk military governor, 18 June 1907.

damp, dark conditions, and the skill and physical strength needed to bore holes in the rock faces.

> The mines were cold and damp and dark to the unaccustomed eye; only, the stench was less than I'd first expected: the fetid water had been drained and the ice on top of the first, filthy layer, already punctured by Semenov's and Rakitin's hacks, was white and pure as sugar . . . "So this is what a mine is!" I thought, shivering from the cold and contemplating in secret fear having to be in this cellar for five or six hours a day.[17]

Iakubovich went on to describe the processes of chiselling at the cliff face by hand, and pounding the blasted holes, and his own ineptness at this task compared to the criminal prisoners around him. His description of the criminal prisoner's physical prowess contrasted with his own feebleness:

> I struck it four times, but my blows were so childishly weak and clumsy that I felt quite ashamed of my efforts and, hearing the general laughter, let the sledgehammer fall to the ground. All the same, I was gasping for air and unsteady on my feet after these four blows. Nogaitsev began pounding after me. I expected something clumsy and ridiculous from his awkward, ursine physique, but to my surprise, I had to admire him as well. His labour, too, displayed an agile, poetic strength, and also summoned up a hero of fabled times . . . I could barely avert my eyes from admiring these 'children of nature'![18]

This contrast between the physically strong and capable criminal prisoners, who were almost all from lower class backgrounds, and Iakubovich, a privileged and educated nobleman, who lacked a robust physique and lacked familiarity with physical labour, was one that was frequently drawn. In this source, Iakubovich may be describing the physical prowess of the criminal prisoners as a means to distance himself from them—their animal strength echoes the 'primitive savage' rhetoric that Iakubovich sometimes employed in his descriptions of criminal prisoners. Regardless of these undercurrents in Iakubovich's prose, a number of sources comment that life in exile was more difficult for those in intelligentsia professions, as they were less versatile in taking job opportunities than industrial workers. They were subject to restrictions from the authorities on practising their professions, as doctors or as lawyers, for example, because of the perceived risk they posed in 'propagandizing' among the native population.[19] There were very limited opportunities for literate work in eastern Siberia's small and underdeveloped towns. Much of it was in white-collar work, as shop assistants, bookkeepers, clerks, and scribes. Though some individuals held one job for their period of exile, many went through between two and five jobs, and all endured unemployment. This instability of occupation beset all levels of occupation. One political exile suggested that employers preferred to employ political exiles, because they worked more quickly and did not get drunk, though I did not see any further evidence for this.[20]

[17] Iakubovich, *In the world of the outcasts: notes of a former penal laborer*, volume 1, p. 63.
[18] *In the world of the outcasts: notes of a former penal laborer*, volume 1, p. 74.
[19] Bagotskii, 'Krakovskii soiuz pomoshchi politicheskim zakliuchennym'.
[20] Cherkunov, 'Zhizn politicheskoi ssylki i tiur'mi po perekhvachennym pis'mam', p. 174.

Exiles with medical training were the exception to the general patterns of unemployment. Significant proportions of pre-1905 political exiles had some sort of medical training, and were welcomed by the Siberian community, as we discussed in chapter 3, because they offered an important service. The more humble backgrounds of the post-1905 generation meant that they included far fewer medics. In our sample of 299 political exiles in Figure 4.1, only ten worked in medical professions. None of these ten were doctors; nine were medical assistants, and one was a midwife. Most of them worked in the medical professions during exile.

Of the eight women categorized as skilled workers in the sample, all were employed in the clothing trade, one as a milliner, and seven as dressmakers. Seven of these eight worked as seamstresses in exile. This reflected the prominence of needlework as a profession for women workers, and the portability and saleability of their trade.[21] It did not imply that they had secure employment in exile—even for free seamstresses in European Russian cities, needlework was a precarious and overcrowded trade, which usually involved lengthy periods of unemployment.[22] Most of these women took piece needlework rather than factory employment. A case study from Yakutsk allows us to develop a more vivid picture of what prospects dressmakers faced in eastern Siberia. Rasha Iakovleva Friedman arrived in Yakutsk on 16 May 1900, to serve a term of four years' exile, along with her husband Ruben, for her involvement in Social Democrat propaganda in Kiev.[23] She was a twenty-four-year-old townswoman. She had 'dark hair and eyes, a sharp nose, a gentle mouth, some missing teeth, a round chin and a clean face.'[24] She became pregnant while in exile, but lost the baby after complications in her pregnancy in 1901.[25] Her appeal to the Yakutsk governor, dated 10 November 1903, gives an insight into the difficulties for exiles in making a living, and hints at the dire poverty she encountered. Friedman explained in her letter that she was initially sent to Olekminsk, but that her husband was sent to Viliuisk in June 1903, and she followed him voluntarily. Her term of exile was due to end on 22 March 1904, but she was unable to survive these last months in Viliuisk, as she had 'been unable to sell any of her possessions' and there was no business for her in her trade as dressmaker. She appealed for permission to return to Olekminsk so that she could earn enough to live through her trade. This permission was granted.[26] For Friedman, and many others like her, exile offered material uncertainty about keeping body and soul together, as well as the dislocation of place and of family.

One case exposed some peculiar intersections between work and punishment. On 26 April 1900, Vladimir Alexandrov Voznesenskii was administratively exiled

[21] Needleworkers made up the largest group of non-industrial women workers apart from domestic servants. See R.L. Glickman, *Russian factory women* (Berkeley, 1984), pp. 61–2.
[22] Engel, *Between the fields and the city: Women, work and family in Russia 1861–1914*, p. 177.
[23] NARS, f. 12, op. 10, d. 22, p. 2, letter from Irkutsk military governor to Yakutsk governor, 16 May 1900.
[24] NARS, f. 12, op. 10, d. 22, pp. 8–9, official report (*stateinyi spisok*) on Rasha Friedman.
[25] NARS, f. 12, op. 10, d. 22, pp. 13–19, letters between Yakutsk governor and Rasha Friedman.
[26] NARS, f. 12, op. 10, d. 22, p. 31, letter from Friedman to Yakutsk governor, 10 November 1903, and response on rear.

to Yakutsk region for five years. He received this punishment for this role in organizing a secret society 'Group of Socialist Revolutionaries' in Petersburg, and distributing illegal literature among students and workers. Voznesenskii was a nobleman, and he worked as a geologist and mining engineer.[27] His wife and eighteen-month-old son accompanied him into exile.[28] He was based in Irkutsk prison for some time, and while he was there the Trans-Baikal railway employed him. He carried out important technical work on the planning of the Trans-Siberian railway's route around Lake Baikal, studying the types of soil on all the lines on the Trans-Baikal railway, and calculating the relationships between drainage work and rock layers.[29] The correspondence between Irkutsk's military governor, Yakutsk's governor, and the overseer of works on the Trans-Baikal railway exposes some profound conflicts over the need to isolate and punish Voznesenskii, and the need for his important technical work, on a state project no less, to continue. The railway manager valued Voznesenskii's work very highly, and arranged for him to have special treatment while in Irkutsk prison so that he could continue his work:

> Voznesenskii does not have what he needs to pursue his work, that is, light, especially in the evening, and a desk, and most of all that he has not been given permission to receive and send papers required, requiring his signatures... this prevents him from continuing his very important work.[30]

The railway's requests to allow Voznesenskii permission to remain in Irkutsk prison until he completed his work were turned down by Irkutsk's military governor.[31] He was moved to Yakutsk in the summer of 1903, and arrived there in September along with his wife and son. Voznesenskii's employer wanted him to continue his work in Yakutsk. The Yakutsk governor was sympathetic to this need, and suggested that Voznesenskii be settled in Yakutsk town, where he would have access to communication networks and living space conducive to his working needs. Irkutsk's military governor would not accept this suggestion, however, and demanded that he be settled in an *inorodtsy* village.[32] In the end, Yakutsk's governor proposed a compromise measure whereby Voznesenskii be settled in the *skoptsy* village of Markhinsk, which was remote, but which, unlike *inorodtsy* iurts, could provide this important worker with the desk, light, and postal service that he needed to be productive.[33] This curious case demonstrates the profound conflicts

[27] NARS, f. 12, op. 10, d. 22, p. 1, letter, from Chancery of Irkutsk military governor to Yakutsk governor, 24 June 1900.

[28] NARS, f. 12, op. 10, d. 22, pp. 6–7, form describing Voznesenskii.

[29] NARS, f. 12, op. 10, d. 22, p. 63, letter from captain of Trans-Baikal railway to Irkutsk military governor, 11 February 1903.

[30] NARS, f. 12, op. 10, d. 22, p. 178, letter from captain of work for the building of the Trans-Baikal railway to Irkutsk military governor, 23 August 1903.

[31] NARS, f. 12, op. 10, d. 22, p. 171, letter from Irkutsk military governor, 20 August 1903.

[32] NARS, f. 12, op. 2, d. 22, pp. 16–18, p. 16; letters between the Trans-Baikal railway captain, Yakutsk governor and Irkutsk military governor, 9 November 1903–18 December 1903.

[33] NARS, f. 12, op. 10, d. 22, pp. 21–2 letter from Yakutsk governor to Irkutsk military governor, 15 January 1904.

that could emerge between punishment and isolation for exiles, which was clearly prioritized by Irkutsk's military governor, and productive work. Voznesenskii's specialist skills were of vital importance for a major state construction project, but the need to punish him seemed in this case to trump the significance of his work.

A small but significant number of political exiles were employed in expedition and scientific work in the northern regions.[34] These expeditions required educated, physically fit people, and were a plum job for the few who secured such work. Expeditions were conducted for a range of scientific, geographic, and infrastructure purposes, including collecting botanic specimens, making geological and mapping surveys, conducting meteorological observations, and carrying out ethnographic work. Political exiles had made significant contributions to the study of the Yakutsk region and its peoples, particularly in the 1880s and 1890s, when the vast majority of the exiles to the region were intelligentsia.[35] The post-1905 generation of exiles to Yakutsk were predominantly of worker and peasant background, and anyhow regarded local cultural work as 'petty affairs'.[36] Despite this, a handful of the post-1905 generation of exiles were involved in scientific work. Political exiles were participants in most of the scientific expeditions in the Northern regions. The six members of the Nel'kano-Aianskaia expedition led by the engineer V.E. Popov in 1903 were all political exiles.[37] In 1907, an expedition was commissioned by Yakutsk region statistical committee to study the Suntarskii saliferous area of Viliuisk region, and to collect materials. This project employed two political exiles, Petr Liudvigovich Dravert, and Pavel Vasilevich Olenin. Both these men participated in a number of other expeditions, and both became prominent scientists in their own right. Dravert published his work on Yakutsk, 'Materials on the ethnography and geography of Yakutsk oblast' in 1912.[38] Dravert had been studying in the maths and physics faculty at Kazan University when he was exiled in 1906 to Yakutsk for five years, for participation in the revolutionary student movement. He participated in a series of botanic, geographical, and scientific expeditions while in Yakutsk. He also wrote poetry and prose. He stayed in Yakutsk region until 1910, when he returned to Kazan for medical treatment.[39]

Pavel Olenin provides us with an example of a political exile who found a niche in Yakutsk society. He had been a student at Moscow University, but was exiled administratively to eastern Siberia for five years. In 1901 he became an assistant to the Yakutsk regional statistical committee, and a conservator at the museum. He was described as an 'amateur botanist'. The Yakutsk governor gave Olenin permission to go north in summer 1902, in order to collect materials for the

---

[34] For an example of exile work on expeditions before our period, see Daniel Beer, 'The Exile, the Patron, and the Pardon: The Voyage of the Dawn (1877) and the Politics of Punishment in an Age of Nationalism and Empire,' *Kritika: Explorations in Russian and Eurasian History*, no. 1 (2013).

[35] Nikolaev, 'Ssylka i kraevedenie; Yakutskii krai', pp. 96–100.

[36] 'Ssylka i kraevedenie; Yakutskii krai', p. 101.

[37] 'Ssylka i kraevedenie; Yakutskii krai', p. 105.

[38] 'Ssylka i kraevedenie; Yakutskii krai', p. 101.

[39] See Petr Liudvigovich Dravert, *Pod nebom Yakutskago kraia* (Tomsk, 1911); A. Maliutina, 'Vospominaniia o P.L. Draverte,' *Enisei*, no. 4 (1973); O.D. Tarmakhanova (ed.) *Pisateli Vostochnoi Sibiri: Biobibliograficheskii ukazanie* (Irkutsk, 1973), pp. 102–3.

museum. He was subsequently involved in a number of important expeditions. He led a big expedition into the Verkhoiansk hills commissioned by the Russian Geographical Society in 1905, and participated in A.V. Kolchak's expedition under the auspices of the Russian Academy of Sciences.[40]

Expedition work was not always romantic exploration of uncharted territories— it could entail much more mundane activities, like counting and measuring livestock. The Menshevik Vladimir Dmitrevich Vilenskii-Sibiriakov worked for Yakutsk's regional agricultural section. He recalled his work:

> When the news of the beginnings of the (February) revolution in Petrograd was received in Yakutsk, I wasn't actually in Yakutsk. At that time, I was one thousand *versts* (662 miles) from Yakutsk in the god-forsaken settlements (*uluses*) of Viliuisk region, where I led an expedition carrying out an inspection of Yakut cattle. I measured Yakut cows, photographed them, counted them, when a Yakut came to me with news of the revolution.[41]

The counterpoise of recording cows and hearing news of the long-awaited revolution is poignant. Cow counting in the distant reaches of Yakutsk region could be regarded as a lucky break when so few exiles found any regular paid work.

UNEMPLOYMENT AND THE URBAN–RURAL NEXUS

This chapter opened with a discussion of the kinds of work that exiles did, but unemployment and occupational transience were the most enduring shared characteristics of work for exiles. Most exiles in eastern Siberia spent at least part of their time unemployed, and most exiles had to pursue multiple different jobs during their time in exile. There was no permanent work in rural areas, except in farming. The seasonal opportunities in rural areas were little better, and included hunter-gatherer activities, agricultural day labour, work breaking and making barges and boats, and help with river haulage in season. Urban areas offered more opportunities, including seasonal building work, dressmaking, and various craftsmen's employment. There were also possibilities for intelligentsia work, as clerks, teachers, printworkers, and so on in urban environments, but these were sometimes denied to political exiles if they were deemed politically unreliable. These poor working opportunities beset political and criminal exiles alike, though criminal exiles were more likely to have the skills required for work in agriculture. The majority of exiles were unable to find paid work, and 'they flailed about like a fish out of water'.[42]

As we discussed in chapter 3, exiles were named specific locations as places of residence, and these locations were almost invariably away from Siberia's urban

[40] Arkhivi Rossiiskoi Akademii Nauk, St-Petersburg Filial, f. 25, op. 001, d. 73, d. 297; letters between Olenin and E.P. Borodin.
[41] Vilenskii-Sibiriakov, 'Poslednee pokolenie Iakutskoi ssylki (1912–1917gg)', p. 137.
[42] Sokolov, 'Sibir i ssylka', p. 44.

areas. The opportunities for paid work in rural eastern Siberia were extremely limited, and the work that existed was usually seasonal. Work in agriculture was an option that was only available to those with prior experience and skills in that area, and was anyhow extremely poorly remunerated, and seasonal. Other alternatives, if permission to move was granted, were work in the various mines across the region, and on railway and road construction. Population density was extremely low across the region, which meant that there was a very limited demand for craftsmen, skilled work, or educated professions. Exiles had to petition for permission to move away from their named place of residence to search for work. They could also request permission to enter urban areas for work. There were multiple ambiguities and contradictions in official attitudes toward exile work. Though permission was usually given to exiles to search for work in the region, they were often barred from entering urban centres. The records give the impression that the administration was keen to give permission for work-related movement, so long as those exiles clearly intended to work, and were not trying to settle in the capitals.[43] The governor of Eniseisk wrote to Leonid Mikhailovich Kniazev, Irkutsk's military governor, in April 1913 to inform him that he gave permission for exile-settlers to move around the districts, with the exception of entry into towns, to prevent the accumulation of exile-settlers.[44]

There is evidence that the regional governors were generally sympathetic to the petitions of those exiles considered politically reliable. Yakutsk's police administration was forced to appeal to the region's administration about permissions to move for work, as they were uncertain as to which categories of prisoner could be given permission to move freely around the region.[45] Practical considerations encouraged regional governors to permit exiles to work. If they did not work, they had to be supported, to some extent at least, by the state.

There are a large number of sources listing the trades and occupations of political exiles, as Siberian governors required monthly reports on the conduct and occupation of administrative exiles and state criminals.[46] Observers' reports on exile conduct included exiles' prior occupations, and what they were currently employed with. This was almost invariably listed as 'no occupation'.[47] These reports provide a useful indicator of the extent of unemployment among political exiles, and confirm

[43] See for example NARS, f. 15, op 21, d. 593; delo about provisional departure of exiles to Irkutsk oblast for paid work, 1916. 15ll.

[44] GAIO, f. 25, op. 6, d. 5385, pp. 407–9; report from Eniseisk governor, to Irkutsk military governor, 1 April 1913.

[45] NARS, f. 15, op. 18, d. 191, pp. 153–4; note from Yakutsk police administration to Yakutsk region administration, 16 September 1908.

[46] These include NARS, f. 15, op. 18, d. 191; list of exiles arriving into Yakutsk in September 1909; NARS, f. 15, op. 22, d. 128, delo about the conduct, form of life and occupation and provisional departures from the region of exiles, 1910 (325 pp.); NARS, f. 15, op. 22, d. 136, delo about the conduct, activities, searches for exiles, 1911, pp. 19–20, 71–5.

[47] See for example, NARS f. 15, op. 21, d. 67, pp. 12–19; pp. 23–34; pp. 39–44, pp. 49–65. NARS f. 12, op. 2, d. 5135, pp. 13–14; 21, 28, 33, 71, 124; NARS, f. 12, op. 12, d. 800, about views of form of life and activities of politicals under observation in Yakutsk region in 1904; gives detailed information about occupation of Yakutsk exiles in 1904; and a number of files in NARS f. 15, op. 22, d. 128, NARS f. 15, op. 22, d. 136, with occupational information.

that urban exiles were uniquely ill-suited to eastern Siberia, where the industrial economy and urban infrastructure was extremely weak. This was particularly the case in Yakutsk region, which was even more sparsely populated than Irkutsk province. In 1903, there were 105 political exiles listed in the region under police observation. All of them received payments from the state, and in answer to their current occupation, all used the formulation: 'I do not have independent means. I am able to work, but there is no paid work in local conditions.'[48]

The majority of political exiles were unemployed, or employed only in temporary labour. Of the fifteen administrative exiles settled in Markhinsk village, Yakutsk region, in 1916, those who were 'fit for peasants' work', like the unskilled worker Sergei Shuzhkin, might work as a hired labourer (*batrak*) on the peasants' fields for one rouble a day. Ivan Mikhailov was a hat maker by trade. He tried two days of fieldwork, but found he was unable to do it. He relied on his small state allowance for his daily needs.[49] This inability to work ensured that exiles were not productive settlers, but a burden both to the region and to the state. Even exiles that managed to find work in an appropriate trade were usually unable to earn enough money to support themselves, and were awarded state allowance as well. Yakutsk's governor warned Irkutsk's military governor in 1911 that since Yakutsk was almost entirely without industry and without significant population points, it had no need for workers and the local population were themselves without work through the long Yakutsk winter.[50]

Opportunities for any paid work were usually restricted to the summer months. Ivan Ivanovich Kraft, the governor of Yakutsk between 1907 and 1913, was explicit about the seasonal nature of available work, and the impact of unemployment on his region, in this report to Nicholas II in 1911:

> At the end of every summer, when all work finishes and comes to a halt, crowds of hungry, ragged, criminal people turn up. Turning out to be in a hopeless position, the exiles steal, rob, go downhill (*ubyvaiut*) and again end up in prison at state expense.[51]

The young urban workers that made up many of eastern Siberia's political exiles after 1905 found little to offer them in the 'dark villages' that they were assigned to. Many formed cooperatives to make paid employment for themselves, but the local market was not big enough for these ventures to be successful, and they usually closed.[52] Artels, which were cooperative associations for trade and craft workers, were formed, and these provided some income for those with skilled trades like joiners, metalworkers, and shoemakers, though they were only successful when on a very small scale. Larger scale efforts were usually scuppered by police intervention,

---

[48] NARS 12.21.48, pp. 2–34. Table of information about giving of state means to political exiles, 4 December 1902–10 June 1906.

[49] NARS, f. 15, op. 18, d. 217, pp. 107–8; Information on administrative exiles settled in Markhinsk village, Yakutsk region, for 1916.

[50] GAIO, f. 25, op. 6, d. 3104, pp. 59–61; Letter from Yakutsk governor to Irkutsk military governor, 3 August 1911.

[51] Kalashnikov, *Istoriia Yakutii v otchetakh Yakutskikh gubernatorov*, p. 117.

[52] Sokolov, 'Sibir i ssylka', p. 33.

or a lack of markets. Joiners and turners' artels could only be successful in larger villages or towns, because they needed customers. Shoemakers' artels often repaired old shoes in the winter, due to a lack of work, and sold them in the summer to Lena workers. Bakeries and sausage shops had limited success; they could only operate if they were near a major road or halting station, and if the quality of their goods was significantly better than what the local peasants could produce.

Agricultural artels, which worked the land and gardens, and occasionally ventured into bird keeping and milk products, were usually successful. As well as these artels designed to provide permanent work, there were a number of ventures organized to exploit specific short-term opportunities. For example, there was an artel for dockers on the Lena, an artel for steamer building, an artel for demarcating land plots, and so on. The permanent artels were heavily reliant on help from outside, as they needed means for their tools and raw materials, and to rent premises.[53] Some workers resorted to foraging, trapping, and hunting. Artels were formed to market and sell nuts and berries that its members collected. They could make around fifty kopeks per day doing this.[54] F. Seniushkin, who was exiled to Ust-Udinsk, Irkutsk province, in 1908, recalled his community's struggle to establish workers' cooperatives. They tried to establish a carpentry cooperative workshop, to sell goods to the local population. The community's women also established a business, making essential oils that were sold to firms in Irkutsk and Moscow. This enterprise went well, but was soon broken up by the authorities, and the organizers were dispersed around the region, accused of agitation among the local community.[55]

Only a handful of exiles had the skills, experience, and commitment to establish themselves meaningfully in their place of exile. One such survivor was Vladimir Dmitrevich Vilenskii-Sibiriakov, known as Vikula. Vikula was born to a peasant family in Tomsk, in western Siberia. He graduated from technical college, and worked as a foundryman in various Siberian factories. He was a very active member of Social Democrat circles in western Siberia, and became a professional revolutionary in 1907, propagandizing around the factories of the region. He was arrested in 1908, and after eighteen months in Krasnoiarsk prison, was sentenced to eighteen months of hard labour, which he served in the Nerchinsk prison complex. On completion of his term, he was sent to exile in Yakutsk. He recalled that as soon as he arrived in Yakutsk, he had to think about work straight away. His first job was rendering a house for a Yakut. This was skilled work, so earned him a few roubles. Subsequently, he spun the wheel for a printing press, on which the paper 'Lena Krai' was printed, and worked as a tinsmith, a joiner, a housepainter, gave lessons, and so on. Vikula recalled that the big question for all the exiles in Yakutsk was whether to stay or to escape. His decision was made for him when his wife arrived in the town. They decided to stay 'till better times'. Vikula opened a carpentry

---

[53] Bagotskii, 'Krakovskii soiuz pomoshchi politicheskim zakliuchennym', p. 191.
[54] Sokolov, 'Sibir i ssylka', p. 34.
[55] F. Seniushkin, 'Zavodchiki (vospominaniia iz zhizni Ust-Udinskoi ssylki),' *Katorga i ssylka*, no. 1 (1921).

workshop, as well as studying literature and the Yakut economy. He also worked with the regional agricultural section collecting statistics on the region. He became closely involved with the higher levels of Yakut administration. The administration was aware that he was a former katorzhan, and therefore deprived of rights, but they worked with him anyway. He was only censured when he tried to set up an artisans' committee.[56] Vikula stayed on in Siberia after the revolution.

One of the most limiting and punishing aspects of Siberia for many exiles were the quotas in place on the numbers of political exiles permitted to settle in urban areas. Unless you were employed in agriculture, or in seasonal hunting and foraging, there was virtually no employment in rural areas. There were numerous requests from exiles for permission to stay in major urban areas.[57] Reponses of governors to these requests varied significantly. Vikula recalled that Ivan Ivanovich Kraft, the Yakutsk governor, was inclined to grant permission to move even to political exiles, because he wanted them to work.[58] Other sources suggested that while criminal exiles were free to move around the region, political exiles had their movement severely restricted.[59] One anonymous exile memoir likened a refusal of permission to settle in town as akin to a death sentence:

> Often, and particularly recently, the administration has not given permission to live and work in the towns; receiving a refusal is the equivalent of receiving a death penalty. From this moment something terrible threatens the *lishentsy* (former katorzhan). They are excluded from the right to live in town, excluded from the honour to work for their own crust of bread, and deserted in under populated and virtually uncultured Yakutsk region, taken from their family and close acquaintances, it seems that *lishentsy* have been abandoned by court order. They have no work, no means, insufficient comradely support, no land allotment... Wandering from one village to another, around the region, to Bodaibinsk gold mines and back, and not finding work for themselves anywhere, even for daily subsistence. There is no work anywhere, either for the unskilled worker, or for the intelligentsia.[60]

This excerpt is part of a lengthy and melodramatic article that was intended to demonstrate the inhumane and impossible conditions faced by exiles in Yakutsk region. We have some individual cases from the archive that go some way towards substantiating our anonymous exile's case. Vasilii Ushakov, for example, appealed for permission to stay in Yakutsk so that he could ply his trade. He was a

---

[56] Vilenskii-Sibiriakov, 'Poslednee pokolenie Iakutskoi ssylki (1912–1917gg)', p. 132.

[57] See for example GAIO, f. 600, op. 1, d. 913; information about political exiles around Irkutsk town, 1915, pp. 709. The vast majority of these pages grant permission for petitioners to stay in Irkutsk for a six-month term, without any explanations. NARS, f. 15, op. 18, d. 186, pp. 7–25; 1908–1912 correspondence regarding requests of Konstantin Dmitriev to settle in Yakutsk town, which were refused, but after they were eventually granted, he escaped. GAIO, f. 25, op. 6, d. 5385, karton 624; regarding petitions of exiles about permission for leave from their place of settlement and other things, 1912.

[58] Vilenskii-Sibiriakov, 'Poslednee pokolenie Iakutskoi ssylki (1912–1917gg)', pp. 132–3.

[59] Bagotskii, 'Krakovskii soiuz pomoshchi politicheskim zakliuchennym'.

[60] GARF, f. 533, op. 1, d. 1178, pp. 5–11, article entitled 'the situation of lishentsy', part of a published leaflet, ed. Oleinikov, *Pervyi literaturnyi sbornik v Yakutske* (published by Yakutsk tipog. VV Zharova, 1908).

coachman.[61] A letter from the wife of Aleksandr Denisov Pliucharev, an exile settled in Olekminsk region of Yakutsk oblast, used work as its central theme in her plea to get permission for the family to settle in Yakutsk town. She pointed out that her husband, a joiner, has not been able to find any work in Olekminsk. Furthermore, the couple's two daughters needed to learn a trade, and this could only happen in Yakutsk.[62]

Gerasim Izmailovich Novikov, an exile-settler in Kansk district, Eniseisk province, petitioned Irkutsk's military governor requesting that he be allowed to settle in Taishet volost, Nizhneudinsk district, in Irkutsk province. His appeal gives a vivid impression of the challenges of finding work:

> I am an exile-settler from Eniseisk, sent here in 1911 having been sentenced in Orlov in 1911 for joining the *Skoptsy* sect. Living here for a year, I am utterly impoverished, so for example, I've spent everything that I had for money, and also all my belongings, including my jacket, shoes and clothes and all this just so that I could live here for one year; and now to live here is just impossible, as I am by profession a clerk and there is only peasant work here that I am not fit for because of my weak health and lack of knowledge. Apart from that, my uncle lives in Taishet township, where he carries out trade; I could stay with him and in such a way defend my future existence.[63]

Novikov's petition was refused; policy towards religious sectarians tended to be extremely draconian, even after the relaxation of religious persecution after 1905, as they were regarded as a contagious risk to their neighbours.[64] There is evidence that the regional governors were generally sympathetic to the plight of those considered to be politically reliable. The case of Aleksandr Novitskii illustrates the contradictions and cruelties of state policy regarding permission to live in urban areas. Novitskii had been living as an exile in Kansk district, Zabaikal region, since 1909, along with his wife and children. He made repeated appeals for permission to move to urban areas, which were refused by the Eniseisk governor. He subsequently appealed to the Irkutsk military governor, who granted him leave to move to urban areas. Novitskii's correspondence is enlightening in the ways it expresses his need to move to urban areas, and his grounds for grievance when he is initially refused. Novitskii recounts that, 'As a person of the intelligentsia professions, I cannot find paid work here . . . When I was sure that I could not feed my family here, I appealed to Eniseisk governor with a request to be transferred to Kansk town.'[65] This, along with subsequent requests for permission to live in the other urban centres of Achinsk and Krasnoiarsk, were turned down, on the grounds that

---

[61] NARS f. 12, op. 2, d. 4693, p. 95; letter from Vasilii Ivanov Ushakov to Yakutsk governor, 28 June 1909.

[62] NARS, f. 12, op. 2, d. 4693, p. 19; handwritten letter from Varavara Fedorovna Pliucharev to Yakutsk governor, 27 June 1909.

[63] GAIO, f. 25, op. 6, d. 5385, p. 489; petition from Gerasim Izmailovich Novikov to Irkutsk military governor, refusal on p. 496.

[64] For a discussion of *skoptsy* in exile, see Laura Engelstein, *Castration and the heavenly kingdom: a Russian folktale* (Ithaca, N.Y., 1999), pp. 118–48.

[65] GAIO, f. 25, op. 6, d. 5385, p. 26; letter from Aleksandr Ignatov Novitskii to Irkustk military governor, 29 November 1912.

there was no outstanding quota for exiles in these areas. Irkutsk's military governor chastised Eniseisk's military governor on Novitskii's case:

> I find, that if the person in charge of exile in the prison inspectorate, with the exception of those individuals who have brought attention of the police upon themselves, then it is inadmissible to not grant permission for exiles capable of work, in particular with families, and those who have lived peacefully in their places of residence and who are known to be trustworthy. Work, providing sustenance for exiles and their families, brings into its midst several reconciliations, and without doubt with all possible observations, saves from the peaceful population to the greatest extent, rather than the maintenance of conditions that are impossible for life, which force them into crime.[66]

This clearly recognized the importance of work, both for the exile community and for the state. Eniseisk's governor was unrepentant in his response, however, pointing out that the regulations clearly required him to abide by the quotas set for urban residence for exiles, and that the problem lay in the excessive numbers of exiles settled in Zabaikal region.[67]

Even in urban areas, there was no panacea offered for unemployment. Exiles dispersed to district towns, and to the mines. Sokolov recalls that 'the district towns were little better than the villages'.[68] Our anonymous exile memoir written in 1914 described the author's struggles to find work in Yakutsk region. Even in Yakutsk town, the most populous and developed settlement in the region, work was difficult to come by and highly seasonal, with construction work stopping abruptly with the onset of the freeze in mid-September.

> Sparsely populated and without any sort of industrial establishments, Yakutsk town doesn't have a great call for working hands, either unskilled workers or intelligentsia. Intelligentsia labour is already occupied, either by regional residents or by administrative exiles. There is unskilled work only in the summer, when the building fever commences, but even this is in insignificant quantities, and Yakut men can often fill working places cheaply. And so, *lishentsy* run all around town in the search for work, only in summer, and with difficulty they find temporary work, three months unskilled labour... Often the intelligentsia, not accustomed to any sort of manual labour, appeal equally along with their comrade unskilled workers, to be bricklayers, stove makers, coalminers; to carry bricks, mix mortar and to do the very heaviest work.

> But this is only summer. And so when the winter's freeze sets in, exiles remain without anything. Only a few professionals are successful in settling down comparatively comfortably. All the remainder, the majority of course, remain without work, for the whole eight months, without any sort of savings, and as a consequence, without a crust of bread. Without warm clothes, without a roof over their heads and without money, the *lishentsy* fall to the most impossible conditions of life. Half starving, with some sort of comradely support, living in the most unhygienic conditions, *lishentsy* alone carry all

---

[66] GAIO, f. 25, op. 6, d. 5385, p. 31; letter from Irkutsk military governor to Eniseisk governor, undated.
[67] GAIO, f. 25, op. 6, d. 5385, pp. 54–5; letter from Eniseisk governor to Irkutsk Military Governor, undated.
[68] Sokolov, 'Sibir i ssylka', p. 43.

the burdens and suffering of the exiles' 'ruinous place' (*giblykh mest'*), and drag out their sorry existence.[69]

This account paints a visceral picture of the ways in which the search for work defined daily existence for many exiles. The weight of requests sent by exiles to regional governors requesting permission to move in order to find work to some extent substantiates the grim picture presented in this extract. It serves as a useful corrective to the numerous accounts of exile as a place of leisure and reflection. This individual's exile life was one of striving, suffering, and fear of starvation.

ROAD AND RAIL CONSTRUCTION

Eastern Siberia witnessed a series of major infrastructure projects in the late nineteenth and early twentieth century. The most significant of these was the development of the Trans-Siberian railway, which provided a route from Moscow to Vladivostok. The Trans-Siberian was constructed between 1891 and 1916, and provided a significant source of employment, drawing on locals, convicts, exiles, and workers from other regions as its labour force. The conditions of work were made exceptionally difficult and unpleasant, because of the unforgiving climate, the frozen ground, and the difficult terrain. The ground was frozen until mid-July, but once it thawed, it turned into a swamp, and 'labourers had to work in up to two feet of water'.[70] The project was unable to attract enough free labour, because of eastern Siberia's sparse population, and prison labour was used extensively.[71] A total of 9,000 prisoners and 4,500 exiles worked on the railroad. The work was appealing to prisoners, because it offered a reduction in sentence, and prisoners were paid at the same rate as free workers.[72] Work outdoors of any sort was attractive to prisoners, while for exiles, as we have seen, work of any sort was necessary, but extremely difficult to come by. The authorities were inundated with requests from prisoners and exiles for permission to work on the railways and roads.[73] The numbers of exiles requesting permission to work on the Amur railroad were such that the Yakutsk governor asked Irkutsk's military governor to send a clarifying order stating that 'only those prisoners sent for general crimes and considered fit for hard work with excellent conduct will be sent'.[74] Many of those who applied for

[69] GARF, f. 533, op. 1, d. 1178, pp. 5–11, article entitled 'the situation of lishentsy', part of a published leaflet, ed. Oleinikov, *Pervyi literaturnyi sbornik v Yakutske* (Yakutsk tipog. VV Zharova, 1908).

[70] Marks, *Road to Power: The Trans Siberian Railroad and the Colonisation of Asian Russia, 1850–1917*, p. 171.

[71] Gran, *Katorga v Sibiri. Izvlechenie iz otcheta o sluzhebnoi poezdke nachal'nika glav. tiurem. upravlenia P.K. Grana v Sibir v 1913 g*, p. 41.

[72] Marks, *Road to Power: The Trans Siberian Railroad and the Colonisation of Asian Russia, 1850–1917*, p. 182.

[73] NARS, f. 12, op. 2, d. 5169, pp. 4–6; lists of those sent for medical inspection from Yakutsk prison for work on the Amur railroad, January 1911, pp. 24–63; further requests from exiles to work on Amur railroad, and medical reports.

[74] NARS, f. 12, op. 2, d. 5169, p. 67; letter from Governor Kraft to Irkutsk military governor, undated.

work on the railroads were turned down on grounds of their weak health. The experience of exiles working on rail and road construction was broadly analogous to the katorga prisoners working there, so I have drawn on extant katorga memoirs to get a sense of working conditions.

Katorga work was widely recognized to be inefficient and expensive, not least because katorga workers were 'bad workers' due to their poor health and lack of vigour. The exception to this was the use of katorga labour on the Ussuri, Amur, Trans-Baikal, and Priamur railroads, especially after 1905, where katorga prisoners cherry-picked for health and reliability proved to be a cost effective and efficient workforce. Prison and exile labour had been used to good effect in the earlier section of railway construction since 1891.[75] Indeed, prisoner labour on the Amur and Trans-Baikal railways was considered such a success that in 1914 suitable prisoners were transferred to Siberia from European katorga prisons for this work.[76] An account of conditions and usefulness of penal labour on the Ussuri stretch of line concluded that the work was hard, but that conditions were better than elsewhere in Russia's penal archipelago, and that penal labour provided a useful and cost-effective labour force.[77]

The Amur railway, which was the final section of the Trans-Siberian to be completed, was constructed between 1907 and 1916. It became a strategic priority for the government after Russia's losses in the Russo-Japanese war in 1904–5, and gave Russia access to a warm water port, as well as enabling rapid transfer of troops. It was built at state expense. The Amur railway spanned 5,225 miles, and linked the western and eastern sections of the Trans-Siberian railway. It was completed in several stages, moving from west to east. Its construction presented some very particular challenges. As well as the harsh continental climate and hilly terrain, much of the route had to be built over permafrost. Katorga labour was used extensively for its construction.[78] The report of the main prison inspector, P.K. Gran, was extremely positive about the conditions and outcomes of prisoner work on the Amur railway. He noted that the relatively good food and accommodation provided for prison workers, along with the one-third reduction in their term that they won for this work, meant that railroad work was relatively attractive to prisoners, and disabled the impact of strikes and runaways from the free workers.[79] A recent work on the construction of the Trans-Siberian also emphasizes the relatively good conditions of work, partly as a corrective to Soviet evaluations of 'unprecedentedly harsh' conditions, and partly in

[75] V.F. Borzunov, *Proletariat Sibiri i dal'nego vostoka nakanune pervoi Russkoi revoliutsii (po materialam stroitel'stva transsibirskoi magistrali, 1891–1904gg)* (Moscow, 1965), p. 32.

[76] *Otchet po glavnomu tiuremnomu upravleniiu za 1914g* (Petrograd, 1916), p. 36.

[77] Andrew A. Gentes, 'Penal Labor on the Trans-Siberian Railroad,' unpublished conference paper, *Villains and victims: Crime and punishment in late Imperial and early Soviet Russia* (University of Nottingham, 2010).

[78] M.A. Vivdych, 'Zheleznodorozhnoe stroitel'stvo na dal'nem vostoke v kontse XIX- nachale XX veka,' *Gumanitarnyi vektor*, no. 3 (2011). See also B.B. Pak, *Stroitel'stvo Amurskoi zheleznodorozhnoi magistrali, 1891–1916* (Sankt-Peterburg; Irkutsk, 1995), pp. 91–6.

[79] Gran, *Katorga v Sibiri. Izvlechenie iz otcheta o sluzhebnoi poezdke nachal'nika glav. tiurem. upravlenia P.K. Grana v Sibir v 1913 g*, pp. 41–53.

drawing an implicit (positive) contrast with the conditions endured by workers in the Gulag system.[80]

A series of memoirs from katorga prisoners working in rail and road construction offer an alternative vision to Gran's positive perspective on working conditions. A number of memoirists described their labour on the Amur cart road, or *Kolesukha*. *Kolesukha* was a road that linked Blagoveshchensk with Khabarovsk, and was completed between 1899 and 1909, using katorga labour almost exclusively. I have used these memoirs in conjunction with accounts of work on the Trans-Siberian railway, because the features of the work and the environment were similar, so can be used to get a grass-roots view of working life on construction projects. These accounts, all roughly contemporaneous, have a number of common features that emerge, though they differ on some of the finer points. The workers were organized into working teams of ten, *desiatniki*. Andrei Sobol' recalled that political prisoners were distributed around the working teams, so that there was only one or two politicals to eight or nine criminal prisoners on each team. F. Vrubelskii openly contradicted this recollection, and suggested that in fact the prisoners formed working teams themselves, and grouped into national and party groups.[81] Each team had a daily quota of earth to shift, a figure described as unachievable. Quotas were increased steadily, maintaining ever-increasing pressure on workers. After a month on site, the foreman announced to the workers that they had consistently failed to meet their quotas, and that if they failed for one week more, they would be on reduced rations. If they failed to meet their targets for a second week, they would be flogged. Pay rates were advertised as good, even for katorga prisoners, at up to thirty roubles per month. In practice, though, because work norms were set unrealistically high, most workers earned a fraction of this, with around twenty to thirty out of 200 earning around five to six roubles per month.[82] Vrubelskii argued that individual experiences of katorga were highly variable. He distinguished three broad categories of experience. Those who were strong and accustomed to physical labour found the regime comparatively easy. A second group included individuals who were physically weaker and less accustomed to physical labour, and they found katorga harder. The third group, incorporating the weak and those not able to do physical labour, found conditions in the Amur hardest of all. He noted that the former soldier and sailor prisoners were in the first group, and usually returned to camp early, having fulfilled their work norms easily.[83]

The workers walked between one and five miles in the morning to get to their place of work, and could drink tea on site, but returned to their barracks for lunch. The work itself was hard manual labour, moving stones, clearing ground, and felling wood. Former Sakhalin administrators found work on the Amur project, as

[80] Marks, *Road to Power: The Trans Siberian Railroad and the Colonisation of Asian Russia, 1850–1917*, pp. 183–4.

[81] F. Vrubelskii, 'Vospominaniia ob Amurskoi kolesnoi doroge,' *Katorga i ssylka* (1923), p. 238.

[82] Bagotskii, 'Krakovskii soiuz pomoshchi politicheskim zakliuchennym', pp. 172–5; 'Iz pisem o Krugo-Baikal'skoi zheleznoi dorogi'.

[83] Vrubelskii, 'Vospominaniia ob Amurskoi kolesnoi doroge', p. 238.

did a significant number of former Sakhalin convicts.[84] The writer and exile Andrei Sobol' evocatively recalled that conditions broke even the hardened Sakhalin lags.[85]

Dubinskii described the conditions at work as terrible, with the team working in waist-deep water, and swamp, and soaked to the skin. The dry days were no better, because then the workers were covered with great clouds of biting mosquitoes.[86] F. Drozhzhin, another katorga prisoner, described similar working conditions, with intense heat, constant thirst, and a plague of blackflies day and night, alongside intensely crowded sleeping quarters.[87] Work was often stopped by rain, and workers had to trail to and from their worksite because of such stoppages.[88] Two memoirs mentioned that they were not issued any boots, and one recalled that many workers went barefoot.[89]

Work finished at seven in the evening. There were insufficient dishes to go round at mealtimes, so the workers had to take turns. After everyone had eaten, there was a roll call, and everyone settled down to sleep, ready to rise in the morning at daybreak or even before the sun rose. There were no mattresses or pillows, so the workers were given a bag to gather herbs, sticks, and hay to sleep on. There was no more than an hour for lunch, including the time taken walking to and from the barracks. The rations included 200 grams of meat, 1,200 grams of black bread, and 400 grams of half-white bread on Sundays. For dinner they received a portion of porridge. A memoirist recalled: 'For such hard work this food was inadequate, but in the first instance we were so tired that we couldn't eat, but now, it is not sufficient.'[90] These complaints are difficult to evaluate in any kind of objective way—the memoirist remembered, or professed to remember, his conditions of life in these ways, but that does not mean that the conditions were qualitatively worse than in other work sites or places of incarceration. On the question of food portions, though, we do have a comparative indicator—prisoners assigned to heavy work were provided with significantly larger rations in Aleksandrovsk prison; they received double the amount of meat, 1,500 grams of black bread, and porridge fortified with chicken and buckwheat for dinner.[91] This indicates that the letter writer's complaint was justified.

There was a bathhouse on the Trans-Baikal railway site, but it could only hold seven or eight men at once, and there were more than 200 men in the party. Some men chose to bathe in the Baikal, but it was far away, and too cold to wash

[84] 'Vospominaniia ob Amurskoi kolesnoi doroge'. Sakhalin ceased to function as a penal colony after half of it was lost to the Japanese in 1905.
[85] Sobol', '"Kolesukha"', p. 101.
[86] E.P. Dubinskii, 'Pobeg s "Kolesukhi",' *Katorga i ssylka* (1922), p. 112.
[87] Drozhzhin, 'Listki iz zabytoi tetradi (Vospominaniia ob Amurskoi kolesnoi doroge)', pp. 68–9.
[88] Bagotskii, 'Krakovskii soiuz pomoshchi politicheskim zakliuchennym,' pp. 172–5; 'Iz pisem o Krugo-Baikal'skoi zheleznoi dorogi'.
[89] 'Krakovskii soiuz pomoshchi politicheskim zakliuchennym', pp. 172–5; Sobol', '"Kolesukha"', p. 100.
[90] Bagotskii, 'Krakovskii soiuz pomoshchi politicheskim zakliuchennym,' pp. 172–5; 'Iz pisem o Krugo-Baikal'skoi zheleznoi dorogi'.
[91] *Polozhenie tiuremnoi chasti i ssylki v Irkutskoi gubernii po dannym dokladov tiuremnago inspektora, 1911–1913gg*, pp. 114–15.

properly in. It was only possible to use the bathhouse on Sundays. There were no facilities for washing underclothes; the men were given a change of underclothes once a fortnight.[92]

A number of memoirists described the convoys as exceptionally brutal and inhumane. Andrei Sobol' recalled,

> There were 100 men in the convoy. They were all penal, and had all forgotten their humanity... The convoy beat the prisoners day and night. You were beaten because you were a Jew, you were beaten, if you wore glasses, had long hair, beaten when you went to work, beaten as an endless lesson... [93]

This account of constant beatings was openly contradicted by Vrubelskii's account, which argued that Sobol' was allowing his artistic licence to run away with him.[94] These discrepancies may be a reflection of diverse individual experiences, or it may be that Sobol' was inclined to the dramatic—he was after all a gifted poet and writer.

Escapes from convoy were relatively infrequent. Collective responsibility was applied to discourage workers from escape attempts. If any one member of a working team attempted escape on the Trans-Baikal railway, all remaining members were shackled and immediately returned to prison. A katorga prisoner escaped from railway work in the early hours of 10 July 1913; he was seen, and two shots were fired, but he did not fall and hid in nearby woodland. He was pursued, and he was apprehended an hour later on the road to Mongolia. He was put in chains, given thirty-five blows with birch rods, and returned to Aleksandrovsk central. There were a number of other escape attempts, but these were mostly unsuccessful.[95] The level of supervision over workers in this context made successful escapes unlikely.

Despite certain inconsistencies, these memoirs present a clear picture of physically challenging working conditions, and norms of labour production that are reminiscent of Gulag working practice. They also make it clear, however, that the economic benefits of the work were recognized, and that while conditions were unpleasant, workers' basic needs were provided for, and they were cared for by the state. The death rates were modest, unlike the execrable death rates witnessed in Soviet forced labour projects.[96]

AGRICULTURAL WORK

The Russian state emphatically failed in its putative goal to make exiles into settlers. Though some exiles did become peasant householders, the majority of exiles

[92] 'Krakovskii soiuz pomoshchi politicheskim zakliuchennym,' pp. 172–5; 'Iz pisem o Krugo-Baikal'skoi zheleznoi dorogi'.
[93] Sobol', '"Kolesukha"', p. 102.
[94] Vrubelskii, 'Vospominaniia ob Amurskoi kolesnoi doroge,' pp. 237–9.
[95] Bagotskii, 'Krakovskii soiuz pomoshchi politicheskim zakliuchennym,' pp. 172–5.
[96] Marks, *Road to Power: The Trans Siberian Railroad and the Colonisation of Asian Russia, 1850–1917*, p. 184. See also Golfo Alexopoulos, 'Destructive-Labor Camps: Rethinking Solzhenitsyn's Play on Words,' *Kritika: Explorations in Russian and Eurasian History*, no. 3 (2015).

reverted to begging and criminal activity, much to the chagrin of Siberia's administrators.[97] The failure of exile-settlers to transform successfully into settler agriculturalists can be summarized simply—there was a shortage of available land, resistance to settlers from already established local dwellers, and a lack of appropriate skills and motivation from the exile-settlers themselves. The vision of Siberia as an empty place, ready to be tilled, worked, and civilized by great armies of Russian settlers, was a mirage. Waves of free settlement, particularly in the early twentieth century, claimed much of the viable agricultural land.

Though eastern Siberia was extremely sparsely populated, much of the empty land was simply unsuitable for farming. Quite apart from the vagaries of the harsh climate, much of the land in northern and eastern Siberia was rocky, with thin soil, or claimed by taiga. The old settlers had long ago appropriated those areas suitable for farming, and they understandably resisted the encroachments of exiles on their land. Zabaikal's governor warned in 1911 that while only three districts in the region remained open for settlement, none of these three could satisfy the necessary quantity of cultivatable land, so that incoming exiles, even if they wanted to, could not farm. There had been petitions for the last four years from local residents about stopping further settlements, because of the crime levels arising from lack of work in the region for exiles.[98] Yakutsk's governor warned Irkutsk's military governor in 1911 that there was not enough land suitable for cultivation available even for the native population.[99]

Those who had the skills and inclination to farm, many of whom were on criminal convictions, were faced with major obstacles despite ostensible state support. Despite the legendary vast emptiness of Siberia, the plots of land available and suitable for agricultural labour were extremely limited. The Irkutsk prison inspector's report in 1914 noted that the material condition for exiles had been getting worse over the last few years, because villages had fixed quantities of land available to them, and there was therefore no spare land available for new exile-settlers.[100] A report from Yakutsk's governor in 1914 clarified the situation:

> Even in those rare cases, where exiles want to get involved in agriculture, they are not in the circumstances to fulfil this intention. All places suitable for working the land, and also those areas that are relatively easy to clear of wood, have long ago been utilised in all inhabited areas of the region, and exiles cannot set up households in the wild taiga.[101]

---

[97] For an excellent analysis of the Russian state's failure to turn exiles into settlers, see Gentes, 'Roads to Oblivion: Siberian exile and the struggle between state and society', chapter 10.

[98] GAIO, f. 25, op. 6, d. 3104, pp. 49–50; letter from Zabaikal governor to Irkutsk military governor, 29 April 1911.

[99] GAIO, f. 25, op. 6, d. 3104, pp. 59–61; letter from Yakutsk governor to Irkutsk military governor, 3 August 1911.

[100] *Polozhenie tiuremnoi chasti i ssylki v Irkutskoi gubernii po dannym dokladov tiuremnago inspektora, 1911–1913gg*, p. 87.

[101] NARS 12, 21, 168, pp. 14–34; letter to the captain of Irkutsk gendarme administration, from Yakutsk governor, 12 July 1914.

The exiles themselves were unpromising material for settlers. Though some criminal exiles had experience of agricultural labour, those who were assigned to eastern Siberian locations had usually already served significant periods in katorga prisons. Work, especially in the mines, damaged their health irreparably, as we will discuss in chapter 5. As well as the handicaps of poor physical health, exile-settlers were constrained by their lack of family support network—the arduous and labour-intensive work of farming required collective effort to be most effective, but the vast majority of exiles were expected to farm either alone, or with a small nuclear family in tow. It was the collective effort of extended families, or communities, that facilitated successful farming in challenging environments.[102] Finally, the background of many of the criminal exile-settlers made them unlikely to succeed as farmers, because of their lack of experience and disinclination for agricultural work. Irkutsk's military governor, Andrei Nikolaevich Selivanov, summed up the problem succinctly in a letter to the Ministry of Justice in January 1909: 'There is no settlement in truth in Siberia, just the creation of a homeless gang of unemployed and recidivists, who live off the local population, and are a thoroughly pernicious influence.'[103]

State policy assumed that agricultural labour would facilitate healthy settlement and integration with the existing population. Agricultural work was widely believed to be healthy and beneficial to criminals' morality and to the regional economy. Criminal exiles were encouraged to take up a landholding and establish themselves as farmers. In a letter from the Ministry of Justice's prison section to Selivanov, Irkutsk's military governor in 1907, the importance of improving possibilities for work were stressed, and the governors were promised funds to get exiles started as farmers.[104] Attempts had been made by the state since the 1820s to facilitate settlement and to domesticize criminal exiles through marriage.[105] Grants were given to exiles that married, and to help establish a new farmstead, for farm equipment and seed corn, in an attempt to further facilitate 'healthy' settlement. We can look at a couple of case studies to see the criteria that the local administration used in making grants. Nilokai Nikitin Petukhov, known as Ivan Nikitin, successfully petitioned for an agricultural grant. Petukhov was thirty years old in 1911 when he petitioned the governor for one hundred roubles to buy seed corn. Petukhov had been exiled to eastern Siberia after a sentence in Tula for vagabondage. He was 173 cm tall, had dark hair and grey eyes, with a beard, a big nose, and a small birthmark on his right cheek.[106] His petition was supported by the settlement (*naslega*) authorities, which confirmed that he had a farmstead and sowed grain

[102] On the functioning of rural Russian life, and the importance of family units, see Christine D. Worobec, *Peasant Russia: Family and community in the post-emancipation period* (Princeton, 1991).
[103] GAIO, f. 25, op. 6, d. 3104, pp. 35–9; letter from Irkutsk military governor to Minister of Justice, 10 January 1909.
[104] GAIO, f. 25, op. 6, d. 3104, p. 1; letter from Ministry of Justice, main prison section, to Irkutsk military governor, 26 October 1907.
[105] Schrader, 'Unruly felons and civilizing wives: Cultivating marriage in the Siberian exile system, 1822–1860'.
[106] NARS, f. 12, op. 2, d. 5619, p. 24; information form (*Stateinyi spisok*).

every year, that his house was dilapidated, and that he owned one horse. He needed grain because of a poor harvest in 1909 and harvest failure in 1910. Yakutsk's regional administration agreed to grant him means, but judged that '20 roubles will be sufficient for a single man'.[107]

Login Smert'ev, another exile-settler, petitioned the regional administration for financial support in January 1911. His letter is eloquent in describing his situation:

> I was sent to Nablosk township on 3 September 1910 . . . I was freed and I settled in the township, I live very poorly, I cannot get any work, and when I find it they refuse me, saying that they do not have any work, that they harvest themselves and prices are rising. I have no family, and no one who could give me help for my unfortunate situation, I want to carry out agriculture but I don't have the means. I appeal to you, your highness, as to a father, and I ask from you help in order to equip myself and carry out farming, I ask for 200 roubles from state funds. With this money I can buy a horse, a cow, field tools and can carry out agriculture. For my honour I want to put forward two homeowners who can vouch for me at a greater sum than that requested from the state. This request I personally hand over to the hands of your highness. By Loginov. (Written for the illiterate Loginov by exile-settler E. Krasov)[108]

We can see that Smert'ev, or perhaps Krasov on his behalf, was very careful to present himself as a supplicant and as a willing settler. He drew on a narrative that he anticipated would tap into state discourses about exile and settlement. Despite these efforts to speak the state's language, Smert'ev's petition was rejected in June 2011:

> There are no grounds for giving Smert'ev this money, and he has no guarantors (i.e. no-one to speak for him), since the petitioner Smert'ev does not have a single place of residence, living in adjacent villages and in Yakutsk town, apparently, he has no inclination towards agricultural work, and so fulfilling the conditions required for the grant are not the petitioner's aim, and he will not use the money for these uses.[109]

In this case, the authorities were profoundly sceptical about Smert'ev's claim to be good settler material. The arrival of exiles with claims to land provoked significant hostility from local communities, who sought to protect their own community's use of viable land. The case of Ivan Kaminskyi gives us a concrete example of exiles' impact within local communities. Kaminskyi received an allotment of fourteen acres of land from the first Modutsky commune in Pavlovsk township. Kaminskyi was decrepit and unable to work this land, so rented out half of it to local Yakuts. His homestead was decrepit, but he did not receive any financial help from the commune.[110]

The land issue often crystallized local communities' resistance and hostility to exiles. A petition sent to the Yakutsk governor on 7 January 1902 from the Yakut

[107] NARS, f. 12, op. 2, d. 5619, p. 27; decree of Yakutsk regional administration, prison section, 29 April 1911.

[108] NARS, f. 12, op. 2, d. 5619, p. 42; petition from Login Ivanov Smert'ev to Yakutsk governor, 3 September 1910.

[109] NARS, f. 12, op. 2, d. 5619, p. 41, report to Yakutsk governor from Yakutsk region police, 12 June 1911.

[110] NARS f. 12,op. 2,d. 5135, p. 138; report from Yakutsk regional police to Yakutsk governor, 14 October 1910.

residents of Batursk settlement (*ulus*) illustrates the grievances of resident Siberians towards exile-settlers. The residents demanded that exiles be removed from the settlement (*naslega*), since they were overloaded with exiles, and that this was unfair, as other settlements in the area had few or no exiles at all.[111] The extract below gives a sense of the burden represented by exile families on the settled population, as well as the ways in which the community manoeuvred with the authorities to maximize their land allocation:

> We, the below signed *inorodtsy-* communal peasants (*obshchestvenniki*) of Batursk settlement (*ulusa*), Betiusk settlement (*naslega*), made a decision at our general meeting (*skhod*), that sending exile settlers to us, totalling 23 people with children, of which five people have a land allotment... several [10] people are absent, and they receive money in return for the land due to them, and the remaining eight people live in the village, but receive money in return for their land, on average 63 roubles for every person per year, and the village also spends 504 roubles a year also on maintenance, feeding and clothing these eight people. Apart from this in 1900 and 1901 part of our land was given to the newly formed Dukhobor[112] village named 'Otrabnoi' on the Angara tract... Both us and also the exiles numbered among us are in extremely constrained situation in relation to land use... cattle rearing is our sole source of material wellbeing, and this is strongly compromised. In view of all this, with long discussion and agreement we unanimously spoke; to as your highness to send all exile-settlers from our village to another village which is rich in land, and to grant us some land from a neighbouring village for our use to compensate for the land lost to the Dukhobor settlement.[113]

The villagers spoke collectively, and drew on a discourse of fairness and justice, emphasizing the material liabilities that they faced as a result of hosting exiles, and their lack of land more generally. This petition emphasizes two important features of life in Yakutsk. First, exiles placed a significant financial burden on local communities. Second, although Yakutsk was a huge and relatively empty landmass, there was still intense pressure on those parts of the land that were suitable for agriculture or cattle grazing. The frustrated governors of Irkutsk and Yakutsk repeatedly made the point to the central authorities that, just because the land mass was big, did not mean that they had unlimited 'space' to accommodate new settlers.

ESCAPE

Of the 72,136 exiles sent to Irkutsk region by 1913, an extraordinary 43 per cent (31,043 exiles) had run away or were absent without explanation.[114] Escape from exile was endemic. Exiles had to move around occupations and places to work, and

---

[111] NARS f. 12, op. 2, d. 1261, p. 1; report from elder of Batursk settlement, Nikita Onudriev, to Yakutsk governor, 7 January 1902.

[112] The Dukhobors were a religious sect whose members were exiled before 1905.

[113] NARS, f. 12, op. 2, d. 1261, p. 2; petition from peasants of Batursk settlement, 29 December 1901.

[114] *Polozhenie tiuremnoi chasti i ssylki v Irkutskoi gubernii po dannym dokladov tiuremnago inspektora, 1911–1913gg*, p. 85.

this placed unmanageable strain on the already overstretched observation and tracking systems for exiles. The state made some efforts to keep track of the activities of exiles, particularly those punished for state crimes or administratively exiled for political reasons.[115] They failed emphatically to do this. The college adviser Sofronov, an employee of the Ministry of Internal Affairs, wrote a scathing report on the state of exile in 1912, which was shared with Irkutsk's Military Governor Leonid Mikhailovich Kniazev. Sofronov was emphatic that both administrative and political exile was failing as a system, primarily because escape was so widespread and straightforward. He laid most of the blame on the total disorganization of exile, and lack of consistent observation of exiles. He was particularly scathing about the quality of police staff in the regions:

> Observation bodies are in the majority of cases made up of barely literate, totally unprepared and not always honourable employees, who in the majority of cases are individuals prone to alcoholism . . . the poor conditions of the system of guard, the lack of observation over them, and lack of leadership from higher administration, leads to 'philistine relations' towards exiles, facilitated by the easy granting of terms of absence, virtually unfettered freedom of movement, and as a result of this, the easiness of escapes and autonomous decisions on their place of residence.[116]

The case of Petr Gorelin's exile provides a vivid illustration of the ways in which exile observation failed. Gorelin was settled around 130 miles from Yakutsk, in the Viliuisk tract. The elder who had been delegated responsibility to oversee Gorelin lived around forty miles away, in Usovsk settlement (*naslega*), and he in his turn had commissioned a local resident, Matvei Ivanov, to observe Gorelin's movements—Ivanov lived just a couple of hundred metres away from Gorelin. The elder reported that he didn't observe Gorelin closely, because 'Gorelin seemed to have very good conduct, often left his place of residence to the town and for hunting and always returned accurately.' Ivanov was unable to dissuade Gorelin from heading to town with Nikolai Luglasov, an indigenous Siberian from a neighbouring settlement. Ivanov was confident that Gorelin would come back as he usually did, so asked a local Cossack to let the police know about Gorelin's absence. He did not submit a report himself, and when questioned by the authorities, said that he did not know that he had to inform the police inspector (*ispravnik*) directly about Gorelin's absence. Gorelin's absence was not reported until the end of July, and searches for him had not started by the end of September.[117]

---

[115] NARS, f. 15, op. 22, d. 172; regarding observations over administrative exiles and those in settlement for state crimes, 1913. There are a large number of requests from Yakutsk governor asking for detailed information about the conduct, form of life, occupation, and so on of political exiles, directed to specific villages (e.g., p. 179).

[116] GAIO, f. 25, op. 6, d. 5385, pp. 35–40; report from college advisor Sofronov to Leonid Mikhailovich Mniazev, regarding state of exile in the region, received in Irkutsk December 1912, pp. 35–6.

[117] NARS, f. 12, op. 12, d. 802, p. 2, Letter from Yakutsk governor to Irkutsk military governor, 22 December 1904.

Sofronov's report questioned the granting of permission for exiles to go into the taiga 'for nut collection':

> It's questionable whether they really spend all their time in the taiga, however for all the time they are in the taiga, there can be no doubt that in that time it's possible to meet a party, to meet necessary people, to transfer or receive from them instructions, and then return to their place of residence.[118]

Sofronov concluded that there were no meaningful restrictions to leaving exile:

> Those who remain in exile are only the ballast of the parties, known locally as 'scum' *(shpana)*; the revolutionary cannon-fodder, not able to run due to lack of means and personal insignificance, or those (and these are very rare) who are of great importance in the [revolutionary movement], who are openly under surveillance, patiently living out their term of exile, for motives that are known only to them.[119]

He made a number of suggestions regarding measures that should be taken to tackle this problem. His key advice was that a special unit should be set up to tackle escape, and that exiles should be more carefully sited. Other sources confirmed the gloomy picture painted by Sofronov. A letter from the chief of police for Zabaikal region in February 1911 confirmed the straightforward nature of escape:

> the inadequate number of police means that escape is easy, and 'a simple stroll for the fully indentured citizen' . . . Those who don't escape are only those who don't want to run away, who lived in Russia worse before katorga than they do now.[120]

The prospects for escape continued to be very good despite the attention paid to the problem by the authorities. Irkutsk's police administration filed a slightly desperate report on the security situation for exiles in 1916:

> As a result of your request of 15 October I have the honour to report that exiles' escapes have become most commonplace events. For escape, exiles need means and the desire. The police cannot hinder escapes of exiles, who have the right to move freely around the province. If the majority of exiles remain in exile, then it is only because they don't find escape a welcome prospect. Some of them feel that it is advantageous to their material condition, that leaving their place of exile would be a greater punishment, others don't have much paid work but find it undesirable to go into illegal existence, and a third group, the poor and those of indifferent abilities, don't go because they don't have the means, and because they are aware that life is no easier in other places. As a result of the small number of police officers, far from all escapes are known of . . . [121]

---

[118] GAIO, f. 25, op. 6, d. 5385, pp. 35–40; report from college advisor Sofronov to Leonid Mikhailovich Mniazev, regarding state of exile in the region, received in Irkutsk December 1912, p. 37.
[119] GAIO, f. 25, op. 6, d. 5385, pp. 35–40; report from college advisor Sofronov to Leonid Mikhailovich Mniazev, regarding state of exile in the region, received in Irkutsk December 1912, pp. 37–8.
[120] GAIO, f. 25, op. 1, d. 3104, p. 147; letter from captain of the police administration in Zabaikal region to director of the police department, 22 February 1911.
[121] GAIO, f. 600, op. 1, d. 1024, p. 537; secret report to the Department of Police, special section, from Irkutsk police administration, 1 November 1916.

Although Yakutsk presented a greater challenge to would-be escapees because of its extreme remoteness, and because the density of exile settlement was much lower than in Irkutsk and Eniseisk regions, the challenges of observing exiles were greater because of the vastness of the territory and the small numbers of police. Yakutsk's governor reported to the Irkutsk police administration in July 1914 that there was absolutely no observation of exiles living among the town population. Even in Yakutsk district, which had the highest density of police employees in the region, there were very few and sometimes no reports at all on exiles. He went on to state:

> These conditions lead to uncontrollable escapes of criminal exiles from the region, persecuted and starved by the local population. The first stage for escapees is secret work in the mines in the dark taiga of Vitimsk and Olekminsk mine systems. From Viliuisk runaways go down empty river tributaries and on to Enisei. Exiles for state crimes cannot, because of the conditions of their former life, bear the deprivations associated with escape through the unpopulated taiga. They run away more rarely... [122]

These official reports make the ubiquity of escape clear. What, though, did escape actually entail for individual exiles? For the majority of exiles, escape did not entail leaving Russia, or even Siberia, altogether. Many exiles were listed as 'escaped' because they had left their place of exile without permission, but were in fact searching for work in the region. The vast majority of 'escapes' were nothing more than that the exile left their place of settlement and went elsewhere in the region in the search for work. These narratives tended not to be recorded in memoirs. A couple of cases from the archives allow us to illuminate these wandering escapes. Nikolai Pavlov Gribov, known as Solov'ev, was convicted of robbery and sent to Yakutsk for four years in May 1907. He ran away from Yakutsk in September 1907, but by January 1908 he was captured in Olekminsk and returned to Yakutsk. From there, he was sent to Khatyn-Iadrinsk and then to Ust-Maisk village in June 1908. He ran away again and was recaptured on 24 August 1908. His place of settlement was changed to remote Verkhoiansk, and he was to be sent there on 4 September 1908. [123] The final act in his file was that, on 8 December 1910, it was reported that he refused to go to his place of settlement in Namsk settlement (*ulus*), and was therefore detained in the transfer section of Yakutsk town prison. [124] Gribov's story suggests that he was not making daring dashes for freedom, but was moving itinerantly through the region.

The case file of Konstantin Josifovich Dmitriev provides us with an insight into the motivations and outcomes of another such 'escapee'. Dmitriev had been sentenced in February 1906 to four years of katorga followed by exile for his participation in a revolutionary committee. He was a machinist by trade, and came from Chernigov province. He was 160 cm tall, and had a 'red face, blonde

[122] NARS f. 12, op. 21, d. 168, pp. 15–16; letter to Irkutsk police from Yakutsk governor, 12 July 1914.
[123] NARS, f. 15, op. 20, d. 84, p. 48; information list (*stateinyi spisok*) on administrative exile peasant Nikolai Pavlov Gribov (Solov'ev).
[124] NARS, f. 15, op. 20, d. 84, p. 71; decree of Yakutsk region police officer, 8 December 1910.

hair, grey eyes, medium sized nose, average build.'[125] He was married, and his wife and family had followed him to Siberia and lived in Verkhneudinsk. His term of katorga was ended early, in 1908, and he seemed to have been transferred to the almshouse in Khatyn-Iadrinsk in September 1909. Dmitriev had asked permission to live in Yakutsk in December 1909, in order to work on a specific construction project, but this request was refused because by the time his letter was considered, the project had already been completed.[126] He made a further request for permission to move on 15 January 1910:

> I have the honour to humbly ask your highness to submit my petition before the governor about permission to receive an annual ticket for the region and Bodaibo, so that I may work in my specialty. All the time I have been employed as a machinist, and on the railroads . . . I humbly ask you to grant me permission to leave Yakutsk town. Signed K. Dmitriev. 15 January 1910. (all in his own hand)[127]

This letter received a positive response from the Yakutsk police inspector (*ispravnik*); he was granted permission to move around the region, and around the mining region to search for work.[128] A letter from Yakutsk's regional administration to the region's police inspector reported Dmitriev as missing on 30 May 1912.

> Konstantin DMITRIEV is hidden somewhere unknown; description of Dmitriev; he is 160cm tall, 40 years old, fair haired, grey eyes, fair moustache, clean face, no special marks. Reporting about this, I ask that by the order of the governor you make an order for a search for Dmitriev, in case of his discovery he is to be directed to his place of residence, and governor to be informed.[129]

No outcome of this apparent escape is on file, but judging from subsequent correspondence, it was not a sinister absence. In August 1912, Dmitriev wrote to the local administration asking permission to move around Siberia:

> Request. In view of this, that I have lived in settlement for four years, three in Yakutsk and a year in Zabaikal region, and in agreement with the regulations about exile, I have the possibility to ask for a passport around Siberia, and so I humbly ask you to give out to me a passport book around Yakutsk region, round Kirensk, Verkhoiansk, and Balagansk districts. I have permission from the Yakutsk governor to move around Olekminsk and Viliuisk as long as I do not enter the towns, and this is where I live now. . . . I have enclosed my old passport from 19 March 1911. Signed Konstantin Dmitriev (this letter is all written in his own hand). 15 August 1912.[130]

Though Dmitriev was not given a right to roam across Siberia as a result of his petition, Irkutsk's military governor gave him permission to travel in order to search for work in the Kirensk, Verkholensk, and Balagan districts of Irkutsk province.[131] Dmitriev's case underlines the geographical mobility of exiles, which was forced

[125] NARS, f. 15, op. 18, d. 186, pp. 7–8; information list (*stateinyi spisok*).
[126] NARS, f. 15, op. 18, d. 186, p. 12.   [127] NARS, f. 15, op. 18, d. 186, p. 19.
[128] NARS, f. 15, op. 18, d. 186, p. 18; letter from Yakutsk regional police inspector to Yakutsk regional administration, 23 January 1910.
[129] NARS, f. 15, op. 18, d. 186, p. 25.   [130] NARS, f. 15, op. 18, d. 186, p. 3.
[131] NARS, f. 15, op. 18, d. 186, p. 13.

upon them by their search for work. While some unauthorized absences from places of settlement were actual escapes, many more reflected the difficulties of tracking and surveying mobile populations.

The memoir literature is predominated by more dramatic escape narratives. Grigorii Moiseevich Kramarov's memoir provided detailed accounts of his multiple escapes from exile. Kramarov was sentenced to four years of katorga in January 1907 for his participation in revolutionary demonstrations. At the end of his katorga sentence in 1910, he was exiled to Barzugin, in Zabaikal region, which was nearly 200 miles from the railway. There were around fifty political exiles in Barzugin, and the authorities tried to prevent their escape by placing a cordon across the only road towards the train station, and by placing two permanent guard posts in Adamovke, the largest neighbouring village. Despite these precautions, escape attempts were frequent. Kramarov makes it clear that his options were determined by financial considerations. He did not have the funding or the political connections to lubricate his passage to freedom.

Kramarov's first attempt to escape was a failure, and marked him for special observations from the authorities, and transfer to the Yakutsk region, from whence escape was extremely difficult. This planned move motivated Kramarov to try again before he was moved to Yakutsk. He befriended another political exile who also wanted to escape, and they made their plans together. The route east through Chita was preferable, but they could not raise the one hundred roubles they needed for this journey. In the end, they waited till the spring, when the thaw was just beginning, and then walked round the edge of the cordon, and picked up the road to Maksimovka, a village about sixteen miles away. The journey took them about three days, and they carried their supplies on their shoulders. They were chilled to the bone from sleeping on the frozen ground, desperately thirsty, and exhausted by their struggle through pathless bog and swamp. When they arrived in Maksimovka, they were sheltered and fed by one Lobanchuk, a political exile who had settled there. From there, they went on foot without difficulty for another sixteen miles, but from there they hired horses, and travelled down to lake Baikal. They then travelled in a little boat relatively quickly and easily to the train station at Verkhneudinsk, where they were able to buy tickets without any trouble, and travelled to Irkutsk. Kramarov stayed in Irkutsk for four months but was rearrested in the summer of 1911. He escaped again while in transit to exile. His successful escape from Barzugin left him well prepared for his next attempt:

> While sitting in Irkutsk prison, I again began to prepare a new escape. Experience had taught me that for success two things were required—selection of time and place of escape, an address where one could prepare to run, a final destination and addresses on the way, money and a passport.

After a series of adventures, Kramarov succeeded in getting to Kharbin, and then over the border to Japan.[132] Kramarov's experiences were marked by independence, extreme physical discomfort, and the need for physical strength and courage, as well

---

[132] G. Kramarov, 'Iz ssylki na voliu (vospominaniia),' *Katorga i ssylka*, no. 4 (1922).

as planning and experience. They give us a hint of what escape might have entailed for exiles without independent means.

False passports and papers seem to have been ubiquitous. There are references to exiles simply forging their papers, but there was no doubt a trade in stolen papers as well. A secret circular from the Irkutsk province police administration on 9 July 1910 reported the theft of fourteen blank passport books from Ashekhabsk township administration, by a group of men armed with pistols.[133]

Escapes that entailed a dramatic dash for the freedom of Western Europe or America generally required significant financial backing. Marie Sukloff's escapes come into the romantic and dramatic category. Kramarov's account is a useful corrective to the tone of Sukloff's escapes, where the only barriers to her freedom were the diligence of the Tsarist authorities. In Sukloff's first escape, from her exile in Aleksandrovsk village, in Enisei region, she simply walked away from her exile village, to the village twenty-eight miles away where the Orloffs, an exiled couple, lived. From there she travelled unimpeded, paying peasants to drive her in stages to Krasnoiarsk, then hopping on the railway to Vilna. She travelled with the Orloff's young son, and this enabled her to evade any police attention.[134] Her second escape was much more dramatic. She was a prisoner in Maltsev hard labour prison between 1906 and 1910, but managed to escape from the hospital in Irkutsk where she was being treated for appendicitis. As a well-known political convict, the authorities exercised themselves in trying to find her, and she had a series of close shaves as she hid in successive not very safe houses around Irkutsk before finally heading east to Shanghai, and from there to Europe by steamer. In both these escapes, Sukloff was financed by funds sent from 'comrades' in the revolutionary movement.[135] Such dramatic tales of derring-do were the exception rather than the norm.

Those who did escape from exile into emigration were often from wealthier backgrounds, and had higher levels of education. The distances and dynamics of leaving the country required significant funds, and were generally restricted to those with sufficient private means to finance such an expedition.[136] Lydia Dan's escape from Olekminsk cost 3,000 roubles, but, 'It was fairly easy. It was largely a matter of money, because escape was very expensive—2000 kilometres by horse.'[137] Of 299 Socialist Revolutionary Party members exiled to eastern Siberia, sixty-two escaped to an overseas destination. Twenty-five of the sixty-two émigrés (40 per cent of the total) who spent time abroad were women. This disproportionate number of women may be a result of the predominance of women from wealthier parental backgrounds. The most popular destination for exiles was Paris, where almost a quarter (fifteen individuals) lived for some time. An organization existed in Paris

[133] NARS f. 15, op. 22, d. 136, p. 635.
[134] Sukloff, *The life story of a Russian exile*, pp. 113–21. See also D.S. Nadel'shtein, 'Pobeg Marii Shkol'nik,' *Katorga i ssylka*, no. 2 (1921) pp. 48–58.
[135] Sukloff, *The life story of a Russian exile*, pp. 198–251.
[136] Clements Evans, *Bolshevik Women* p. 116, recounts the flight of Evgeniia Bosh, and her lover Iurii Piatikov from Siberia to Switzerland in 1914, financed by money sent to them by their families.
[137] Haimson, *The making of three Russian revolutionaries*, p. 174.

specifically for the assistance of Russian former prisoners and exiles.[138] Apart from Paris, a range of destinations was frequented roughly equally by the exiles, all over the globe. The most popular of these were France, the United States of America, and Switzerland. Paris and Geneva were, historically, centres for Russian exiles, and had a thriving Russian community to embrace the new arrivals. Zurich in particular sheltered a long-standing and well-developed émigré colony. The University of Zurich's policy allowing women to enrol on an equal basis with men particularly drew women émigrés.[139] In Paris Social Democrats and Socialist Revolutionaries ran separate Russian libraries, and there was a non-party club, where social events were held and political questions discussed. The exiles of the post-1905 period were mostly lower class, and they lacked the money, linguistic skills, and cultural understanding that greased the wheels of life in a new country, unlike the cosmo-politan intelligentsia that had made up the bulk of the pre-1905 émigrés.[140] Those who knew a trade were able to find work, but even this was difficult, because of unfamiliar working practices.[141] One former Paris exile, Iadov, described a 'sedi-ment' of the Russian emigrant community, who worked in factories and other industrial enterprises. It was apparently a running joke in the city that that all Paris chauffeurs spoke Russian, because so many Russian émigrés worked in the city as chauffeurs.[142]

CONCLUSIONS

Work was the central defining factor in everyday experience of exile. It was a key concern of the state, of local administration, and of exiles themselves. Work encapsulated some of the most fundamental contradictions of the exile system—if exiles were to be productive settlers, rather than an economic burden, then they had to work. The sparse population and infrastructure of eastern Siberia precluded the possibility of mass productive work, however, and ensured that this destination was unsuitable for productive and self-sufficient exile precisely because of the characteristics that identified it as a suitable punitive destination, namely its remoteness and its sparse population. Many of the best-known depictions of exile in eastern Siberia present only a very partial account of lived experience, which do not reflect the realities of daily life for the majority of exiles who lacked private means or external financial support, and who had to rely on their own skills, tenacity, and resourcefulness to survive.

This chapter has tried to interrogate the question of work and escape from two main perspectives. It has prioritized the experiences of exiles themselves. By exploring the career trajectories of exiles, and the nature and conditions of the work

---

[138] *Politicheskaia katorga i ssylka*, p. 618. P.I. Strokov lived in Geneva and Paris until 1917, and worked in an organization for the assistance of Russian prisoners and exiles.

[139] Alpern Engel, *Mothers and Daughters*, p. 127.

[140] Iadov, 'Parizhskaia emigratsiia v godi voini,' *Katorga i ssylka* (1923), p. 196.

[141] 'Parizhskaia emigratsiia v godi voini', p. 197.

[142] 'Parizhskaia emigratsiia v godi voini', p. 198.

that they took, we have been given insights into the course of daily life for exiles, and the challenges of sustaining body and soul in these remote locations. The narratives of exiles' working lives emphasize the centrality of movement around the eastern Siberian landscape in their search for work. This mobility made exiles difficult to supervise, oversee, and monitor. Escape was ubiquitous, but for many exiles, escape was a term that occluded their lived experience, which was actually of unauthorized movement across the region in search of work.

This chapter has explored the ways in which work and employment for exiles intersected with the administrative challenges of mass exile. Local authorities faced a morass of conflicting priorities. They had to oversee and monitor exiles. They had to try to enable exiles to work, so that they did not constitute a burden on the region, and in order that they could live a reasonable life. They had to try to protect and to respond to the concerns of native Siberians, both ethnically Russian and indigenous, whose own daily lives had to go on alongside the mobile exile population. Exiles could be construed as making a positive contribution to the region, bringing a skilled workforce and even cultural and political enlightenment. In practice, though, it was their negative contributions to the region that were emphasized in the narrative here, as exiles contributed to land hunger, criminality, and unemployment.

Escape brings the problem of administering exile to its fulcrum. The local administration was responsible for monitoring exiles and controlling their movement, but they had insufficient means and resources at their disposal to complete this function. Though in principle exile worked as a prison without walls, in practice the boundaries of exile locations were entirely porous, and exiles effectively moved freely through the Siberian landscape, and beyond.

5

Illness and Death in Siberian Exile

To Yakutsk governor, from transfer prisoner Mikhail Komolov, 2 April 1910. Request. I humbly request that I, Komolov, 60 years old, as a result of weak health and illness I am not fit for physical labour, so I don't have any means for my life. In view of this I humbly appeal to you to authorise me [to be moved] from my place of settlement to Khatyn Iadrinsk almshouse (*bogadel'no*), I have a hope that my request will be satisfied. I submit my petition through the prison captain. This request has been written at my personal request by Andrei Chipachev.[1]

This chapter aims to interrogate the subjective experience of illness for prisoners, and the distinctions prisoners made between legitimate and illegitimate forms of punishment. The chapter also explores state policies towards sick prisoners, and explores how different levels of the Tsarist administration and local Siberian society dealt with the challenge of sick and decrepit exiles. We also illustrate and develop three of the key paradoxes that have emerged repeatedly through this book. First, the state's dual goals in using exile as both punishment and as a means of settlement was particularly problematized by the ill health of exiles, as this ill health was often a direct outcome of the goal of punishment. Second, by focusing on the health of the punished, we highlight that the state's use of work both as punishment and as a productive economic activity was deeply problematic.[2] Finally, this chapter once again explores the evident disparities between what the state professed that it would do, that is, policy intentions and statements, and the real state of local conditions and practice.

For the state, the care of decrepit (*driakhlyi*) prisoners and exiles was paradoxical. The state sought to punish criminals, yet also to make use of their productive potential through forced labour and settlement in some of the harshest and most forbidding regions of the empire. A significant proportion of prisoners were however rendered unfit to look after even themselves. The state was forced to expend time and resources providing care to the very individuals it punished. By the early twentieth century, a range of measures were brought in to try and restrict the numbers of decrepit prisoners and exiles sent to eastern Siberia. Convicts had to be passed as fit to be sent. After 1904, those over seventy were excluded from

---

[1] NARS, f. 12, op. 2, d. 5279, l. 21.

[2] These challenges are also evident in the Gulag system. See Dan Healey, 'Lives in the Balance: Weak and Disabled Prisoners and the Biopolitics of the Gulag,' *Kritika: Explorations in Russian and Eurasian History*, no. 3 (2015).

katorga labour, and those over sixty were excluded from exile in settlement.[3] These measures to exclude the elderly and infirm from Siberian exile were motivated by pragmatic rather than humanitarian considerations.[4] Ultimately, their success was very limited, because even where limits were placed on who was to be sent to Siberia, prisoners had their health compromised by the journey to Siberia itself, and by the conditions in katorga and eastern Siberian exile once they got there. Even those who were fit at the start of their journey to exile ran a high risk of mental and physical illness by the time they reached their destination.

I found only fragmentary evidence on the medical treatment, illness, and mortality rates of exiles, and significantly more information on sickness and treatment in prisons. The statistical information presented here is drawn mainly from prison inspectors' reports and the official, published statements of the Main Prison Administration. These sources are problematic, as both could be charged with trying to present the state of the prisons in the best possible light. The prison inspectors' reports acknowledged multiple failings of the system, however, and stressed the need for reform, which indicated that they did not present an entirely unrealistic representation of the prisons. Where statistics are utilized in this chapter, they are used as indicators of what we might be able to infer about exile illness.

There is a developing field of literature relating to sickness and healthcare in late Imperial Russia, but it has focused more on epidemiology, and on the experiences of healthcare workers as professionals, as activists, and their relationship with the state.[5] Adele Lindenmeyr's work on charity and welfare provision in late Imperial Russia focused on public welfare and private giving, and deals only in passing with the recipients of this welfare.[6] My focus on local experience indicates that, in accordance with this literature, there was a gulf between policy direction and proclamation at the centre, and its implementation in the regions. The policies of differentiation through punishment that Schrader demonstrated in her work are not discernible in the treatment and care of the sick and infirm.[7]

As we know, supervision over exiles once they had been transported to their place of exile was of the most nominal sort. The main disincentive to escape was the expense and difficulty of extended travel, not state imposed boundaries. The corollary to this lack of supervision from the state, however, was a corresponding lack of support. Chapter 3 explored the challenges of life in exile, and the importance of interpersonal relationships in making these challenges more bearable. For the aged and infirm exile population, the absence of established community and family networks heightened the pains of old age and decrepitude.

[3] G. Gol'shukh, 'Prizrenie driakhlykh ssyl'nikh v Irkutskoi gubernii,' *Tiuremnyi vestnik* (1910).
[4] Schrader, *Languages of the Lash: Corporal Punishment and Identity in late Imperial Russia*, p. 185.
[5] Nancy M. Frieden, *Russian physicians in an era of reform and revolution, 1856–1905* (Princeton, 1992); Mary Schaeffer Conroy, 'Health Care in Prisons, Labour and Concentration Camps in Early Soviet Russia, 1918–1921,' *Slavic Review*, no. 7 (2000); Charlotte E. Henze, *Disease, health care and government in late Imperial Russia: Life and death on the Volga, 1823–1914* (Abingdon, 2011); S.G. Solomon and J.F. Hutchinson, *Health and society in revolutionary Russia* (Bloomington, 1990); John F. Hutchinson, *Politics and public health in revolutionary Russia, 1890–1918* (Baltimore, 1990).
[6] Lindenmeyr, *Poverty is not a Vice: Charity, society and the State in Late Imperial Russia.*
[7] Schrader, *Languages of the Lash: Corporal Punishment and Identity in late Imperial Russia.*

TYPES AND RATES OF ILLNESS

Mortality rates are high for prisoner populations in general, and late Imperial Russia was no exception to this. We have some statistical information for prisoners in prisons, but information for those in exile is extremely limited. Statistics on mortality rates support anecdotal evidence that prison conditions worsened dramatically after 1906 because of overcrowding and a hardening of the regime.[8] Using mortality rates in different types of prisons, and comparing them to an adjusted national mortality rate, one study showed that there were very significant improvements made in prison mortality from the 1880s to 1906, but that after 1906 mortality rates rocketed. Mortality rates were worse for katorga prisoners than any other category of prison. This was partly a reflection of the longer terms usually served by katorga prisoners. Between 1906 and 1914, mortality rates in all prisons were three to four times higher than mortality rates among the general population. In katorga prisons, mortality rates peaked at 67.4 per thousand in 1911.[9] To put this figure into context, mortality rates for men between the ages of twenty and forty in the period 1908–10 were 38.8 per thousand.[10] Mortality rates in Siberia during 1926 were 25.6 per thousand.[11] These broader figures obscure irregularities in mortality rates between different institutions, and different categories of prisoner, at different times. As we have seen in other chapters, different places of punishment had distinct microclimates defined by the number and type of prisoners, by the physical geography of the place, and by the character of the administration. To give an extreme example of what this could mean in real terms, of 330 political prisoners sentenced to katorga sentences between 1861 and 1893, more than a third of them (118) died either in katorga prisons, or in exile.[12] This extremely high death rate would have to be interrogated through a closer inspection of the particularities of those prisoners and their places of punishment.

We can infer from high mortality rates in prison that prisoners experienced relatively high incidence of sickness and disability. The rate of traffic through the outpatients' section of Aleksandrovsk, Irkutsk's katorga prison, gives an indication of the incidence of illness among prisoners. In 1908 alone, the prison outpatients' section recorded a total of 53,138 outpatients, and 945 inpatients. The average number of resident patients in the hospital on any day was 138, out of a total katorga population of 2,140.[13] The proportion of prisoners fit to work offers another indicator of illness levels among prisoners. Nerchinsk, the complex of katorga prisons in the east of the Zabaikal region, was the destination for most long-serving katorga prisoners in Siberia. In Nerchinsk in 1896, only 42 per cent of

[8] E. Eikhgol'ts, *Tiuremnyi vrachi i ego patsienty* (Petrograd, 1916).

[9] Wheatcroft, 'The crisis of the late Tsarist penal system', p. 41.

[10] Adolf G. Rashin, *Naselenie Rossii za 100 let (1813–1913)* (Moscow, 1956), table 155.

[11] F. Lorimer, *The Population of the Soviet Union, History and Prospects* (Geneva, 1946), table 30.

[12] Margolis, *Tiur'ma i ssylka v Imperatorskoi Rossii. Issledovanie i arkhivnye nakhodki*, p. 191.

[13] Khrulev, *Katorga v Sibiri: Izvlechenie iz otcheta nachal'nika glavnago tiuremnago upravlenie S.S. Khruleva o sluzhebnoi poezdke, v 1909 godu, v Irkutskoi gub. i Zabaikalskuiu obl.*, p. 13.

the 1,159 prisoners were medically fit to work, mainly because of poor food and conditions.[14] This figure had not improved substantially by 1909, when 30 per cent of the prisoners in the Nerchinsk complex were either too weak to work, or in the almshouse. Of 3,767 prisoners, 1,133 were deemed weak and unfit to work or were in the almshouse and categorized as unfit to care for themselves.[15]

Nerchinsk was by far the most overcrowded of Russia's katorga prisons in the early twentieth century. By 1914, it had places for 1,572 prisoners, but held 3,560 residents.[16] Overcrowding is one of the single most compelling indicators of a poor environment in prisons.[17] Other factors, such as the attitudes of the prison administration, or the relationships between prisoners, are harder to quantify than overcrowding, but were also important. We have a number of vivid memoirs from former inmates of Nerchinsk describing conditions there. The character of the prison governor was represented as extremely important in shaping prisoner health and experience.

Women prisoners were more likely to be ill than men. Among the prison population in 1908, it was reported that 7 per cent of the male prison population were sick, compared to 11 per cent of the female prison population. This was accounted for by the incidence of 'women's conditions', in particular, childbirth and illnesses arising from childbirth.[18]

What kinds of illness predominated amongst prisoners? There is some patchy evidence concerning the types of illness prevalent among prisoners in Siberia, but the absence of *zemstva*[19] in Siberia means that there is little comparative data available for the free Siberian population. The most common illnesses, and those illnesses causing most deaths, were respiratory illnesses and gastrointestinal illnesses.[20] Figure 5.1 shows the incidence of illness among all Russian prisoners in 1914, and Figure 5.2 shows reported illness in Irkutsk prisons between 1905 and 1913. Figure 5.2 gives some clear indicators about the prevalence of different conditions, though the amalgamation of multiple conditions into the catch-all of 'general infectious diseases' limits the extent of our knowledge. Two-thirds of deaths came from this category (918 of 1,367 reported deaths), and around one-third of illnesses (10,262 of 29,070 reported illnesses). This category included deaths from epidemics including typhus, malaria, and cholera. Despite some

[14] Malinovskii, *Ssylka v Sibir. Publichnaia lektsiia. Chitaniia v Tomske v Noiabre 1899 goda.*

[15] Khrulev, *Katorga v Sibiri: Izvlechenie iz otcheta nachal'nika glavnago tiuremnago upravlenie S.S. Khruleva o sluzhebnoi poezdke, v 1909 godu, v Irkutskoi gub. i Zabaikalskuiu obl.*, pp. 49–50.

[16] *Otchet po glavnomu tiuremnomu upravleniiu za 1913g*, p. 32.

[17] See Meredith P. Huey and Thomas L. Mcnulty, 'Institutional Conditions and Prison Suicide: Conditional Effects of Deprivation and Overcrowding,' *The Prison Journal*, no. 4 (2005).

[18] *Otchet po glavnomu tiuremnomu upravleniiu za 1908g*, p. 93.

[19] *Zemstva* were organs of local government established in 1864 as part of Alexander II's 'Great Reforms'. They were not established in the empire's western and eastern regions. The *zemstva*, among their many other functions, compiled rich and wide-ranging statistics on conditions of life, economy, and agriculture in their regions.

[20] *Polozhenie tiuremnoi chasti i ssylki v Irkutskoi gubernii po dannym dokladov tiuremnago inspektora, 1911–1913gg*, pp. 17–27, 83–7.

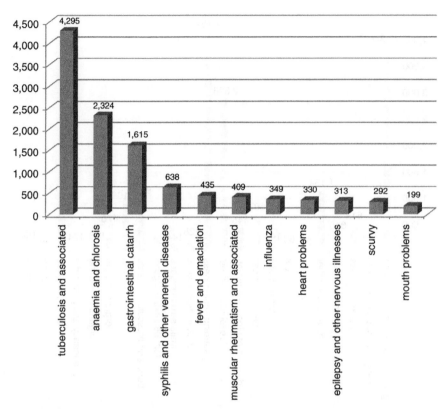

Figure 5.1. Average daily number of patients in Russian prisons in 1910, by illness[21]

improvements to diet, scurvy continued to be a significant disease among prisoners, with around 5,000 cases annually in 1909 and 1910.[22]

Tuberculosis was the main disease causing adult death among the free population in town and village alike. There were 35,808 cases of tuberculosis in the general population of Russia in 1913.[23] Tuberculosis was also overwhelmingly the most prevalent condition in prisons, with an average of 4,295 patients daily in Russian prisons in 1914.[24] Tuberculosis was believed to be hereditary for much of the nineteenth century. We can infer that a significant proportion of the deaths and illness reported in non-infectious diseases would have been accounted for by tuberculosis. There are numerous accounts of deaths from tuberculosis in the memoir literature. One exile wrote in 1915–16 of the death of one of their community, 'Semion died from rapid consumption. His death left an extremely

[21] *Otchet po glavnomu tiuremnomu upravleniiu za 1910g*, p. 36.
[22] *Otchet po glavnomu tiuremnomu upravleniiu za 1910g*, p. 82.
[23] R.B. Kaganovich, *Iz istorii bor'by s tuberkulezom v dorevoliutsionnoi Rossii* (Moscow, 1952), pp. 64–5.
[24] *Otchet po glavnomu tiuremnomu upravleniiu za 1909g*, p. xiv.

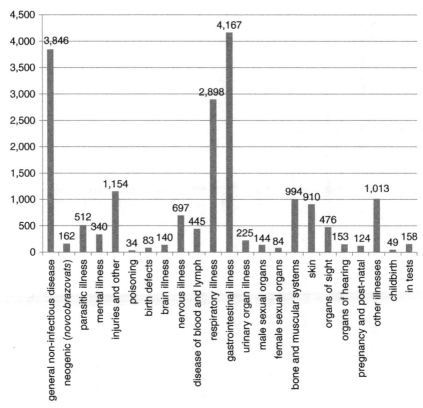

Figure 5.2. Illness in Irkutsk prisons, 1905–13, excluding general infectious diseases[25]

heavy impression on all of us. Our commune is orphaned!'[26] The death of Anatolii Kriltsov in the final chapters of Tolstoy's *Resurrection* in some respects epitomizes the suffering of exiles with tuberculosis.

> He tried to continue, but turning red he began coughing, worse than before, and a stream of blood rushed from his mouth. Nabatov ran to get some snow. Mary Pavlovna brought valerian drops and offered them to him, but, breathing quickly and heavily, he pushed her away with his thin white hand, and kept his eyes closed.[27]

Kriltsov's suffering is a background theme of the latter part of *Resurrection*. His death towards the end of the novel is used by Tolstoy as a final indictment of the pointless evils of Russia's penal system.

A significant proportion of the illnesses listed in Figure 5.2 can be linked to prison conditions. Overcrowding, poor ventilation, weak nutrition, and repeated

[25] *Polozhenie tiuremnoi chasti i ssylki v Irkutskoi gubernii po dannym dokladov tiuremnago inspektora, 1911–1913gg.*

[26] Bagotskii, 'Krakovskii soiuz pomoshchi politicheskim zakliuchennym,' pp. 172–5.

[27] Tolstoy, *Resurrection*, p. 445.

prison transfers all facilitate the spread and development of tuberculosis and other infectious diseases.[28] The prevalence of gastrointestinal illnesses and respiratory illnesses both indicate that poor ventilation and weak nutrition were significant factors in prisoners' illness.

Exiles' petitions provide insights into individuals' lived experiences of illness. Innokentyi Aleksandrovich Brinev had been sentenced to a six-year term of katorga followed by exile in Yakutsk region for his participation in military organizations. His fiancée Anisia Ivanova Kurbatova, a townswoman from Kirensk district, petitioned Leonid Mikhailovich Kniaezev, Irkutsk's military governor, that his place of exile be changed from Yakutsk to one of the southern districts of Irkutsk. Her justification for this petition was the very poor state of Brinev's health. While in katorga, Brinev 'succumbed to a whole range of illnesses, as a result of which his health was very weak'. In 1911 he contracted typhoid, and he had already suffered from gastrointestinal problems. Because of the typhoid infection, he was sent from Akatui (in Nerchinsk) to Irkutsk, where he had two operations, including the removal of his appendix. He also suffered from chronic catarrh (breathing difficulties). He did not recover well from surgery, and required constant medical attention and a special diet. The administration granted his petition for exile to Irkutsk, as they recognized that Brinev was not fit to be sent to Yakutsk.[29] Brinev's case provides us with an example of the ways in which the illnesses dispassionately listed in Figure 5.2 actually manifested themselves on the bodies of individual prisoners.

ENVIRONMENTAL FACTORS INFLUENCING SICKNESS AND HEALTH

A number of factors explain high rates of illness among prisoners. First, life in eastern Siberia was in itself detrimental to health for the whole population, whether free or punished. Data from the 1920s indicates that in general, levels of health deteriorated as one moved across the Russian Empire from west to east, north and south-east, and levels of health tended to be worse in areas occupied by non-Russian nationalities.[30] Irkutsk and Yakutsk accounted for some of the Russian Empire's most distant eastern and north-eastern outposts. Extreme cold, isolation, very limited medical facilities, dampness, a short growing season, and tough fieldwork conditions provided serious challenges to maintaining a healthy body and mind. Whilst there was a severe shortage of medical personnel in prisons

---

[28] For recent works on the history of tuberculosis, see Thomas Dormandy, *The white death: a history of tuberculosis* (London, 1999); Helen Bynum, *Spitting blood: the history of tuberculosis* (Oxford, 2012); P.K. Yablonskii et al., 'Tuberculosis in Russia. Its History and Its Status Today,' *American Journal of Respiratory and Critical Care Medicine*, no. 4 (2015). For comment on TB in prisons in contemporary context, see 'Tuberculosis in prisons', available at http://www.who.int/tb/challenges/prisons/story_1/en/index.html (accessed 23 September 2015), World Health Organization.

[29] GAIO, 25, 6, 5385, pp. 111–12; letter to Irkutsk military governor from Anisia Ivanova Kurbatova, Kirensk townswoman, Irkutsk province, 20 December 1912, and response from administration.

[30] Lorimer, *The Population of the Soviet Union, History and Prospects*, p. 86.

nationally,[31] Siberia as a whole suffered from a paucity of medical support.[32] The shortage of health care facilities was particularly acute in Yakutsk. By 1903 there were 7 hospitals and 17 doctors serving the whole region. Each doctor's practice covered a massive territory of between 95,000 to 628,000 miles. There were periodic epidemics of smallpox, bronchial typhus, malaria and measles. The First World War accentuated the shortage of doctors as medical staff were mobilised for the war.[33] As we saw in chapter 4 on work, political exiles in eastern Siberia with medical training found their services in great demand, as medical personnel were in very short supply.

As well as these general factors that affected health in Siberia, a number of features particular to the exile community made them particularly susceptible to ill health. First, as we have seen in chapter 2, the process of travel to eastern Siberia was in general long, arduous, and injurious to health. Conditions in the transit prisons and transfer buildings were notoriously vile. Poor quality food, exposure to vermin, infectious diseases, extreme cold, emotional dislocation, and exceptionally unsanitary conditions in transit accommodation, all took their toll on even the hardiest of constitutions. Many exiles arrived at their point of settlement already in very poor health.[34] A significant proportion of new batches of exiles arriving in Yakutsk had to be sent to the ever-expanding almshouse, as they were not fit to work or even to care for themselves.[35] The case of Leonid Aleksandrov Remizov provides us with an illustration of this. Remizov arrived in Yakutsk in June 1909, and was assigned to settle in Amginsk township, Yakutsk district. He wrote to Yakutsk's governor asking that he be transferred directly to an almshouse. Unusually, he wrote this petition in his own hand:

> I am a cripple on both legs, I lost four toes from my left leg from frostbite, and have a defective foot, and I lost my big toe on my right leg, apart from this I suffer from chronic rheumatism of the legs and weakness of eyesight, so that I am not fit for any sort of physical labour, and the regional doctor concluded that I was doomed to various deprivations and beggary on being sent to a place of residence. That is why I find myself placed under your defence and protection, and humbly ask if I can be settled in an almshouse, and not be sent to Amginsk township. 23 June 1909.[36]

The physical outcomes of katorga on the bodies of exiles provided another important factor explaining the high rate of illness among exiles in Siberia. Most of the prisoners sent to this region had a term of katorga included in their sentence. Apart

---

[31] Gran, *Katorga v Sibiri. Izvlechenie iz otcheta o sluzhebnoi poezdke nachal'nika glav. tiurem. upravlenia P.K. Grana v Sibir v 1913 g*, pp. 13–14.

[32] Zhukovskaia, *Istoriko-kul'turnyi atlas Buriatii*, p. 212.

[33] Ivanov, *Istoriko-kul'turnyi atlas Yakutiia*, p. 314.

[34] For example, NARS, f. 12, op. 21, l. 119, p. 87; regarding the illness of part of the party of political exiles, which prevented them from continuing on their journey with the rest of the party, 1907.

[35] NARS, f. 15, op. 18, d. 191, ll. 313–4; list of exiles arriving in Yakutsk town in party of 12 September 1909. Forty-one names, five to be sent straight to almshouse.

[36] NARS, f. 12, op. 2, d. 4693, p. 96, letter from Leonid Aleksandrov Remizov to Yakutsk Governor, 23 June 1909.

from road and rail work, katorga labour was used in the gold and coalmines of the region. Numbers of katorga sentences increased dramatically after 1907, from 7,779 in 1907 to around 32,000 in 1912.[37] The steadily rising prison population after 1906 meant that prisons became increasingly overcrowded, and Siberian prisons were disproportionately affected. In 1909, there were 6,646 katorga prisoners in Siberia, split between Aleksandrovsk transfer and katorga prisons, Tobolsk, and Nerchinsk.[38] By 1914 the number of katorga prisoners in Siberia had risen to 7,452, leaving Siberian katorga prisons 58 per cent over capacity. In January 1914, for example, Aleksandrovsk central katorga prison had 1,975 inmates, but was meant to hold a maximum of 1,500 inmates. Of the twenty-three katorga prisons distributed around the Russian Empire in 1913, the vast majority had fewer inmates than they had places for. Moscow transfer prison and Orlovsk provisional katorga prison were the only oversubscribed prisons outside Siberia, and their level of overcrowding was much lower. The gross overcrowding indicates that conditions in Siberian katorga prisons were worse than elsewhere in the empire.[39] Overcrowding reduced the air quality in prisons, and in particular increased rates of tuberculosis.

The sources are emphatic on the physical outcomes of katorga, particularly if it took place in the mines. The bodies of prisoners were often irredeemably broken by these experiences. Exile-katorga labour was most often employed in the hardest unskilled labour, like wood cutting, land clearance, rock breaking, and so on.[40] The state asked the prison authorities to screen all workers carefully so that only the morally and physically fit were selected for work. Significant categories of the punished population were in principle excluded from this work, including those convicted of serious, primarily political, crimes.[41] In practice, these exclusions were not always maintained. Many of those who applied for work on the railroads were turned down on grounds of their weak health. A prison doctor in Shlissel'burg recalled the vetting process:

> A large party of healthy prisoners was collected for sending to work on the Siberian, Amur and Transbaikal railroads. The doctor must select only the healthiest, youngest and strongest element for this work. Those selected by a doctor are verified by a commission and sent to work on the roads, cutting wood . . . the doctor must be very careful, in order that mistakes are not made. The thing is, the majority of prisoners are unacquainted with the difficult conditions of labour in Amur, but they try to get there in order to shorten their term [of punishment]. Thanks to this, those with pulmonary illnesses throw out their chests and take big breaths in order to hide their defects and try everything to hide their flaws. Even just as the inspection ends, those that are

---

[37] Gran, *Katorga v Sibiri. Izvlechenie iz otcheta o sluzhebnoi poezdke nachal'nika glav. tiurem. upravlenia P.K. Grana v Sibir v 1913 g*, p. 4.

[38] *Otchet po glavnomu tiuremnomu upravleniiu za 1909g*, p. 39.

[39] *Otchet po glavnomu tiuremnomu upravleniiu za 1913g*, p. 32.

[40] Borzunov, *Proletariat Sibiri i dal'nego vostoka nakanune pervoi Russkoi revoliutsii (po materialam stroitel'stva transsibirskoi magistrali, 1891–1904gg)*, p. 35.

[41] NARS, f. 12, op. 2, d. 5169, p. 1; circular from Ministry of Justice to all provincial commissars, 18 November 1910.

rejected make a request to the captain of the prison to be looked over again, and if the doctor refuses their request, the prisoner regards this as a great injury.[42]

F. Drozhzhin, a political katorga prisoner, was sent to the Amur railroad construction site in 1907 in a party of 150. He recalled that the work was heavy manual labour, and that they often could not finish their assigned tasks. He was allocated to a convoy of ten men. They had to walk five miles to their work site. Because of a leg injury, Drozhnin was unable to walk, so was carried by his convoy. He continued to work despite a problem with his hand. The medical assistant (*feldsher*) supervising the camp carried out two operations on his hand, but without success. Drozhnin was eventually unable to work because of the problem with his hand, so he stayed at the camp and did domestic work. He recalled that

> there wasn't a single doctor for the whole section. The doctor came once a year to look over the workers. A medical assistant looked after each section. The medical assistants split sick from healthy according to a high temperature, (though they never believed the first reading) . . . many workers had bloody diarrhoea, but they were never exempted from work.[43]

Another former katorga prisoner, E.P. Dubinskii, recalled his illness while working on the Amur road, known as *Kolesukha*. He described nominal medical support for the sick. The only medicines available for him were castor oil and powdered quinine. Dubinskii did not fully recover from this illness, and was eventually reassigned to work in a village as a scribe instead.[44]

High levels of illness and mortality among prisoners cannot be explained solely by the physical challenges of life in Siberia, travel to exile, and conditions of katorga labour. A prison doctor noted that despite sanitary improvements, despite the absence of alcohol and venereal risks, and despite prison conditions that in some cases were 'significantly better than in the ordinary life of a proletarian', prison mortality rates were significantly higher than among the free population.[45] The psychological impact of social dislocation and the loss of free will are impossible to quantify but certainly significant. For exiles, the absence of extended family and community networks, alongside the physical dislocation of exile, and the psychological sense of forcible disconnection from one's own past, all represented significant challenges to well-being. The ageing process accentuated these challenges. This excerpt from a political exile's letter, written from Verkholensk district in 1912, gives us a sense of the impact of isolation and dislocation on individuals:

> I don't want to hope, that it will come to me to live a long time here, I don't want to feel myself at home, I don't want to feel myself properly [at home] in this cursed place, where you only think about when you will be away from this god forsaken hole . . . and depression, like on the stages, and striving for ideals, but the whole thing is not seen,

---

[42] Eikhgol'ts, *Tiuremnyi vrachi i ego patsienty*, pp. 64–5.

[43] (F. Drozhzhin, 'Listki iz zabytoi tetradi (Vospominaniia ob Amurskoi kolesnoi doroge)', *Katorga i ssylka* I (1921), 64–70.)

[44] Dubinskii, 'Pobeg s "Kolesukhi"', pp. 114–15.

[45] Eikhgol'ts, *Tiuremnyi vrachi i ego patsienty*, p. 103.

where you are. Now I understood, that this is what exile is. Before I thought differently. I thought that is was all the same freedom. But the main thing was to be away from prison. Yes, there is no prison, and I have will, and that is pleasing to me. But when you think, there is nothing to do. Remember this—there is nothing to be done. And that is terrible. Like in prison. And it is worse, that you don't see your enemies. There it was all clear—who to mix with, there the bars and observers stood out, the jailers ... and it was clear, who to mix with and who was your enemy. But here there is nothing. There is simply nothing to do until you are sick with it. [*do toshnoti*]. (Znamensk, Verkholensk district, Irkustk province)[46]

This letter's conversational tone reinforces an impression of 'authentic' recollections and reflections on life. While this chapter so far has discussed the varied aspects of exile that contributed to physical health, this letter encourages us to consider the impact of exile on mental health, a less tangible but centrally important aspect of well-being.

MENTAL HEALTH

But in spite of my numerous occupations, there were periods and intervals in my life that I feared more than anything else. An unbearable, painful, deadly loneliness would suddenly seize my soul and everything would drop out of my hands. A sense of utter isolation from the world so dear to me would pierce my brain like a needle, causing me almost physical suffering ... What a waste! What a silence! The thoughts of the thousands of miles and many long months of travel separating me from the world in which I lived heretofore would breed thoughts of death. (Vladimir Zenzinov, describing his emotional state while in remote Siberian exile)[47]

Such poignant descriptions of depressive episodes are rare in the memoir literature emerging from early twentieth-century exile. Zenzinov's recollections offer a powerful evocation of the emotional challenges posed by acute isolation and exile.

Trying to evaluate the mental health of exiles is a particularly challenging area. Numerous accounts testify to heightened levels of emotional disturbance, trauma, and mental health difficulties, up to and including suicide, among prisoners. We can use the limited statistical evidence available to give us an impression of suicide rates, and levels of psychosis and mental disorder among the prison and exile population in Siberia. Our challenges, however, in discussing mental health, are manifold. By peering into the murky waters of what it is to be sane, and what it is to be mentally ill, we probe into the essence of the lived experience, and pry into the prisoners' very souls. Our ability to do this is conditioned by the ways in which prisoners described themselves, the extent to which they recorded their feelings,

---

[46] Cherkunov, 'Zhizn politicheskoi ssylki i tiur'mi po perekhvachennym pis'mam', p. 173. Cherkunov collected letters from 'the archives' (no references were given), and published them in this article without further referencing.
[47] Zenzinov, *The road to oblivion*, p. 80.

and our own parameters of understanding normalcy and deviance in mental health. We rely entirely on ego-documents, many produced years after the events they describe, as sources for these feelings. Relatively few memoirs refer in the first person to anxieties, depression, and mental illness. This may well be because these aspects of internal life were often not discussed, and would have been avoided or even denied by those exiles that experienced such things. We can see from the statistics, and from the observations of others, that suicide and mental breakdowns were disproportionately experienced in exile life. We have to extrapolate from a rather limited evidence base how and why this mental anguish manifested itself.

We can find circumstantial evidence of high levels of suicide, anxiety, and even, possibly, mental health disorders, among political exiles. We cannot, however, extrapolate any firm conclusions about diagnosis of these reported symptoms, or indeed causes for these symptoms, from the evidence that we have. One work on terrorists in early twentieth-century Russia used the circumstantial evidence of individuals reported to be unbalanced or insane to argue that many political terrorists were actually psychologically imbalanced or 'insane' by modern stand-ards.[48] This approach tapped into some of the contemporary discourse around degeneracy and abnormality, but without subjecting it to the necessary critical distance, and it failed to acknowledge the importance of historical context in evaluating mental health. We cannot evaluate the extent to which an individual's suicidal behaviour and psychosis/neuroses were innate in the individual, to what extent a product of exceptionally harsh and unpleasant conditions of punishment, and to what extent they were a rational response to a repressive political regime.

One aspect of mental health that was recognized and reported, and which therefore offers us some basis for speculation, was suicide. A longer-term statistic indicated that of 330 political exiles sentenced to a hard labour sentence between 1861 and 1893, 118 died in katorga prisons and exile. Of these, twenty-six killed themselves (seventeen in katorga), and twenty-five went mad.[49] There are no compiled statistics available on suicide among the exile population, but the prison administration compiled statistics on suicide among prisoners.[50] Suicide among the imprisoned population between 1903 and 1906 was stable at around four suicides per 10,000 prisoners. The relative number of suicides doubled between 1907 and 1914, to seven or eight per 10,000.[51] The prison authorities suggested that this increase reflected an increase in suicides among the free population in this period. We have evidence from other sources that conditions and overcrowding worsened

---

[48] Geifman, *Thou Shalt Kill; Revolutionary terrorism in Russia, 1894–1917*, esp. pp. 167–72.

[49] Margolis, *Tiur'ma i ssylka v Imperatorskoi Rossii. Issledovanie i arkhivnye nakhodki*, p. 191.

[50] Suicide here refers to both attempts at suicide, and successful suicides. The statistics are given separately for some years, and amalgamated in others, so I have left them together in order to provide a comparison.

[51] Statistics drawn from data collated by the prison administration in their annual publication between 1907 and 1917 (*Otchet po glavnomu tiuremnomu upravleniiu za 1908g; Otchet po glavnomu tiuremnomu upravleniiu za 1909g; Otchet po glavnomu tiuremnomu upravleniiu za 1910g; 'Otchet po glavnomu tiuremnomu upravleniiu* za 1912g'; *Otchet po glavnomu tiuremnomu upravleniiu za 1913g; Otchet po glavnomu tiuremnomu upravleniiu za 1914g* (Petrograd, 1916); *Otchet po glavnomu tiuremnomu upravleniiu za 1915g*).

significantly in prisons. If we look at various breakdowns of prison suicides by region, these show that between 1906 and 1909, Irkutsk province had by far the highest numbers of suicides (twenty-four). In subsequent years, the suicide rates in Irkutsk were not exceptional, and were far outpaced by suicides in Moscow and St Petersburg/Petrograd. These figures give us a baseline indicator that suicide rates were significantly raised in our period. The statistics obscure very significant variations in suicide rate from one province to another, and these rates changed from year to year, depending on the microclimate of particular prisons at a particular time.

The prison authorities commented on this dramatic increase in suicides, but were reluctant to speculate on explanations for these rises, and for the hot spots in Irkutsk and other cities at various times. The only suggestion made by official sources was that a higher suicide rate was predicated on increased numbers of intelligentsia or 'semi-intelligentsia' individuals, who were more inclined to take their own lives than prisoners from the illiterate part of the population.[52] This comment alludes to the influx of political prisoners associated with the repressions in the aftermath of the 1905 revolution. One scholar suggested that the wave of suicides in Irkutsk prisons were a result of the failure of escape attempts, and the cessation of escape attempts, after 1908. In fact, suicide rates in Irkutsk lowered very significantly after 1909, so there is no correlation between inability to escape and suicide.[53]

It is a challenge to place these figures in any kind of comparative context. There were no official Russian national statistics on suicide rates in this period, although a number of observers attempted to collate Russia's suicide rates based on a range of data sets, including press reports.[54] The Russian press dwelled on the theme of a suicide epidemic in the early twentieth century, and, suggested some extraordinarily high rates of suicide from five to eleven suicides per 10,000 of the population.[55] If these were accurate, they would suggest that the rates of suicide in Russian prisons accorded with suicide levels among the free population. Other statistical evidence we have on suicide indicates significantly higher rates of suicide among the imprisoned population than among the free population.[56] The rise of suicide was seen both as a marker of alienation and disaffection caused by urbanization and industrialization, and as inextricably linked to the national political situation.[57]

[52] *Otchet po glavnomu tiuremnomu upravleniiu za 1910g*, p. 58.
[53] Bykova, 'Istoriia Aleksandrovskago tsentrala', p. 166.
[54] Kenneth Martin Pinnow, *Lost to the collective: suicide and the promise of Soviet socialism, 1921–1929* (Ithaca NY, 2009), p. 36.
[55] D. Zhbankov, 'O samoubiistvakh v poslednie gody (Statisticheskii ocherk),' *Russkoe Bogatstvo*, no. 5 (1908). For a critical reading of Zhbankov's source base and approach, see Irina Paperno, *Suicide as a cultural institution in Dostoevsky's Russia* (Ithaca; London, 1997), pp. 95–6, 236, footnote 89.
[56] Male suicide rates in contemporary Britain sit at around 1.6 per 10,000 (according to the Office for National Statistics: http://www.ons.gov.uk/ons/taxonomy/index.html?nscl=Suicide+Rates#tab-data-tables [22 January 2016]). Suicide rates in prison ranged from six per 10,000 (1985) to twelve per 10,000 (2004), according to statistics compiled by the Howard League (http://www.howardleague.org/suicide-in-prison [22 January 2016]).
[57] Susan K. Morrissey, *Suicide and the body politic in Imperial Russia* (Cambridge, 2006), pp. 212–14; Pinnow, *Lost to the collective*, p. 32.

Educated society understood suicide to be a symptom that afflicted the Russian population after the first Russian revolution, and was in the same camp as political violence, sectarianism, and 'decadence'.[58]

We have various reports of high levels of suicide among exiles, but not conclusive figures. Yakutsk was considered the harshest destination for exiles, and it was notorious for a high suicide rate; death by suicide was referred to as 'the Yakutsk process'. Of 122 political exiles that died in Yakutsk region between 1830 and 1917, twenty of them (16 per cent) committed suicide, and a further eight (6.5 per cent) died as a direct result of mental illness.[59] A number of factors contribute to high suicide rates among exiles. The isolation and dislocation from known social networks that exile entailed was in itself conducive to depressive states. A number of reports point to a high incidence of alcohol abuse among exiles that was both indicative of and a risk factor for mental health problems. One memoirist recalled dryly that, 'There were a number of incidents of drunkenness and lack of morals from exiles'.[60] The northern location of many sites of Siberian exile meant that winters were extremely long and dark, and summers short and hot. Suicide rates internationally are much higher in northern provinces, even those, like Finland, Norway, and Sweden, which have a high GDP and a good overall quality of life for citizens.

Another complicating factor is that some suicides were construed as political statements from the individual who committed suicide, and therefore not necessarily an indicator of mental illness. Suicide was explicitly politicized in the late Imperial period, and commentators dwelled on the relationship between suicide and the repressive regime.[61] Prison suicide 'became a symbol for both the extremes of tsarist tyranny and the heroism of Russia's political martyrs.'[62] There was also a connection between revolutionary terrorism and suicide, since both represented a sacrifice of self for 'the cause'.[63] The suicide of Egor Sazonov in Nerchinsk in 1910 was part of a mass suicide attempt made by prisoners. This collective action was a response to the harsh prison regime initiated by prison governor Vysotskii, who had taken over Nerchinsk in 1910, and attempted to impose a strict regime on the prison complex. Sazonov was a totemic figure in the revolutionary movement; he had been sentenced for his part in the assassination of Viacheslav von Plehve, Russia's Minister of the Interior, in 1904.[64] Sazonov's death provoked fear from the

[58] Paperno, *Suicide as a cultural institution in Dostoevsky's Russia*, p. 101. See also Morrissey, *Suicide and the body politic in Imperial Russia*, chapter 10. On the moral climate, see also Laura Engelstein, *The Keys to Happiness. Sex and the Search for Modernity in Fin-de-Siecle Russia* (Cornell, 1992); J. Neuberger, *Hooliganism. Crime, culture and power in St. Petersburg, 1900–1914* (London, 1993).

[59] Kazarian, *Iakutiia v sisteme politicheskoi ssylki Rossii 1826–1917 gg*, appendix 3.

[60] Sokolov, 'Sibir i ssylka', p. 45.

[61] Pinnow, *Lost to the collective*, p. 24; Morrissey, *Suicide and the body politic in Imperial Russia*, chapter 10.

[62] *Suicide and the body politic in Imperial Russia*, p. 277. Chapter 10 covers the question of political suicides in detail.

[63] *Suicide and the body politic in Imperial Russia*, pp. 288–9; Oleg Budnitskii, *Istoriia terrorizma v Rossii v dokumentakh, biografiiakh, issledovaniikh* (Rostov-na-Donu, 1996), pp. 162–5.

[64] See A.F. Savin (ed.) *Eto ia vinovat ... Evoliutsiia i ispoved' terrorista: Pis'ma Egora Sozonova s kommentariiami* (Moscow, 2001).

authorities of mass suicides of the political prisoners, in grief and protest.[65] These suicide attempts were construed as explicitly political acts.

V.K. Reisner, a katorga prisoner in Zerentui, was sentenced to birching and a stay in the dark punishment cell because he refused to respond when he was addressed in the informal first person as '*ty*' (*thou*). Questions of personal dignity and status sometimes brought the relationships between prisoners and the prison administration to breaking point, and this is epitomized in the struggles over terms of address. One of the most common demands in urban workers' petitions in the late nineteenth and early twentieth century was that they be addressed politely—only close friends and children ought to be addressed in the informal first person.[66] Reisner responded to the visceral humiliation of corporal punishment by attempting suicide—he slit both his wrists, and lost a lot of blood, but survived.[67] In another, related incident, a katorga prisoner, Kris Makarov, was sent from Zerentui to Aleksandrovsk central, because of his persistent refusal to submit to the Zerentui regime (*kak nepodchiniaioshchiisia rezhimu*). On the journey to Aleksandrovsk, Makarov was beaten up by the convoy guards, and in response he killed himself.[68] In the cases of Sazonov, Makarov, and Reisner, the infliction of corporal punishment was a key factor in their decision to commit suicide. Corporal punishment was widely regarded as the ultimate humiliation, a violation of body that constituted a total subjugation of self.[69] The journalist Vlas Doroshevich wrote of an encounter with a young criminal prisoner on Sakhalin, Ivanov, who attempted suicide after being threatened with birching by the warden. Doroshevich visited him after his suicide attempt, and reported that he was distraught by the prospect of the humiliation inflicted by corporal punishment:

'But the thing is...I...I didn't think...I already thought, that I, as I am, that I now...in his very last words...(to send me to) the mare! (*bench for corporal punishment* SB) But anyhow, I am a man (*chelovek*).' He began to cry.[70]

This aversion to corporal punishment, which is a connecting thread in a number of political suicides, was present in civilian society too. A contemporary doctor noted

---

[65] V. Pleskov, 'Pamiatnie dni,' *Katorga i ssylka*, no. 3 (1922), p. 48. Morrissey, *Suicide and the body politic in Imperial Russia*, p. 280, describes the attempted group suicides in Kara, a part of the Nerchinsk complex, in 1889. These collective suicide attempts were a response to Nadezhda Sigida's sentence of one hundred lashes for insubordination.

[66] For a discussion of this, see for example, Gerald D. Surh, *1905 in St. Petersburg: Labor, society and revolution* (Stanford, 1989), p. 181.

[67] Bagotskii, 'Krakovskii soiuz pomoshchi politicheskim zakliuchennym', pp. 168–9, 'letter from Zerentui' (undated, but from 1912–1914 period).

[68] 'Krakovskii soiuz pomoshchi politicheskim zakliuchennym', 'the visit of Gran', p. 169.

[69] See Schrader, *Languages of the Lash: Corporal Punishment and Identity in late Imperial Russia*; Stephen P. Frank, 'Emancipation and the birch: The perpetuation of corporal punishment in rural Russia, 1861–1907,' *Jahrbucher fur Geschichte Osteuropas*, no. 3 (1997); Ben Eklof, 'Worlds in Conflict: Patriarchal authority, discipline and the Russian school, 1861–1914,' *Slavic Review*, no. 4 (1991). One work suggests that corporal punishment was actually a preferred method of punishment, but other evidence seems overwhelmingly to contradict this position (Adams, *The Politics of Punishment. Prison Reform in Russia, 1863–1917*, pp. 13, 36–7).

[70] Vlas Doroshevich, *Katorga-3 'Sakhalinskoe Monte-Karlo'* (Moscow, 2001), p. 144.

that peasants who were subject to corporal punishment often subsequently committed suicide.[71] Suicides were not necessarily indicators of mental illness. Though some cases were no doubt the outcome of mental illness, some suicides might be constituted as a rational political act, or as an act of desperation in response to degrading and humiliating punishment.

L. Kleinborg, an activist who was arrested in 1903, wrote a florid memoir recounting the sacrifices of revolutionaries. He described a rash of suicides by political prisoners and exiles in the early twentieth century. Some of these suicides were represented as desperate responses to impossible living conditions. The suicide note of Liudovik Ianovich, however, who was sent to Yakutsk province after thirteen years in Shlissel'burg, positioned the suicide as a statement against the regime as well as a suicide of desperation. Ianovich's suicide note read:

> No-one should be found guilty in my death. The reason for my death was nerve disorder and tiredness, as a result of my lengthy imprisonment and exile (18 years) in the most difficult conditions. In essence, the Russian government killed me. Let the responsibility for my death fall on them, and equally for the death of countless numbers of my comrades. 17 May 1902. Liudovik Ianovich.[72]

As the historian Susan Morrissey pointed out, this note, which drew on many themes of earlier political suicides, was represented as a state execution, but an execution that the exile administered himself. Suicide, then, offered the prisoner a chance to reclaim agency over his or her own body, and to publicly indict the Tsarist regime. In a further suicide note to another political prisoner, A.E. Ergin, Ianovich dwelled on his own mental state, and indicated that in fact his suicide was predicated heavily on the deterioration of his mental health: 'My nerves are completely shot. Mere trifles cause hysterics in me. I have become an unfit milksop'.[73] This case reaffirms the difficulties of making glib generalizations about mental health, and about causes for suicide. Iakovich's suicide may have been accountable by his abnormal state of mind, or it may have been a conscious political gesture. It was most probably a combination of these factors. Aaron Failevich Faibis'iak is a similar case. Faibis'iak hanged himself in Aleksandrovsk's punishment cell in 1913. He had been sentenced to the death penalty, later commuted to life in katorga, for political offences. He had been sent to the punishment cell for slandering a prison official. His suicide was a protest against both the punishment itself, and the katorga regime more broadly.[74] The prevalence of images of political suicides and the lionizing of martyrs that was prevalent in late Imperial Russia certainly provided a climate that enabled suicide, while an interpretation of mental illness and degeneration offered the chance to deny political suicides any political meaning. This narrative was well developed in the early twentieth century, as

[71] Schrader, *Languages of the Lash: Corporal Punishment and Identity in late Imperial Russia*, pp. 176–7. Male peasants were subject to corporal punishment until 1904.

[72] L. Kleinborg, *V tiur'me i ssylke* (Petrograd, 1917), p. 25. This suicide is also reported by Morrissey, *Suicide and the body politic in Imperial Russia*, pp. 283–4.

[73] L. Ergina, 'Vospominaniia iz zhizni v ssylke,' *Byloe*, no. 6/18 (1907).

[74] Bykova, 'Istoriia Aleksandrovskago tsentrala', p. 165.

explanations for prison suicides pivoted around explanations of personal strength and integrity, and personal weakness and degeneration.[75]

A.P. Stanchinksii, a Menshevik political exile who spent some time in Algacha, part of the Nerchinsk complex, discussed the distinctive challenges for prisoners in retaining their morale and sense of self. On the one hand, they needed to preserve their strength for the revolutionary struggle to come, and to try and secure small ameliorations to the struggles of daily life. On the other hand, this could leave them morally bankrupted, and left them emotionally drained and losing all sense of self. By seeing themselves as prisoners of war in an ongoing struggle with autocracy, political prisoners committed themselves to a steady battle with the prison administration. Stanchinskii argued that this position was taken partly to uphold prisoners' psychological health.[76] Not all political prisoners subscribed to Stanchinskii's approach, however. Prokopii Diomidovich Klimushkin was a peasant teacher from Samara who became involved in the Socialist Revolutionary Party's terrorist wing, and was sentenced to twelve years of katorga in 1907. He served ten years of his sentence at Zerentui before he was freed by the amnesty of 1917.[77] Klimushkin described the regime in Nerchinsk just before the revolution, and suggested that the majority of 'comrades' worked in prison shops, and focused their energies on how they could get transferred to settlement more quickly, or to the free command. These thoughts occupied all their attention. 'Everything was calm and clear on our horizon'.[78] Klimushkin emphasized that prisoners sought to protect and preserve their physical and mental health while incarcerated, through resignation and preparation. This discordance of approaches to the mental exercise of retaining sanity in prison settings confirms that mental health was highly specific to the individuals concerned, and that it is impossible to generalize a common approach or response to the problem.

The incidence of mental health problems and suicide was high in exile locations as well as in prison. Alexander Dobrokhotin-Baikov left us an unusually rich and penetrating insight into the impact of exile, and solitude, on his mental health. He provided an overview of exiles' mental health:

> The days are very short in the northern winter, and the nights are endless... The silhouettes of comrade exiles who you know or who you heard about stand in the memory, in this settlement (*ulus*) comrade X shot himself with a Yakut hunting gun; he had a screw loose, said comrade Ia, K finally lost his mind; the poor thing was sent to Yakutsk to the psychiatric section of the hospital, from where there has not returned.

---

[75] Morrissey, *Suicide and the body politic in Imperial Russia*, p. 297–301.

[76] Stanchinskii, 'V Algachakh', p. 5.

[77] Klimushkin was one of the revolution's survivors. He joined the Socialist Revolutionary Party in 1905. In 1917, he was politically active in the Duma and Soviets of Samara. He was elected as a member of the Constituent Assembly, and subsequently took part in the organization of Komuch. He emigrated to Paris in 1920, but was deported from Czechoslovakia to the Soviet Union in 1945. He was sentenced to ten years in a labour camp for anti-Soviet activities. On completion of his term, he returned to Czechoslovakia in 1956, where he later died (Protasov, *Liudi Uchreditel'nogo sobraniia: portret v inter'ere epokhi*, p. 310).

[78] Klimushkin, 'K amnestii 1917 g', p. 9.

S-kii, a student technologist from Kiev, had private means and so drank vodka day and
night, and his life decayed. The nervous system of comrade L (female) shook her head
and her whole organism broke down.[79]

This dramatic picture of fracturing sanity is reinforced by other accounts.
L. Simanovich was exiled to Kirensk district. In his description of exile, he argued
that few political exiles were able to remain sound in mind and body. He saw the
exiles around him changed because of isolation, loneliness, and desperation. While
some engaged in trade and became difficult to distinguish from the 'dark peasants'
surrounding them, others resorted to drunkenness and became alcoholics. Many of
the alcoholics became 'broken down' (*polurazvalini*) through a range of chronic
illnesses, including heart defects, tuberculosis, and from nervous disorders. Simanovich's attempts to escape came in part from his desire to escape such fates.[80]
Another exile, also from Kirensk district, described a not dissimilar process:

> You hear different stories of ours (exiles); one is hungry for whole days, others are
> drunk from the horror, and a third part actually go mad (*ugorelye*), and cannot find rest
> in their souls; and I see and live through all this . . . oh horrors![81]

Dobrokhotin-Baikov offers us a wonderful insight into the torments of isolation
and loneliness—in his memoir, he described his inner world and his descent into
depression and despair:

> In the middle of the winter my comrades finished their terms and left. I remained alone
> in the empty iurt, alone standing by the little rivers, by the snowy ravines . . . Depression
> began to overwhelm me, to have no neighbours to chat to, nowhere to go; no work to do;
> to light the fire and sitting whole hours by it, occasionally throwing something onto the
> bright flames. The wood for fuel had already been prepared together with the comrades
> at the start of the winter. There was sufficient frozen meat and bread . . .
>
> Unasked, unused thoughts in my head—there is no sun, the night goes long, long, and
> there is no end. Sitting in the iurt, like a beast in a cage, [I had] no strength to struggle
> with depression. Washing, jumping out of the darkness, and going into the fresh air in
> quick steps around the dwelling, going till I cannot go any further. Nothing disturbs
> the silence. The silent polar snowy emptiness under the clear sky with bright but cold
> stars. Not a sound. Quiet!
>
> I struggled with inactivity and depression, but in the end everything was worrying.
> Thoughts about suicide, formerly hidden in (my) heart, came to the surface and began
> to dominate all other remaining thoughts . . . 'On finishing exile,' I thought, I will go at
> once to Moscow, meet with my close old comrades, and then we will begin an
> atrocious terror . . .
>
> All these ideas weakened, [my] brain wearied of one through, [my] memory was
> clouded as if in foggy thoughtlessness, and I, if it is possible to so express it, sank
> into a coma; for whole days I sat by the fireplace in a torpor. I don't remember, if I had

---

[79] Dobrokhotin-Baikov, 'V Yakutskoi ssylke (zapiski rabochego)', p. 190.

[80] Simanovich, 'Ocherki iz zhizni v ssylke (Kirenskoi uezd, Irkutsk gub)', p. 243.

[81] N.E. Teterin, '"Sukhaia Gil'otina" (Ocherk o polozhenie ssyl'nikh),' *Katorga i ssylka* (1924),
p. 194.

any thoughts at all, or if I didn't have any. I dimly recall- there was some sort of grey emptiness; so dragged our days and weeks. My organism weakened...

And in such a weak light my life glittered—until spring. I sometimes went to the local administrative centre, ten miles from my residence, received a letter there from distant Moscow, from acquaintance comrade print-workers, and also from several members of our group, living our exile in different grim places of European and Asiatic Russia.

Lack of money tangibly oppressed me. I had no relatives—they had already retired from the struggle of life in the Vagan'kovskyi cemetery in Moscow. I was sent that winter a solid package of different books from some kind soul in the name of the editors at *Russkaia mysl'*. In the beginning of the spring I received a little money and some garden vegetable seeds, cucumbers, carrots and so on. I began to prepare for sowing. I spoke with Yakuts about rent and use of land, situated not far from my dwelling.

It began to feel, at last, closer to northern beauty—spring. The snow began to melt quickly. Lots of birds flew over. The lake opened. The distant hills were blue... As the spring came alive I began to come round from my winter torpor. [*he described planting his seeds, and the lightening of his heart along with the arrival of the summer sun*...]

The summer days went very quickly; I read, strolled, bathed and lived, absorbed in the interests of my garden and field. I got up extremely early, I felt cold, went out of the yurt, and was horrified; my shoots were killed by the night frost... Great hunger awaited me in the winter, and it was possible that I would die of starvation... I don't know how I would survive for longer in my situation; it was possible that winter would carry me to my forefathers, or carry me to Yakutsk in a lunatic asylum.[82]

Baikov's insights emphasize the natural world that surrounded him, the climate and the landscape, juxtaposed with his feelings of isolation and fear of deprivation. The personal and even intimate nature of these recollections sets Baikov's writing apart from most other exile memoirs. It was almost unheard of for memoirists to reflect on their internal lives in this way, apart from an odd throwaway sentence here and there. Baikov's final collapse in his dark and lonely place was averted by a recall to Yakutsk town from the governor of the province. He recalled that: 'I collected my things quickly and in half an hour left with the Yakut and Cossack, on the back of the Cossack's horse, leaving my garden and my poor field forever.'[83]

Baikov's poignant and detailed account of his own mental state in exile, and the importance of isolation in inducing a state of depression and anxiety, is unusual, and cannot of course be generalized into any kind of 'common' exile experience. It does, however, offer us a personal insight into the mental strains of exile. Mental health cannot be easily counted and quantified, or even pathologized. But that does not mean that we should ignore it. This attempt to evaluate elements of mental health problems faced by exiles helps us to understand the challenges that exiles faced, and the shape of their world.

[82] A. Dobrokhotin-Baikov, 'V Yakutskoi ssylke (zapiski rabochego),' in N.F. Chuzhak (eds.), *Sibirskaia ssylka: Sbornik pervyi* (Moscow, 1927), pp. 190–4.
[83] Dobrokhotin-Baikov, 'V Yakutskoi ssylke (zapiski rabochego)', p. 193.

TREATMENT AND CARE OF PRISONERS

Much of the ill-health suffered by prisoners was a direct result of the conditions of their punishment. The state sought to punish criminals, and to make economic use of their labour in a region that was short of working hands. The state also recognized a duty of care to those made ill by their punishment. Siberia's small but lively civil society and a reluctant indigenous population also played a role in ministering to the needy. Exiles themselves sometimes provided support to those among them who needed care. The poor conditions facing prisoners in Siberia were not so exceptional in their Russian context. Despite some attempts at reform, a comprehensive poor relief system failed to develop in Russia, and there was a heavy reliance on private charitable organizations, and on individuals' almsgiving in Russian poor relief. The Russian Imperial government recognized as late as 1911 that public poor relief was inadequate, chaotic, and obsolete.[84] Poor relief across Russia for the free population was patchy, and conditions in almshouses were routinely dismal.[85] Almshouses and hospitals had historically been overburdened because of the power of communes in other parts of Russia to exile their members for non-specific crimes against the collective right up until 1917. Communes may have used this power to rid themselves of elderly, infirm, and disabled individuals.[86]

The influx of sick prisoners and exiles into eastern Siberia placed significant further pressure on local resources. Prisoners had better access to support when they were sick than exiles did. There were doctors and medical assistants serving the prisons, and the larger prisons had their own hospital wings. Memoirs recalled that the prison hospitals were often inadequate, because of lack of medicines, extremely poor standards of hygiene, poor quality food, and the personal qualities of the doctors themselves—one of the serving doctors, for example, was a renowned drunk.[87] E. Krivorukov recalled dryly that: 'Every day eight to ten sick people went from the cells to the hospital—true candidates for the prison mortuary.'[88]

The hospital at Aleksandrovsk prison was built in 1890. It was situated less than a mile from the prison itself, and was surrounded by taiga. It had five barracks with places for ninety-six people, but was enlarged in 1909 with an extra two barracks and places for 130 patients. By 1913, the barracks had special sections for psychiatry, syphilis, surgery, therapy, and infectious diseases.[89] The seventh barrack was built as an isolation ward for patients with tuberculosis, and was meant to be a destination for all prisoners that were suffering from tuberculosis in the region.[90] Nerchinsk katorga prisons had fifty-five dedicated hospital places at Zerentui, and a

[84] Lindenmeyr, *Poverty is not a Vice: Charity, society and the State in Late Imperial Russia*, p. 95.
[85] Henze, *Disease, health care and government in late Imperial Russia: Life and death on the Volga, 1823–1914*, p. 121.
[86] Gentes, *Exile, murder and madness in Siberia, 1823–1861*, pp. 30–5.
[87] Bykova, 'Istoriia Aleksandrovskago tsentrala', p. 58.
[88] Krivorukov, 'Bor'ba s "Ivanami" v Aleksandrovskoi katorge (po lichnym vospominaniiam)', p. 94.
[89] Bykova, 'Istoriia Aleksandrovskago tsentrala', p. 44.
[90] Gran, *Katorga v Sibiri. Izvlechenie iz otcheta o sluzhebnoi poezdke nachal'nika glav. tiurem. upravlenia P.K. Grana v Sibir v 1913 g*, pp. 13–14.

further ninety places at Maltsev for weak prisoners and those with tuberculosis. The prison inspector recommended that Akatui, which had been used as a women's prison, be converted into a one-hundred-bed station for prisoners with tuberculosis.[91] Exiles did not have access to these prison hospitals.

For prisons without dedicated sick beds, as in Yakutsk, the town hospital was used for the treatment of both prisoners and exiles. The records of Yakutsk town civilian hospital give some indication of the burden placed on the town's hospital by treating exiles. In 1909, a broadly representative year, every month there were between fourteen and thirty exiles resident in the civilian hospital, staying for a total of 4,364 days over the course of the year.[92] Some of these criminal patients presented a risk to the other patients, and required special supervision. In October 1909, the Yakutsk governor had to request a military guard for the hospital to oversee two criminals being treated in the psychiatric section.[93] In March 1910, the prisoner Petr Terentev Alekseev was treated in the psychiatric section. He was deemed so dangerous that he was to be placed in a specially adapted building, as he presented a risk to the safety of those around him.[94] Prisoners who were chronically sick and decrepit remained in prison alongside healthy prisoners, clogging up beds for the acutely sick. Some chronically sick patients in prisons or hospitals had actually finished their terms, but remained in prison as there was nowhere else for them to go. Five of the Yakutsk hospital patients were long-term residents, and two had been admitted in 1884.[95]

There was a gulf between the principles laid out in the state's proclamations and practice on the ground. The prison report for 1909 noted that former katorga prisoners in exile who were decrepit or unfit were to be taken into an almshouse (*bogadel'no*) or other similar institution, where they would be maintained from capital earmarked for exiles. After ten years, or in some cases six years, of being named in exile, the settlers were to be transferred to the peasant estate, with permission to join peasant or townsmen communities in Siberia, subject to the community's invitation.[96] In practice, sick and decrepit exiles were often left to fend for themselves due to inadequate provision of almshouses, and the lack of incentive for village communities to take on decrepit exiles. Some communities of political exiles came together to

[91] *Katorga v Sibiri. Izvlechenie iz otcheta o sluzhebnoi poezdke nachal'nika glav. tiurem. upravlenia P.K. Grana v Sibir v 1913 g*, p. 28.

[92] NARS, f. 12, op. 6, d. 2914, pp. 2–67; list of exiles from Yakutsk region in Yakutsk civilian hospital for the treatment of illness, January–December 1909; NARS, f. 12, op. 12, d. 881, pp. 2–3; office of Yakutsk civilian hospital, about political exiles receiving inpatient treatment in the hospital, January–May 1908.

[93] NARS, f. 12, op. 2, d. 4693, p. 147, letter from Yakutsk governor to Irkutsk military region captain of the staff, 9 October 1909. See also NARS, f. 12, op. 2, d. 4820, pp. 2–3, 6–7, 3; information from the controller of Yakutsk civilian prison about the treatment of exiles as inpatients in the hospital in the course of 1909; NARS, f. 12, op. 2, d. 8077, p. 38; information about the number of exiles using inpatient treatment in the clinic, second doctor's section, Yakutsk region, for 1912–1914.

[94] NARS, f. 12, op. 2, d. 4693, p. 274; report to Yakutsk governor from Yakutsk police, 2 March 1910.

[95] NARS, f. 12, op. 6, d. 2914, p. 63; list of exiles from Yakutsk region in Yakutsk civilian hospital for the treatment of illness, November 1909.

[96] *Otchet po glavnomu tiuremnomu upravleniiu za 1908g*, p. 32.

support and care for those among them who were sick, invalids, or with large families. Such support placed a significant strain on these small communities. One exile letter from 1915–16 recounted, 'Things go really badly for us. We send a request for help. We have several tuberculosis sufferers and invalids, who need constant assistance. . . . In order to find these means, we deny ourselves the necessaries'.[97]

While the State Treasury was committed to paying for one Siberian almshouse, in practice there was no official almshouse in Irkutsk until 1909. The care of invalid exiles was left largely to the village communities that harboured them. It was rare for invalid exiles to reach the town hospitals where they were meant to be cared for, because of the expense and difficulties of travel. Some communes allocated a small sum for the maintenance of decrepit exiles, and others set up unofficial almshouses, using bathhouse buildings in the summer and firefighters' depots in the winter. These facilities were rudimentary, and were notorious for their high death rates.[98] This exile's letter gives a sense of the hopeless position decrepit exiles were left in:

> To the inspector of Irkutsk provincial prison, from katorzhan Peter Rybalkin. REQUEST. I am due to finish my term on 22 February 1904, and from there I will be sent to one township or another. I am old, 66 years old, and furthermore from illness I always lie in the prison hospital. And so when I am freed, I cannot walk and cannot work, and I must be put in a country far from my homeland, not known to me. In view of this I humbly ask if you can find a possibility to place me in an almshouse, where I can live part of my life, not subject to hunger and cold, I ask you like my father not to refuse the request of an old man. 15 January 1904. (Written in a neat hand by a scribe, signed in a very wobbly hand by Rybalkin himself)[99]

For men like Rybalkin, the exile that faced him at the end of his hard labour term seemed to be a fate beyond endurance. While in prison, though he may have experienced difficult conditions, he was at least provided with a place to sleep and food to eat. In exile, he was vulnerable and exposed. Lindenmeyr notes that the sparseness of almshouses in European Russia reflected the role of family in caring for the decrepit, and that the needy did not congregate in ways that shocked 'respectable citizens'.[100] The network of family and community support was absent for exiles, and the presence of large numbers of decrepit and disabled exiles in urban centres attracted attention from the state and from local residents. Regional governors in Irkutsk and Yakutsk were emphatic about the need for almshouses to service decrepit prisoners and exiles, but they struggled to obtain financial support and approval from central authorities.

Irkutsk's regional administration proposed the building of six village almshouses for exiles in 1903, with places for up to 215 residents, but the scheme was not approved. The Minister of Justice wrote to Irkutsk's military governor in 1907

---

[97] Bagotskii, 'Krakovskii soiuz pomoshchi politicheskim zakliuchennym'.

[98] Gol'shukh, 'Prizrenie driakhlykh ssyl'nikh v Irkutskoi gubernii', p. 1601.

[99] GAIO, f. 32, op. 5, d. 8644, p. 43; petition from Peter Rybalkin, 15 January 1904. On p. 45 of the same file, an official note confirmed that Rybalkin had done six years of katorga work, and that he was now ill and not fit for work.

[100] Lindenmeyr, *Poverty is not a Vice: Charity, society and the State in Late Imperial Russia*, p. 67.

proposing a number of reforms to Siberia's prison systems, including the establishment of almshouses for the decrepit.[101] Irkutsk's military governor briskly rebuffed many of his proposals, but on the question of almshouses, all seemed agreed that these were urgently needed.[102] Eventually the Main Prison Administration agreed to build an almshouse in Irkutsk, though it specified that places would only be available to katorga prisoners unfit to work. The almshouse was opened in the village of Tel'min, around twenty miles from Aleksandrovsk prison, using the buildings of a disused stage post. It was described as a nice healthy place, with excellent air quality.[103] It received its first residents in February 1910. By September 1910 it had eighty-five residents. While this facility took pressure off the prison hospital by removing the chronically infirm, it did nothing to resolve the problem of care in the community. By 1913, it had between thirty and forty residents, indicating that its role in taking pressure off the prison hospitals and the community was extremely limited.[104] Reading between the lines here, we see a struggle between the regional administration, who sought to open almshouses for decrepit exiles in order to take pressure off the local population, and the national administration, which was unwilling to provide funds for such ventures.

The establishment and history of the Yakutsk almshouse confirms this reading of a tussle between regional administrators and the centre. Ivan Ivanovich Kraft was appointed the new governor of Yakutsk province in 1907. He set about his new post with gusto, making a survey of conditions in the region, and identifying possible problems. He regarded the plight of unfit exiles as one of the primary burdens on the region. In a telegram to his immediate senior, Andrei Nikolaevich Selivanov, Irkutsk's military governor, received on 6 April 1907, Kraft wrote in his characteristically forthright manner:

> By journeying around the region I personally saw that the decrepit and maimed criminal exiles based in the villages of Yakutsk nomads place a heavy burden on the local population who have to support them in turn; exiles move from house to house, from *iurt* to *iurt*; the three rouble payment provided for them is not sufficient in local conditions for those exiles needing an almshouse, I personally established that there are around 100 [exiles in need of an almshouse place], but the current almshouse cannot accommodate more than 15 people; it is impossible to further burden the local population; it is unlawful as the responsibility to give means to exiles lies with the state, in agreement with statute 373. I find it necessary from 1 May 1907 to broaden the current almshouse to 100 places... [105]

---

[101] GAIO, f. 25, op. 6, d. 3104, l. 1; letter from Ministry of Justice to Irkutsk military governor, 10 November 1907.

[102] GAIO, f. 25, op. 6, d. 3104, pp. 35–9, for full details of Irkutsk military governor's response. But pp. 10–12, sees Irkutsk prison inspector emphatic on the need to build an almshouse.

[103] Bykova, 'Istoriia Aleksandrovskago tsentrala', p. 50.

[104] *Polozhenie tiuremnoi chasti i ssylki v Irkutskoi gubernii po dannym dokladov tiuremnago inspektora, 1911–1913gg*, p. 22.

[105] GAIO, f. 25, op. 6, d. 3136, pp. 4–5; telegram from Yakutsk governor Kraft to Irkutsk military governor.

Kraft's statement was beyond his jurisdiction, and demarcated the boundaries of his power and authority. Both the military governor of Irkutsk and the Ministry of Justice chastised him for his direct action, and refused to authorize the funds that he had peremptorily requested.[106] Despite these teething problems, the almshouse he proposed was established. A former *skoptsy* village, Khatyn-Iadrynsk, was bought on 25 April 1907.[107] Preparations were made quickly, and the almshouse was opened on 15 May 1907, with all residents moved from Yakutsk by steamer on 25 May.[108] In its first year, from 1 June 1907 to January 1908, it had sixty-five residents, which was full capacity. Numbers quickly expanded, however, with ninety-three residents by September 1908, and 101 by October 1908.[109] There was no accommodation for these extra residents, and the almshouse administration requested in September 1908 that no further residents be sent until means for a new building had been secured.[110] The almshouse's existence did not ultimately resolve the problem of care for sick exiles. Numbers continued to escalate so that by 1911 the almshouse was severely overpopulated, with 133 residents, and conditions there deteriorated accordingly.[111] By 1915, the building had 'fallen into decay and almost unusable condition'.[112] While the problem of sick and disabled exiles had been removed from Yakutsk town, the almshouse did not resolve the burden, but rather shifted it. The problem of sick and decrepit exiles had been moved away from the public eye, but it continued to exist, and it continued to demand public funds. Neighbouring residents wrote complaints and petitions complaining about the almshouse and its residents. The peasants of the neighbouring Khatyn-Iadrynsk commune petitioned bitterly that the almshouse be moved away from their region, as the carelessness of its residents had led to a succession of very destructive fires breaking out.[113]

What human flotsam drifted up in these almshouses, the last shores of exile? I have surveyed a number of the personal files of those convicts who ended their terms in Khatyn-Iadrinsk. These case studies offer us small insights into the lives of these men and their families. Many were older men, and most were recidivists whose original sentences had been increased exponentially by their repeated attempts to escape from Siberia. Abram Pinson's records give some indication of the path to the almshouse for

[106] GAIO, f. 25, op. 6, d. 3136, pp. 25–6; letter of support from Irkutsk governor to Ministry of Justice regarding Kraft's plan, pp. 27–8; Kraft's letter to Ministry of Justice and Irkutsk military governor requesting funds, and their replies refusing funds.

[107] NARS, f. 15, op. 8, d. 41, p. 1; outline of the cost and exact details of the properties purchased in former *skoptsy* village Khatyn-Iadrinsk, 25 April 1907.

[108] NARS, f. 15, op. 8, d. 41, p. 17; letter from Yakutsk regional police inspector to Yakutsk town police, 12 May 1907.

[109] NARS, f. 206, op. 1, d. 563, pp. 1–2; information on the question of the transfer to Yakutsk guardians' prison committee the management of Yakutsk settlers' almshouse.

[110] NARS, f. 206, op. 1, d. 604, p. 1, letter from Khatyn-Iadrinsk almshouse to the prison committee, 28 September 1908.

[111] GAIO, f. 25, op. 6, d. 3136, p. 71; letter from Yakutsk governor to Irkutsk military governor, 7 December 1911.

[112] GAIO, f. 25, op. 6, d. 3136, p. 73; letter from Yakutsk governor to Irkutsk military governor, 23 September 1915.

[113] NARS, f. 206, op. 1, d. 604, p. 4; petition from residents of Khatyn-Iadrinsk village commune, 27 October 1908.

convicts. A member of the townspeople (*meshchanstva*) class in Vitebsk town, he was exiled without rights to a village in Verkholensk. He escaped from exile and ran to Viatka in 1895, where he was sentenced for his escape from Siberia to forty lashes and three years of katorga work. He was considered fit to work at the time of this sentence. He left his family behind in European Russia. Pinson's katorga term ended in June 1896, and he was sent to Aleksandrovsk in October 1896. His term was reduced by a third in the 1894 amnesty. He received his forty lashes on 28 December 1896. A persistent escapee, he was punished with a further thirty lashes in 1898, and another nine months of katorga work, for failing to go to his place of settlement in Yakutsk. From katorga, he was sent to Viliuisk, one of Yakutsk's remoter regions, and from there, he was settled in the almshouse.[114] Three years of bodily punishment, by the lash and by work, had clearly broken Pinson's body, and made him an invalid, and a financial burden on the region.

Another persistent escapee who ended up in the almshouse was Iskender, known as Mashadi. He was described as an illiterate Muslim Tatar peasant from the Caucuses, who spoke no Russian. He was swarthy and strongly built, his face pockmarked and his black beard slashed with streaks of grey. His twenty-five-year-old wife and their three small children did not follow him to Yakutsk, but remained behind in Elisavetpol'sk province.[115] He arrived at the almshouse shackled and unable to walk. His initial crime had been in 1906, but his repeated attempts to escape condemned him to katorga, and settlement in Yakutsk region.

Another case was Boris Ivanov Klimov, who arrived in the almshouse manacled but able to walk, and was slated for special observation. He was a literate peasant from Saratov, born in 1875, so was only thirty-six when he entered the almshouse. His wife and four small children were left behind in Saratov. He was first sentenced in 1905 and sentenced to four years of katorga work, but he escaped in 1907, and was recaptured in 1910. He was then sentenced to a term of solitary confinement followed by a further six years of katorga work. He arrived in Yakutsk in 1913, and was transferred to the almshouse soon after.[116]

Innokenty Sinitsyn was sentenced to a year of imprisonment in 1895 for a robbery in Irkutsk, and to the loss of all rights and property. When he completed his term of punishment, his village commune issued a declaration that they would not accept him back into their midst, which meant that instead of going home, he was sent to Yakutsk province to settle in 1897, along with his wife Aleksandra and his four young children. He suffered severe frostbite on both hands in 1905. In 1912, when he was only forty-five years old, he was committed to the almshouse as not fit to do any sort of physical work.[117]

These cases offer insights into the lives of these men on the margins of tsarist society, and offer an example of the interactions between the state and the 'broken

---

[114] NARS, f. 15, op. 10, d. 2445, pp. 35–6; information form (*stateinyi spisok*) for Abram Pinson.
[115] NARS, f. 15, op. 10, d. 2445, pp. 70–1; information form (*stateinyi spisok*) for Iskender.
[116] NARS, f. 15, op. 10, d. 2445, pp. 73–4; information form (*stateinyi spisok*) for Boris Klimov.
[117] NARS, f. 15, op. 10, d. 2445, pp. 13–15; information form (*stateinyi spisok*) for Innokenty Sinitsyn.

punished'. The punishments of these broken men went beyond their intended bounds as their physical health deteriorated. Their infirmities were apparently direct results of their punishment, through work, or corporal punishment, or frostbite incurred in Siberia's harsh climate. We have first-hand accounts of the attitudes of prisoners towards their own health, in the form of their appeals to the region's governors. The petitions to regional authorities made by prisoners often requested permission to reside in urban centres for health reasons.[118] Exiles complained of a range of ailments, including deafness, respiratory illnesses, and tooth problems. Illness was used to request what was in effect a mitigation of sentence. Settlement of exiles in non-urban areas was one of the explicit terms of most punishments. This indicates that prisoners did not regard illness as an intrinsic part of their punishment, but rather as an additional and unrelated aspect of their being, which justified their requests for more lenient treatment. Prisoners regarded the suffering of their bodies as something that needed to be resolved, even if they accepted their punishment of exile for their crime. They held up their illness as cause for leniency and special treatment from the authorities. For example, Andrei Donskoi, writing to the Yakutsk governor Ivan Ivanovich Kraft in 1910, complained that the conditions in transit to exile had ruined his health, and that this necessitated a milder location for his final point of exile. He suffered from chronic rheumatoid arthritis, but contracted scurvy in Aleksandrovsk because of the bad food. His letter emphasized the outrage and injustice done to his body, and even demanded that an investigation be made into the cause of his illness.[119]

Other prisoners appealed for support from the state, or for a change of their named place of residence, because of their state of health. Nikolai Perfilev wrote two letters to the governor in September 1908, one on his own behalf, and one for a cell mate, Nikon Tsytsarev. His formulations stressed their desire to avoid the almshouse, and an awareness of the redemptive power of labour:

> To Yakutsk governor, from exile settler currently in Yakutsk prison cell, Nikolai Perfilev. Request. Your highness, please be so good as to not refuse the humble request of this unfortunate exile, sent to such a distant and harsh region, without any means for existence, with weak and impaired health, weakened by the efforts of katorga labour. My term of hard labour has already been ended for 10 months, at last the Zabaikal administration gave permission for me to be sent to settlement in Yakutsk oblast, where I was sent from Algachinsk mines, Nerchinsk katorga in the beginning of May, and arrived in Yakutsk only on 5 September... The harsh northern winter is beginning, so they say, and I am left absolutely without means for existence. I don't know when or where I will be sent to settlement. Work is ending, and will be off for the whole winter, and I am excluded of the possibility of wages, however only in entering into work as a peasant (*illegible line* SB) there will be no harvest. As a result of all this I ask you to name for me a monthly or even one off sum of means, and to name my place of residence. I don't want to be confined to an almshouse, but want to take a path

---

[118] GAIO, f. 25, op. 6, d. 5385, karton 624; regarding petitions of exiles about permission for them to leave their named places of residence and other matters, 1912 (760ll).

[119] NARS, f. 12, op. 2, d. 5135, l. 75; letter from Andrei Donskoi to Yakutsk governor, 30 May 1910.

of honourable labour for the satisfaction of my means of existence. Signed exile-settler Nikolai Perfilev, 19 September 1908.[120]

Perfilev's request indicates that he accepted his punishment per se, but sought to ameliorate its impact by appealing on the grounds of their health. Both this letter and the one he wrote for his fellow prisoner Tsytarev stressed the men's willingness to work and be productive, a common trope. They also emphasized that their health impeded their ability to settle successfully. Mirza Sufieva had been exiled to Balagansk district, Irkutsk province, but had been sentenced to three years katorga work in Aleksandrovsk as punishment for her attempt to escape from that place. Her new place of exile settlement was named as Yakutk region, and she was to be sent there as soon as the Lena was navigable. She appealed to the Irkutsk military governor on 25 November 1912, asking that she be permitted to serve her exile in her former location, Balagansk district. Her justification for this amelioration of sentence was her health; 'in view of my weak health, severe deafness in both ears, and complete incomprehension of the Russian language'. Her request was refused without comment beyond a reference to the regulations governing exile.[121] We need to ask if these letters, and others like them, really reflected the prisoners' thoughts and feelings, or if they were formulaic presentations of grievances, that used accepted modes of language and complaint in order to appeal for leniency.[122] Based on the examples I have seen, convict petitions were often extremely specific in their nature, and while they utilized some formulaic language, overall they expressed very real concerns.

VOLUNTARY FOLLOWERS

For those exiles who were accompanied to exile by dependants, the ill-health of their spouses and children lent additional resonance to their punishment. When dependants accompanied an exile, the family unit experienced the conditions of punishment, and contributed to the scale and impact of the punishment for the convict. A significant minority of prisoners was accompanied by their family; between one and two thousand 'followers' were recorded annually for prisoners and exiles between 1900 and 1912. This figure excludes the significant numbers of individuals exiled on administrative grounds. The tsarist authorities sought to ameliorate the suffering of these innocents; the exiles' punishment was not intended to encapsulate their families as well. The letters, appeals, and requests of prisoners to the authorities show that this emphasis on the unjust suffering of the

---

[120] NARS, f. 15, op. 18, d. 191, p. 176, request from Nikolai Perfilev to Yakutsk governor, 19 September 1908.

[121] GAIO, f. 25, op. 6, d. 5385, pp. 2–3; letter to Irkutsk military governor from Irkutsk province prison inspector, 11 December 1912.

[122] Pyle, 'Peasant strategies for obtaining State aid: A study of petitions during World War One'; Andrew Verner, 'Discursive strategies in the 1905 Revolution: Peasant petitions from Vladimir province,' *Russian Review*, no. 1 (1995).

family was a common theme in convict complaints. The authorities often responded positively to requests from exiles, where the emphasis was laid on amelioration of
family suffering.

The case of Aleksandr Novitskii provides an illustration of the authorities'
willingness to consider families. Novitskii had been living as an exile in Kansk
district, Zabaikal region, since 1909, along with his wife and children. He had
appealed repeatedly to the governor of Eniseisk for permission to live in one of the
urban centres of the region, as his wife was ill, and he was unable to find suitable
work outside urban areas. He was moved to appeal to the Irkutsk military governor,
who oversaw the whole Siberian region. Novitskii's letter articulated the importance of his family's plight in his unfortunate situation:

> I don't know of any motives for my refusal, if in the course of all my years of exile I had
> in any way broken any of the laws governing exile, but I have not. Can the governor
> not see my hungry family? This is not stated in laws about exile, or even in any
> circulars. So, what is there left for me to do? I only know that for a long time I haven't
> been able to feed my hungry family. This summer I lost one of my children, as
> I couldn't provide either medicine or good food. So now I appeal to you to permit me
> to transfer either to Kansk or to Achinsk.[123]

Novitskii clearly regarded the sickness and death of one his children as a direct
consequence of his punishment, and his language here points up the injustice of
this unreasonable punishment. He was willing to serve out his sentence, but argued
that the punishment wreaked upon his family was disproportionate. Leonid
Mikhailovich Kniazev, Irkutsk's military governor, agreed with him. He chastised
the Eniseisk military governor regarding Novitskii's case, pointing out in particular
that exiles who lived peacefully and had families to support ought to be allowed
opportunities to work and to support their families.[124]

Lia Girshevoi Eshtovich, an exile's wife, appealed to Irkutsk's military governor
in 1912 that her husband be allowed to return from Turukhansk krai, where he had
been sent on suspicion of plans to escape. The language and justification that
Eshtovich used in her petition confirms the prevalence of the family narrative
appeals about exile conditions:

> ...After the birth of our child, we were given permission in December 1912 to go to
> Mina village. My husband had work there, and sufficient wages to feed the three of us.
> But in February he was suddenly sent to Gaivkin village, Vybrinsk township, and from
> there over the course of a few days was sent to Turukhansk region, where he is
> currently I, with a baby in arms, and poorly to boot, remain almost without any
> means for existence. I could have petitioned the Eniseisk governor for permission to
> join my husband in Turukhansk region, but I could not take such a measure. Though
> I could go myself, I could not decide to take my sick child there, where the climate is
> harsh, there are no medical points, and there's no paid work for my husband, it would

---

[123] GAIO, f. 25, op. 6, d. 3585, p. 26; letter from Aleksandr Novitskii to Irkutsk Military
Governor, 19 November 1912.
[124] GAIO, f. 25, op. 6, d. 5385, p. 31; letter from Irkutsk military governor to Eniseisk governor,
undated.

kill him (the child). I hope that you will investigate this, and it will be confirmed that there was a misunderstanding, as my husband never prepared to escape. And once again, I hope that you will permit him to return to his family.[125]

Lia Eshtovich, as the supplicant, takes on the rhythms of speech and the themes of extraordinary need that were characteristic for late Imperial petitions. Her petition, though, is clear in its expectation that her husband's family situation ought to mediate the extent of his punishment, and the suffering to be endured by both her and her child need to be ameliorated by the state.

CONCLUSIONS

We can draw some conclusions from this study of illness among the exile community of eastern Siberia. Conditions in Siberian prisons were, in general, worse than those in European Russian prisons in the post-1906 period. We can speculate that the experience of exile in eastern Siberia placed it as among the most difficult location for exile. This question highlights one of the fundamental ambiguities of the system of Siberian punishment in late Imperial Russia. Ostensibly intended to provide Siberia with Russian settlers as well as removing undesirable elements from mainland Russia, in practice the process of punishment damaged many potential settlers to the extent that they were unable even to provide for themselves. The state's responses to the challenges raised by the damaged bodies and minds of prisoners are ambiguous. The nature of the punishment in itself caused much of the physical damage to prisoners. Two main responses can be identified. First, as with Kraft and his almshouse, the illness of prisoners was responded to not as a result of humane considerations, but because the illness of exiles was a major contributing factor to the burden that the exiles represented to the local population. Second, though, we also see in other examples of state responses, particularly in relation to the suffering of family followers, a basic humane response, as state representatives sought to ameliorate the suffering of wives and children. The gulf between often well-meaning tsarist policy and reality was often stark. The prison system provided adequate healthcare for sick prisoners, reflecting a range of reforms and improvements made in the late nineteenth and early twentieth century. Exiles, however, seemed to fall through the gaps of medical provision. The state, despite recognizing some duty of care to these men, was reluctant to provide for sick and decrepit exiles. The almshouse in Yakutsk was only established due to the efforts of a particularly intransigent and lively regional governor, who was willing to confront the centre for funds. There seems to have been no connection made between the costs incurred by the state in caring for the broken punished, and the conditions of their punishment that resulted in ill-health.

---

[125] GAIO, f. 25, op. 6, d. 5385, p. 71; letter to Irkutsk military governor from Lia Girshevoi Eshtovich, undated.

Exile illness was a significant factor in making exiles more of a burden than a benefit to Siberia's native population. Individuals broken by the conditions of their punishment, sparse local facilities, and inadequate support from the regional authorities combined to make Siberian exiles an onerous burden for the local community. While there is evidence of local sympathy for the plight of the women and children that accompanied the convicts, local charity towards sick exiles was limited. The position of exiles' families shows how categories of free and forced, convict and innocent, punished and unpunished, were profoundly blurred when face-to-face with the realities of daily life. Those families that followed prisoners into exile often lived in conditions as bad, or even worse, than those of their spouse. The provision of care for these families was often set up using prison buildings and facilities, ensuring that the distinction between convict and innocent was fundamentally undermined. Prisoners seemed in general to regard their state of health as distinct and not an integral part of their punishment. The body's physical suffering could be used to demand an amelioration of sentence. Neither state nor prisoners themselves regarded illness an integral part of punishment. This evidence indicates, however, that illness did form an important component of the overall experience of punishment. We can conclude that the prevalence of illness and disease compounded the cruelty of sentences. The image of Siberian exile as a living death sentence can be supplemented by the notion of Siberian exile as a slow death sentence.

Afterword: Endings and Beginnings

At last, at 6pm (on 3ʳᵈ March) we received an answer, 'In Petrograd great
events have occurred. A new government is formed. The Minister of Foreign
Affairs is Miliukov, the Minister of Justice is Kerensky. We await a general
amnesty.' We clearly understood, that something great and grandiose had
happened in Petrograd.... We threw down our work, our occupations; we
devoted ourselves to crazy, impetuous joy.

> (Recollections of P. Klimushkin, a prisoner at Gornyi Zerentui
> katorga prison, Nerchinsk, on the news of the February revolution)[1]

The February revolution brought an abrupt end to exile for many of our protagonists. In Petrograd, several thousand miles away from eastern Siberia, a series of
workers' demonstrations and military insurrections at the end of February 1917 set
in motion the final collapse of the Romanov regime. As news of the disturbances in
the capital spread, waves of disorders reverberated across the regional capitals of the
empire. Local prisons were often the revolutionary protestors' first targets. All over
the empire, the incarcerated population received unprecedented attention, as
protestors sought to break down the walls of their own Bastilles. Significant
numbers of criminals and soldiers under court martial were freed, along with the
odd political prisoner. Zinovii Magergut, a Socialist Revolutionary Party activist
from Sormovo, wrote a pathos-ridden description of released prisoners in Nizhnii
Novgorod in April 1917, which offers a good example of the sort of sympathy and
interest expressed to all political prisoners:

> The comrades from katorga arrived. Their bodies were still stung by chains. But they
> did not feel it. They fixed their eyes on the red flag, on the clear sun, the bright sky.
> They were carried aloft by the crowd, threw up their arrested caps, echoing the people
> 'LONG LIVE THE REVOLUTION'. And then one comrade arrived, bending under
> the burden of a long imprisonment. He moved slowly, his feet covered with wounds,
> eyes that could not get accustomed to the blue light, ears could not carry the roar
> (*SHUM*) of the rejoicing crowd. For almost 10 years he had been oppressed in solitary.
> He said: 'Comrades, thank you, I am glad that I lived to witness liberty... take me
> away, I need to calm down'... his voice trembled and his feet did not hold even his
> decrepit body. The years forced, they did their business... [2]

---

[1] Klimushkin, 'K amnestii 1917 g', pp. 10–11.
[2] RGASPI, f. 274, op. 1, d. 26, p.104; excerpt from Zinovii Magergut's memoir, entitled 'writings-
recollections of a member of the Sormovskii organisation of the PSR, from April 1916 to April 1917'.

Nicholas II was unable to muster any meaningful support in civil or military circles, and he abdicated on behalf of himself and his son on 2 March 1917. The Provisional Government took over the aegis of state authority. The Minister of Justice was Alexander Feodorovich Kerensky, a member of the old State Duma, a committed socialist, and a well-known attorney who had acted as defence counsel in a number of high-profile trials of revolutionaries and striking workers. One of his very first orders as Minister of Justice was to the governor general of Irkutsk, and the governor of Eniseisk, on 2 March, demanding that the exiled State Duma deputies be immediately released and returned to Petrograd.[3] On 6 March 1917, the Provisional Government issued a general political and religious amnesty.[4] This was followed by an order on 17 March from Prime Minister Prince Lvov that all criminal offenders would receive a cancellation or reduction of their sentence.[5] On 26 April 1917, deportation to Siberia was formally abolished as a punishment.[6]

For the tens of thousands of individuals imprisoned and exiled for political offences, news of the February revolution was met with suspended disbelief, followed by unbridled joy, trailed with more uncertainty as misinformation and rumours swirled around. The news of revolution came to urban centres first. Prisoners in transfer and katorga prisons heard the news of the regime change and their imminent change of status long before those in distant exile locations. Exiles' journey home from distant locations was delayed by the practicalities of travel in these regions. There were around 350 political exiles in the Yakutsk region in March 1917. Those settled in the region's more remote locations of Viliusk, Verkhoiansk, and Kolymsk were initially transferred to Yakutsk. From Yakutsk, they travelled down the Lena to Irkutsk. Several of them left the region in April, but most left in May and the first part of June when the ice on the Lena broke, and steamers started to travel downriver. The newly freed exiles received financial support for their journeys. A single person making the journey from Olekminsk received seventy-five roubles, while a family of four departing from Yakutsk was provided with 245 roubles.[7]

Criminal exiles were also given the right to travel home at state expense after the abolition of Siberian exile on 26 April. Some 2,000 criminal exiles gathered in Yakutsk by the beginning of May, to prepare for their journeys home. One can imagine the impact a group this size would have had in a town of just over 7,000 people. A panicky telegraph from the regional Commissar, G.E. Petrovskii, to the Provisional Government's Ministry of Internal Affairs on 3 May warned that the local government had no means available to finance the journey of these exiles.

---

[3] Robert P. Browder and Alexander F. Kerensky (eds.) *The Russian Provisional Government of 1917; documents* (Stanford, 1961), volume 1, chapter 5, p. 191, doc. 160.
[4] Browder, *The Russian Provisional Government of 1917; documents*, volume 1, chapter 5, pp. 196–8, doc. 170.
[5] Browder, *The Russian Provisional Government of 1917; documents*, volume 1, chapter 5, pp. 198–9, doc. 172.
[6] Browder, *The Russian Provisional Government of 1917; documents*, volume 1, chapter 5, pp. 207–8, doc. 186.
[7] Kazarian, *Iakutiia v sisteme politicheskoi ssylki Rossii 1826–1917 gg*, pp. 274–5.

A group of 771 exiles accompanied by 521 family members left by the beginning of June 1917.[8] These journeys put an enormous strain on the region's finances. Most of the political and criminal exiles had left the Yakutsk region by the end of September 1917, and the departure of the remaining few dragged on until the end of 1918. These long waits for freedom are remarkable, and testament to the difficulties and expense of the long road back to European Russia.

Some of the exiles streamed back to their homelands, mainly in European Russia. A significant number stayed on in Siberia, and developed the political and social networks that they had established while in exile. Some of those who remained went on to play important roles in revolutionary politics in Siberia. In Krasnoiarsk, exiles were among the most important individuals in the city's socialist parties, and some of the key figures in the Soviet throughout 1917.[9]

Political exiles returning from Siberia carried a special political and social cachet in 1917.[10] The narrative of mythologization developed by the revolutionary political elite seemed to intersect with popular sentiment, at least for a few months in 1917. Some political exiles, particularly women, had attracted significant popular sympathy and interest before 1917.[11] Both Maria Spiridonova and Ekaterina Breshko-Breshkovskaia, for example, caught the attention of the national press, and were portrayed even by the moderate press as 'martyrs to the cause'.[12] They were mythologized, Spiridonova as a young warrior for justice and Breshkovskaia as the 'grandmother of the revolution'.[13] The work of Sally Boniece on Spiridonova shows how Spiridonova exemplified the myth of the revolutionary-martyr-heroine.[14] The importance of 'suffering for the cause' in the pre-revolutionary period, which was particularly manifested in the Socialist Revolutionary Party, found full expression in 1917. There were distinct religious overtones in the new revolutionary narrative, particularly in the use of martyrdom and familiar ethical and religious concepts.[15] To have been exiled or imprisoned for the revolutionary cause lent

[8] *Iakutiia v sisteme politicheskoi ssylki Rossii 1826–1917 gg*, pp. 275–7.

[9] For a detailed evaluation on Krasnoiarsk city's politics in 1917, and the role played by exiles, see Alistair Dickins, 'Krasnoiarsk, 1917: The Making of Soviet Power in Central Siberia' (PhD dissertation, University of Manchester, 2015), especially chapters 1–3.

[10] Badcock, *Politics and the people in revolutionary Russia: A Provincial History*, pp. 46–9.

[11] For an analysis of this question, see forthcoming work by Ben Phillips, 'Political Exile and the Image of Siberia in Anglo-Russian Contacts Prior to 1917' (PhD dissertation, University College London, 2017).

[12] See Alexander Rabinowitch, 'Spiridonova,' in *Critical companion to the Russian revolution*, ed. Edward Acton, V.Iu. Cherniaev, and William G. Rosenberg, Spiridonova (Bloomington, 1997), p. 182. For further evidence of the public sympathy received by Spiridonova, see V. Vladimirov, *Maria Spiridonova* (Moscow, 1906).

[13] Breshkovskaia was described as such by V.P. Antonov-Saratovski, *Pod stiagom proletarskoi bor'by: Otryvki iz vospomininanii o rabote v Saratove za vremia s 1915g do 1918g* (Moscow and Leningrad, 1925), p. 92. On Breshkovskaia's iconic status in Russia and abroad by 1917, see Jane E. Good and D.R. Jones, *Babushka: The life of the Russian revolutionary E.K. Breshko-Breshkovskaia* (Newtonville, 1991).

[14] A fascinating exploration of the creation of Spiridonova's 'myth' can be found in Boniece, 'The Spiridonova case, 1906: Terror, myth and martyrdom'.

[15] Boris I. Kolonitskii, 'The Russian Idea and the ideology of the February revolution,' in *Empire and Society: Approaches to Russian history*, ed. Teruyuki Hara and Kimitaka Matsuzato (Sapporo, 1997), p. 52.

individuals significant cachet, and massive public sympathy. The physical distress of released political prisoners offered a real physical manifestation of the evil oppressions of tsarism.

It was not only the 'celebrities' of the revolutionary world, like Spiridonova, that attracted public sympathy and interest in the post-revolutionary months. The political prisoners freed from the town prison in Nizhnii Novgorod at the start of March attended the first meeting of the Nizhnii Novgorod soviet of workers and soldiers' deputies. When they entered the hall, all those present rose to their feet in silent acclaim, and the speech of one of their number was received rapturously. Many of those present in the stalls were only there to catch a glimpse of the freed political prisoners.[16] The greeting these men received reflected their high status in the new revolutionary climate. Returnees from political exile were reported triumphantly in the local press.[17] The lead article in *Kazanskaia rabochaia gazeta* on 16 April was devoted to a discussion of the importance of the return of émigrés, and expressed gratitude to the British government for facilitating returns.[18] Special committees were set up to assist Russia's returning exiles, and numerous appeal funds were set up for the families of 'victims of the revolution' and for former exiles and political prisoners.[19] At the first post-revolution meetings, there were often prayers spoken, songs sung, and collections taken in the name of the revolution's victims. Iadrinsk district's first revolutionary meeting on 12 March, for example, included an interlude when all stood in memory of Russia's glorious freedom fighters, and '*Vechnaia Pamiat*' (Let their memory be eternal) was sung.[20]

While many of these meetings and written reports were orchestrated by the national or local political elites, the level of support shown by ordinary people for collections and at meetings indicate that the sufferings of exiles had struck a popular chord. There was a special meeting in Kniagininsk town, Nizhegorod province, on 15 March to 'commemorate those who had fallen in the struggle for freedom'. A requiem was held, and numerous speeches made in memorial of events. More than 246 roubles were collected at the close of the meeting specifically for these 'victims of revolution'.[21] These donations of funds for former political prisoners offered the public a means to identify with the revolutionary struggle. Yet even given the symbolic resonance in donations to the revolutionary cause generally, ordinary people had a choice of causes they could donate to, and many chose to donate their money to the 'victims of the revolution'.[22] As of the 16 March, the Nizhnii Novgorod soviet of workers' deputies had received donations of 7,462

[16] P.E. Shul'gin (ed.) *Za vlast sovetov: Vspominaet uchastniki bor'bi za vlast v Nizhegorodskoi gubernii* (Gor'kii, 1967), p. 31; Ikonikov's memoir.

[17] See for example, *Izvestiia soveta rabochikh i soldatskikh deputatov* 6, 9 April 1917, p. 4.

[18] *Kazanskaia rabochaia gazeta* 7, 16 April 1917, p. 1.

[19] GARF, f. P-3349, op. 1, d. 72; *Society for the assistance of freed political prisoners (1917–1918)*.

[20] NART, f. 1246, op. 1, d. 46, p.133; journal of public meeting chaired by Iadrinsk district commissar, 12 March 1917.

[21] GANO, f. 1887, op. 1, d. 28, p.7; letter from Kniagininsk district commissar to Nizhegorod provincial executive committee, 23 March 1917.

[22] Diane Koenker argued that workers' contributions to political causes were more telling indicators of their political attitudes than resolutions passed. In her assessment of Moscow workers' donations to

roubles, the vast majority of which, 6,114 roubles, had been given to the 'fund for the assistance of freed political prisoners'. The second most heavily supported fund that the soviet ran was the fund for the assistance of victims of the revolution, which attracted donations totaling 709 roubles.[23] Soviet records show that this level of support continued; in the period 20 March–8 April, 1,604 roubles, which constituted a quarter of the Soviet's income, was donated to the fund for the assistance of freed politicals, and a further 1,493 roubles was donated to the fund for victims of the revolution.[24]

While our knowledge of the journey home and reception of political exiles is relatively rich, our awareness of the fate of criminal exiles and prisoners is much looser and more provisional. Prisoners of all categories were often released from the empire's prisons, and the criminal justice system was in utter disarray in 1917. All of Petrograd's prisons were 'liberated' in the first days of 1917. Shlissel'burg, a notorious prison housing many political prisoners, was just twenty-two miles from Petrograd, so the revolution's reverberations hit the prison early, on 28 February. Great crowds of people, including workers from the gunpowder factory nearby, gathered around the prison and demanded that the political prisoners be freed.[25] Sixty-six prisoners were freed immediately. One prisoner freed that day recalled the greeting he received from the worker delegate,

> We came to you to say in the name of 12,000 workers of the Shlissel'burg gunpowder factory, we have surrounded the fortress and are waiting for you to join us in freedom! Your torments are ended! Come, comrades, to freedom![26]

V. Simonovich was another of the prisoners in the first tranche of freed politicals. He recalled the rapturous welcome they received:

> We were met by a crowd of many thousands with red flags and revolutionary songs and with cries of 'Hurrah!' I was overcome by an inexpressible, incommunicable feeling of joy, my heart hammered, it was ready to burst and fly away, to be engulfed by this whole mass of people and never to be separated from them, to merge with them and to be a small insignificant part of them. The people were dressed in their celebration clothes, their faces were joyful, cheerfully and ceaselessly singing revolutionary songs and shouting 'Hurrah! Long live the revolution!' Thousands of people embracing us, enveloping us, kissing us, shaking our hands, and they gave us coats, hats, shoes, shawls, they vied with each other to try and give us our things.[27]

While Simonovich's emphasis on collective feeling may in part be a reflection of the expectations of his censors and his audience when he published this account in 1934, it nevertheless captures something of the spontaneous outpouring of

political causes, the fund for victims of the revolution was one of the best supported. (Diane P. Koenker, *Moscow workers and the 1917 revolution* (Princeton, 1981), chapter 7, esp. pp. 274, 286.)

[23] *Izvestiia soveta rabochikh i soldatskikh deputatov* 3, 19 March 1917, p. 2.
[24] *Izvestiia soveta rabochikh i soldatskikh deputatov* 9, 25 April 1917, p. 4.
[25] Gernet, *Istoriia tsarskoi tiur'mi v piatikh tomakh*, v. 5, pp. 244–5.
[26] *Istoriia tsarskoi tiur'mi v piatikh tomakh*, v. 5, p. 246.
[27] V. Simonovich, *V novom Shlissel'burge* (Moskva, 1934), p. 187.

goodwill towards former political prisoners. While the political prisoners were the crowds' target, tens of thousands of criminal prisoners were also released. When the first sixty-six prisoners were released from Shlissel'burg, one memoirist recalled that the criminal prisoners shouted from their cell windows, 'Don't forget about us! See here, Don't forget us!'[28] The criminals were not forgotten. Toshi Hasegawa, in his landmark study of the February revolution in Petrograd, related that up to 70,000 criminals were released into the city's streets.[29] Even for those criminals who were not purposely freed in the early days of revolution, escape from prisons in 1917 was widespread, as many prisons ceased to meaningfully function.[30]

A number of studies referred to a crime wave in 1917, driven in part by escaped or amnestied criminals, who formed powerful criminal gangs in cities across the empire. Some reports have indicated that there was a criminal element among revolutionary activists, as criminals and revolutionaries both targeted the same symbols of oppression.[31] In Petrograd, the numbers of robberies, thefts, and murders increased dramatically, and left the capital 'on the verge of collapse'.[32] In Odessa, a port city that had always attracted a significant number of professional criminals, the amnesties of 1917 enabled the development of large and powerful criminal gangs. These gangs terrorized the city, and organized systematic raids on homes, shops, and offices in broad daylight. The professional criminals were well armed and well organized.[33] In Voronezh criminals donned military uniforms during 1917 to participate in acts of crime and violence in the town.[34] These tales from Russia's cities indicate that criminal associations and networks developed in urban space, and were peopled by escaped or freed prisoners and exiles. We know very little of how these criminal subcultures functioned. The intersections between the end of the Imperial carceral state, revolutionary violence, and social disorder is a story that has been hinted at but has not been fully explored.

The end of exile, and of a punitive carceral state, was short-lived. The Bolshevik seizure of power in October 1917 initiated a long and bloody civil war in Russia. This civil war provided a basis of violence and terror for the Soviet administration

---

[28] Gernet, *Istoriia tsarskoi tiur'mi v piatikh tomakh*, v. 5, p. 247.

[29] Tsuyoshi Hasegawa, *The February revolution: Petrograd 1917* (Seattle, 1981), p. 289.

[30] Michael C. Hickey, 'The Provisional Government and Local Administration in Smolensk in 1917,' *Journal of Modern Russian History and Historiography*, no. 9 (2016). See also Michael Jakobson, *Origins of the gulag: the Soviet prison camp system, 1917–1934* (Lexington, 1993), pp. 3, 16–17.

[31] Boris I. Kolonitskii, *Simvoli vlasti i bor'ba za vlast: K izucheniiu politicheskoi kul'tury Rossiiskoi revoliutsii 1917 goda* (St Petersburg, 2001), pp. 32–3.

[32] See Tsuyoshi Hasegawa, 'Crime, police and mob justice in Petrograd during the Russian revolutions of 1917,' in *Revolutionary Russia: New Approaches*, ed. Rex A. Wade, (New York, 2004). Also, see Hasegawa's forthcoming book, *The Crowd in the Russian Revolution: Crime, Police, and Mob Justice in Petrograd, 1917–1918* (Harvard, 2017).

[33] See Tanya Penter, 'The Unemployed Movement in Odessa in 1917: Social and National Revolutions Between Petrograd and Kiev,' in *Russia's home front in war and revolution, 1914–1922, vol. 3, book 1: Russia's revolution in regional perspective*, ed. Sarah Badcock, Liudmila G. Novikova and Aaron B. Retish (Bloomsburg, 2015), pp. 283–7.

[34] See Stefan Karsch, 'Voronezh: Revolutionary violence and Bolshevik victory,' in *Russia's home front in war and revolution, 1914–1922, vol. 3, book 1: Russia's revolution in regional perspective*, ed. Sarah Badcock, Liudmila G. Novikova and Aaron B. Retish (Bloomsburg, 2015), p. 336.

that rose from its ashes. The new regime demonstrated an enthusiasm for political oppression from its inception, which was fuelled in part by the desperate exigencies of the civil war.[35] For the Bolsheviks' socialist opponents, this meant that after years of prison and exile imposed by the Romanov dynasty, they faced persecution from the new state too. The Bolshevik state systematically represented the socialist opposition as enemies of the state.[36] Many of the exiles that feature in this book returned to prison and exile under the Soviet regime.

There are some clear intersections between late Imperial and Soviet systems of punishment. Both systems occupied the intersections between colonization, repressive politics, and resource extraction.[37] The Gulag scholar Lynne Viola commented that 'However much a monstrosity the Gulag was, an aberration in its scope and radicalism, it nevertheless shared its basic desiderata with the Tsarist state.'[38] Both states based their penal systems around forced labour and internal exile, and kept only a small minority of convicts in prisons. This use of Russia's geography as punishment provided an answer to the challenge of extracting natural resources from Russia's remote and hostile environments, and provided people to colonize its peripheries. All the large Gulag camps and colonies were located in the northern and eastern parts of the Soviet Union, in remote and inhospitable places.[39] The choice of these locations was determined by considerations of economic utilization of resources and isolation of prisoners. The Soviet state's ambitions for the use of forced labour were far greater that anything seen in late Imperial Russia. The Soviet system was based on a principle of self-sufficiency, and punished labour had a central role in state plans for economic development. For both states, the economic utility of forced labour and exile was not realized. Recent research has exposed the Gulag as economically inefficient and wasteful, despite the state's grandiose ambitions.[40]

In both cases, banishment and exile ultimately failed in its objective of isolating prisoners and preventing escapes. The Gulags were porous, and in fact, recent scholarship has conceptualized the whole of Soviet space as embroiled with its carceral institutions and iterations.[41] Significant numbers of camp inmates and settlers escaped, and urban networks developed symbiotically alongside carceral settlements.[42]

[35] See Alexander Rabinowitch, *The Bolsheviks in power: The first year of Soviet rule in Petrograd* (Bloomington, 2007).

[36] For a superb treatment of this, see Scott B. Smith, *Captives of revolution: the socialist revolutionaries and the Bolshevik dictatorship, 1918–1923* (Pittsburgh, Pa, 2011).

[37] See for example, Nick Baron, *Soviet Karelia: politics, planning and terror in Stalin's Russia, 1920–1939* (New York, NY, 2007).

[38] Lynne Viola, 'Historicising the Gulag,' in *Global Convict Labour,* ed. Christian G. De Vito and Alex Lichtenstein (Leiden: Boston, 2015), p. 376.

[39] Paul R. Gregory and V.V. Lazarev, *The economics of forced labor: the Soviet Gulag* (Stanford, 2003), p. 19.

[40] Viola, 'Historicising the Gulag', p. 368.

[41] For a brilliant analysis of the place of the Gulag in Soviet space, see Kate Brown, 'Out of Solitary Confinement: The History of the Gulag,' *Kritika: Explorations in Russian and Eurasian History,* no. 1 (2007).

[42] On relationships between Soviet carceral space and surrounding free settlements, see Alan Barenberg, *Gulag town, company town: forced labor and its legacy in Vorkuta* (New Haven, 2014);

This picture of escape and interaction with local communities resonates with what we have learnt of late Imperial exile. The failure of exile to function effectively as a means to rehabilitate and manage socially undesirable elements in late Imperial Russia is also echoed in the Soviet experience, as this comment from the Ministry of Internal Affairs in 1927 exemplifies:

> The exile of socially dangerous elements ... the only result is to shift these elements from one province to another. They are unable to find work in their place of exile, and so they immediately return to their criminal or suspect activities.[43]

This complaint about the failings of exile could have been written in 1907. As with late Imperial Russia, neglect and negligence caused more suffering in the Gulag system than strict regimes and harsh oversight.[44] While we can find a range of resonances and continuities between late Imperial and Soviet penal systems, however, the scale and ambition of the Soviet state's carceral policies dwarfed anything imagined by Russia's late Imperial rulers. The Gulag system picked up some threads from the punishments that we have described, but took these methods, of isolation, incarceration, transportation, forced labour, and the pains of neglect to new and terrible extremes. The scale of Soviet repressions meant that not just tens of thousands, but millions of people were imprisoned, executed, and forcibly displaced. Penal labour in late Imperial Russia was an afterthought, weakly conceived and partially implemented. Penal labour in the Soviet system took on a central role in economic development.

While we can identify certain continuities and dislocations between late Imperial and Soviet penal policies, it is more challenging to conceptualize a comparative understanding of the lived experiences of these punishments. In my introduction, I forswore the notion of 'hierarchies of suffering', and I continue to struggle with these concepts. While the Soviet system exceeded the late Imperial system in terms of scale, ambition, mortality rates, and sheer callousness, when we focus down to the level of individuals and understandings of their own lives, comparisons are much more difficult to draw.

This book has concentrated on an exploration of everyday life in eastern Siberian exile. What themes emerge from this study? One of the overarching organizing questions for this book have been the relationships between state objectives and policy implementation, and the nature of the relationship between individual subjects, or citizens, and the state. The state exercised less control than one would expect in the context of the 'late Imperial police state', but this did not entail less punishment for the state's subjects. On the contrary, the inadequacy of state control and intervention could mean more suffering for those punished. It is a central paradox that the punished had more autonomy than you would expect, but

---

Judith Pallot, 'Forced Labour for Forestry: The Twentieth Century History of Colonisation and Settlement in the North of Perm' Oblast',' *Slavic Review*, no. 7 (2002). On escape rates, see Viola, 'Historicising the Gulag', p. 369.

[43] Nicolas Werth, *Cannibal Island: death in a Siberian gulag* (Princeton, N.J., 2007), p. 18.

[44] Viola, 'Historicising the Gulag', p. 371.

also that punishment entailed incidental and arbitrary suffering that was not controlled and ordained by the state. The incidental suffering of those who accompanied exiles reinforces the sense that punishment was not rational, or controlled. The tsarist regime did not finely orchestrate punishment, and was often unable to define the movement and treatment of its punished subjects.

Movement is integral to the exile experience. The very nature of exile is an involuntary movement, from the familiar to the unknown. Exile entails the forced removal of the individual from his or her social, economic, and cultural ties. Space is itself used as a punishment. The severity of punishment is delineated by the degree of distance travelled and isolation endured. Our study of lived experience in exile shows us that movement within the exilic space was indeed a central feature of the experience of exile as punishment. As well as the movement to a final destination, exiles were highly mobile once they reached their place of settlement. The need to roam once in exile complicates our understanding of what this punishment entailed. The process of movement towards exile destinations could entail long periods of stasis, as we see in chapter 2. The integration of prison experience into the narrative of what exile entailed demonstrates that exile incorporated multiple modes of being. The uniting feature of this movement and stasis was that it was unfree.

The loss of personal and social networks through exile is another integral part of exilic punishment. Our study of exile experience shows us that while exiles did lose the support of many of their familiar and most intimate relationships, they also built new networks while in exile. Human relationships continued to develop and grow. Some were built on foundations that had been established independent of the carceral space. Exiled soldiers and sailors retained their collective loyalties in prison, and acted as part of a discrete military community. Party activists used their political affiliations as the basis for the social and political networks that they developed in prison and exile. Other exile relationships formed from within the carceral space. The grey area of criminal association and subculture indicates that the prisons themselves provided the arena for the development of a distinct social hierarchy, with complex and well-articulated social codes. Some exiles developed bonds based on their national or religious affiliations, and some developed friendships and relationships based on their shared experience in prison and transit. Women were imprisoned separately from men, and developed their own distinctive networks and subcultures while incarcerated. These multiple, complex networks of communities are testament to the ways in which humans navigate social space together. The exile communities that developed ultimately abnegated the state's objective to isolate exiles.

This study has drawn out some of the fundamental paradoxes of Siberia's use as a place of exile. The dual goals of punishment and settlement were fundamentally inconsistent in a space that already had a settled population. Exiles had to interact with the local communities if they were to live productively. This is particularly apparent when we look at exiles' working lives. The state's hope that exiles would be productive members of Siberian society was at odds with the state's need to isolate and punish exiles. To participate in the region's economic life, exiles had to participate in its social and cultural life as well.

This study provides us with a reminder that an autocratic state is not necessarily a powerful state. Russia was acutely undergoverned. Though there were few legal checks and balances on state power, the ability of the state to manage individual lives was circumscribed by its thin infrastructure. The late Imperial state had limited oversight and knowledge of the individuals in its jurisdiction. The state's struggle to manage its punished populations at the geographical peripheries of the empire illustrates its relatively short reach. Though the state had the power to exile individuals, both through legal and administrative means, it struggled to monitor and to control exiles once they reached their destinations. Just as the state struggled and ultimately failed to 'know' the free population, its punished subjects remained similarly 'unknown'. The 'unknowability' of the punished population engages with fundamental questions on the nature of relationships between subjects and citizens and the state in the late Imperial period.

Have I come to know eastern Siberia's exiled population? To return to the theme with which I concluded my first book, I would like to emphasize that I have written another messy history. By looking more closely at the intricacies of daily lives, we encounter a welter of personalities and individual experiences that are beyond classification. We found that the definition of political prisoners was in fact a very broad one. It included the committed party activists who came to dominate the discourse of what political prisoners were. It included the soldiers and sailors who had been punished for their involvement in mutinies during 1905, and whose collective action challenged the criminal hegemony, and whose songs made the walls of the prison ring, and brought tears to the eyes of overseers on their marches. It included urban lower class people from all over the empire, many of whom had little in common except shared carceral experience. The criminal convicts are ultimately much harder to know, because they left so little written record of themselves. We did snatch glimpses of individuals and their lives, however. We encountered the criminals who sought to lose themselves in great literature while they sat out their prison terms, and the criminal whose comic prose had the whole prison roaring with laughter. We read their appeals to the state, for permission to work, to move, to provide support for their children and families, and for mercy at the end of their lives. This kaleidoscopic set of experiences was many-hued and variegated. Taken together, they provide an exemplar of human endurance, tenacity, and adaptation.

Bibliography

ARCHIVAL SOURCES CONSULTED

The National Archive of the Sakha Republic (NARS)
F. 12, Yakutsk regional administration.
F. 15, Yakutsk regional police administration.
F. 306, Yakutsk regional medical inspector, list 2, 1865–1919.
F. 317, op 1, Verkhoiansk regional doctor, 1891–1913.
F. 509, op 1, The Council of guardians for the orphan children of arrestees and exile settlers, 1902–1917.
F. 169, Yakutsk police.
F. 205, Yakutsk prison cell.
F. 206, Yakutsk region prison committee.

The State Archive of Irkutsk Oblast (GAIO)
F. 25, The Chancery of the Irkutsk Governor-General.
F. 32, Irkutsk provincial administration.
F. 34, Irkutsk province prison inspection, 1864–1920.
F. 90, About the search for the political prisoner Victor Krunatovskyi, escaped from Nerchinsk prison in 1906.
F. 91, Irkutsk police administration.
F. 98, Verkholensk district police administration.
F. 226, Aleksandrovsk central katorga prison, 1875–1920.
F. 394, Balagansk district police administration.
F. 455, Kirensk district police administration.
F. 466, Kirensk township administration, 1902–1919.
F. 600, Administration of the corpus of gendarmes, Irkutsk province.

The Russian State Archive of Social and Political History (RGASPI)
F. 274, Central Committee of the Socialist Revolutionary Party, 1901–1923.
F. 459, Krakov union for the assistance of political prisoners and exiles, 1910–1917.

The State Archive of the Russian Federation (GARF)
F. 102, Department of police, Ministry of Internal Affairs, 1880–1917.
F. 533, Society of political prisoners and exile-settlers.
F. 1463, Collection of separate private documents, 1858–1933.
F. 5800, op. 1; The Russian political émigrés" club in Nagasaki.
F. 9599, Collection of documents on the history of the revolutionary movement in Russia, 1823–1934.
GARF, f. P-3349, Society for the assistance of freed political prisoners.

State Archive of the Russian Far East (GADV)
F. 1, Primor' regional administration.
F. 714, Prison inspectorate of Amur region, Blagoveshchensk town.
F. 3108, Khabarovsk exile-katorga prison.

F. 1318, Khabaorvsk section of Primor' regional committee of guardians about prison society.

F. 1394, Administration of Akatui prison.

F. 1544, Kharbin prison cell.

F. 1607, Khabarovsk regional administration of the Russian society, Red Cross, Khabarovsk town.

The State Archive of Nizhegorod region (GANO)

F. 1887, Nizhegorod province Executive Committee of the Provisional Government.

The National Archive of the Republic of Tatarstan (NART)

F. 1246, Chancery of the Provisional Government commissar for Kazan province.

NEWSPAPERS CONSULTED

Izvestiia soveta rabochikh i soldatskikh deputatov (Nizhnnii Novgorod, 1917).

Kazansakaia Rabochaia Gazeta (Kazan, 1917).

Tiuremnyi Vestnik: Izdanie Glavnago Tiuremnago Upravleniia (St Petersburg/Petrograd, 1893–1917).

PUBLISHED SOURCES CITED

Adams, Bruce F. *The Politics of Punishment. Prison Reform in Russia, 1863–1917* (De Kalb, 1996).

Alatortseva, A.M. 'Zhurnal "katorga i ssylka" i ego rol v izuchenii istorii revoliutsionnogo dvizhenie v Rossii.' *Istoriia SSSR*, no. 4 (1982) 100–14.

Alekseev, E.E. *Po puti pol'nago ukrepleniia vlasti samikh trudiashchikhsia* (Yakutsk, 1970).

Alexopolous, Golfo. 'The Ritual Lament: A Narrative of Appeal in the 1920s and 1930s.' *Russian History*, no. 24 (1997) 117–29.

Alexopoulos, Golfo. 'Destructive-Labor Camps: Rethinking Solzhenitsyn's Play on Words.' *Kritika: Explorations in Russian and Eurasian History*, no. 3 (2015) 499–526.

Anderson, Clare. *Subaltern lives: biographies of colonialism in the Indian Ocean world, 1790–1920* (Cambridge, 2012).

Antonov-Saratovski, V.P. *Pod stiagom proletarskoi bor'by: Otryvki iz vospomininanii o rabote v Saratove za vremia s 1915g do 1918g* (Moscow and Leningrad, 1925).

Applebaum, Anne. *Gulag: A History* (Westminster, MD, 2004).

Ascher, Abraham. *The Revolution of 1905: A short history* (Stanford, California, 2004).

Badcock, Sarah. *Politics and the people in revolutionary Russia: A Provincial History* (Cambridge, 2007).

Badcock, Sarah, Liudmila G. Novikova, Aaron B. Retish, (eds.), *Russia's home front in war and revolution, 1914–22, vol. 3, book 1: Russia's revolution in regional perspective* (Bloomington, Indiana, 2015).

Bagotskii, S. 'Krakovskii soiuz pomoshchi politicheskim zakliuchennym.' *Katorga i ssylka*, no. 9 (1924) 99–193.

Baikalov, Anatole. 'Siberia since 1894.' *The Slavonic and East European Review*, no. 11 (1933) 328–340.

Barenberg, Alan. *Gulag town, company town: forced labor and its legacy in Vorkuta*, (New Haven, 2014).

Barnes, Steven. *Death and redemption: the Gulag and the shaping of Soviet society* (Princeton, NJ, 2011).

Baron, Nick. *Soviet Karelia: politics, planning and terror in Stalin's Russia, 1920–1939* (New York, NY, 2007).

Basharin, G.P. *Romanovskii vooruzhennyi protest* (Yakutsk, 1964).

Bassin, Mark. 'Russia between Europe and Asia: The Ideological Construction of Geographical Space.' *Slavic Review*, no. 1 (1991) 1–17.

Beer, Daniel. 'The Exile, the Patron, and the Pardon: The Voyage of the Dawn (1877) and the Politics of Punishment in an Age of Nationalism and Empire.' *Kritika: Explorations in Russian and Eurasian History*, no. 1 (2013) 5–30.

Beer, Daniel. 'Penal Deportation to Siberia and the Limits of State Power, 1801–1881.' *Kritika: Explorations in Russian and Eurasian History*, no. 3 (2015) 621–50.

Bell, Wilson T. 'Gulag historiography: An introduction.' *Gulag Studies*, no. 2–3 (2009–10) 1–20.

Berenshtam, Vladimir. 'Yakutskaia oblast'' i ssylka.' In *Za pravo! Soderzhanie sbornika*, 187–231. (St Petersburg, 1906).

Bieiere, Daina. *Istoriia Latvii XX vek* (Riga, 2005).

Billington, James H. *Fire in the minds of men: origins of the revolutionary faith* (New York, 1980).

Bitsenko, Anastasia. 'V Mal'tsevskoi zhenskoi Katorzhnoi tiur'me 1907–1910 k kharakteristiki nastroenii.' *Katorga i ssylka*, no. 7 (1923) 192–208.

Boniece, Sally. 'The Spiridonova case, 1906: Terror, myth and martyrdom.' *Kritika*, no. 3 (2003) 571–606.

Boniece, Sally. 'The Shesterka of 1905-06: Terrorist Heroines of Revolutionary Russia.' *Jahrbucher fur Geschichte Osteuropas*, no. 2 (2010) 172–91.

Breshko-Breshkovskaia, Ekaterina K. *Hidden Springs of the Russian Revolution* (London, 1931).

Breshko-Breshkovskaia, Ekaterina K., and Alice Stone Blackwell. *The little grandmother of the Russian Revolution: reminiscences and letters of Catherine Breshkovsky* (Boston, 1917).

Breyfogle, Nicholas B., Abby M. Schrader, and Willard Sunderland (eds.) *Peopling the Russian periphery: Borderland colonization in Eurasian history* (London, 2007).

Brokgauz, F.A., and E.A. Efron. *Entsiklopedicheskii slovar Brokgauza i Efrona, volume XV* (St Petersburg, 1895).

Brokgauz, F.A., and E.A. Efron. *Entsiklopedicheskii slovar Brokgauza i Efrona, volume XXI* (St Petersburg, 1897).

Bronnikov, Arkady. *Russian criminal tattoo police files, volume 1* (London, 2014).

Brooks, Jeffrey. *When Russia learned to read: Literacy and popular literature, 1861–1917* (Princeton, NJ, 1985).

Browder, Robert P. and Alexander F. Kerensky (eds.) *The Russian Provisional Government of 1917; documents* (Stanford, 1961).

Brown, Kate. 'Out of Solitary Confinement: The History of the Gulag.' *Kritika: Explorations in Russian and Eurasian History*, no. 1 (2007) 67–103.

Budnitskii, Oleg. *Istoriia terrorizma v Rossii v dokumentakh, biografiiakh, issledovaniikh* (Rostov-na-Donu, 1996).

Burbank, Jane. 'An imperial rights regime—Law and citizenship in the Russian empire.' *Kritika: Explorations in Russian and Eurasian History*, no. 3 (2006) 397–431.

Bykova, Nina Nikolaevna. 'Istoriia Aleksandrovskago tsentrala (1900–Fevral' 1917gg.).' (Kandidatskii Nauka, Irkutsk State University, 1998).

Bynum, Helen. *Spitting blood: the history of tuberculosis* (Oxford, 2012).

Chatterjee, Choi. 'Imperial Incarcerations: Ekaterina Breshko-Breshkovskaia, Vinayak Savarkar, and the Original Sins of Modernity.' *Slavic Review*, no. 4 (2015) 850–72.

Cherkunov, Aleksandr Nikolaevich. 'Zhizn politicheskoi ssylki i tiur'mi po perekhvachennym pis'mam. Po materialam Irkutskago gubernskago zhendarmskago upravleniia do 1912 g.' *Katorga i ssylka* vol. 26, no. 1 (1926) 171–85.

Chernyshevsky, Nikolay Gavrilovich, and Michael R. Katz. *What is to be done?* (Ithaca, 1989).

Chudovskii, K. 'Istoriko-etnograficheskoi ocherk Irkutskoi gubernii.' *Zapiskii Sibirskogo otdel Imperatorskogo russkogo geograficheskogo obschestvo* vol. 8, no. 2 (1865) 77–98.

Conroy, Mary Schaeffer. 'Health Care in Prisons, Labour and Concentration Camps in Early Soviet Russia, 1918–1921.' *Slavic Review*, no. 7 (2000) 1257–74.

Corrado, Sharyl M. '"The end of the Earth": Sakhalin island in the Russian Imperial Imagination, 1849–1906.' (PhD dissertation, University of Illinois at Urbana-Champaign, 2010).

Cossins, Annie. *Female criminality: infanticide, moral panics and the female body* (Basingstoke, 2015).

Dal', V.I. *Poslovitsy russkogo naroda: sbornik* (Moskva, 1957).

Daly, Jonathan W. *Autocracy under siege security police and opposition in Russia, 1866–1905* (DeKalb, 1998).

Daly, Jonathan W. 'Political crime in late Imperial Russia.' *Journal of Modern History*, no. 1 (2002) 62–100.

Daly, Jonathan W. 'Russian punishments in the European mirror.' Ch. 10 In *Russia in the European context: A member of the family*, edited by Michael Melancon and Susan McCaffray. 161–88. (Basingstoke, 2005).

Dickins, Alistair. 'Krasnoiarsk, 1917: The Making of Soviet Power in Central Siberia.' (PhD dissertation, University of Manchester, 2015).

Diment, Galya, and Yuri Slezkine. *Between heaven and hell: The myth of Siberia in Russian culture* (New York, 1993).

Dobrokhotin-Baikov, A. 'V Yakutskoi ssylke (zapiski rabochego).' In *Sibirskaia ssylka: Sbornik pervyi*, edited by N.F. Chuzhak. 181–94. (Moscow, 1927).

Dormandy, Thomas. *The white death: a history of tuberculosis* (London, 1999).

Doroshevich, Vlas. *Katorga-3 'Sakhalinskoe Monte-Karlo'* (Moscow, 2001).

Dravert, Petr Liudvigovich. *Pod nebom Yakutskago kraia* (Tomsk, 1911).

Drozhzhin, F. 'Listki iz zabytoi tetradi (Vospominaniia ob Amurskoi kolesnoi doroge).' *Katorga i ssylka*, no. 1 (1921) 64–70.

Dubinskii, E. P. 'Pobeg s "Kolesukhi".' *Katorga i ssylka*, no. 3 (1922) 95–120.

Dvorianov, V. N. *Sibirskoi dal'nei storone . . . (Ocherki istorii politicheskoi katorgi i ssylki. 60-e gody XVIIIv.- 1917g.)* (Minsk, 1985).

Eikhgol'ts, E. *Tiuremnyi vrachi i ego patsienty* (Petrograd, 1916).

Eklof, Ben. *Russian peasant schools: Officialdom, village culture, and popular pedagogy, 1861–1914* (Berkeley, 1983).

Eklof, Ben. 'Worlds in Conflict: Patriarchal authority, discipline and the Russian school, 1861–1914.' *Slavic Review*, no. 4 (1991) 792–806.

Ely, Christopher David. *This meager nature: landscape and national identity in Imperial Russia* (DeKalb, 2002).

Engel, Barbara A. 'St. Petersburg prostitutes in the late nineteenth century- A personal and social profile.' *Russian Review*, no. 1 (1989) 21–44.

Engel, Barbara A. *Between the fields and the city: Women, work and family in Russia 1861–1914* (Cambridge, 1994).

Engel, Barbara Alpern. 'Peasant Morality and Pre-Marital Relations in Late 19th Century Russia.' *Journal of Social History*, no. 4 (1990) 695–714.

Engelstein, Laura. *The Keys to Happiness. Sex and the Search for Modernity in Fin-de-Siecle Russia* (Cornell, 1992).

Engelstein, Laura. *Castration and the heavenly kingdom: a Russian folktale* (Ithaca, N.Y, 1999).

Ergina, L. 'Vospominaniia iz zhizni v ssylke.' *Byloe*, no. 6/18 (1907) 52–60.

Evtuhov, Catherine. *Portrait of a Russian province: Economy, society, and civilization in nineteenth-century Nizhnii Novgorod* (Pittsburgh, Pa, 2011).

Fabrichnyi, P. 'Gramota i kniga na katorge.' *Katorga i ssylka*, no. 3 (1922) 189–207.

Fedorov, Vasilii. *Yakutiia v epokhu voin i revoliutsii* (Moscow, 2002).

Figner, Vera. *Memoirs of a revolutionist* (DeKalb, 1991).

Figner, Vera (ed.) *Na zhenskoi katorge: Sbornik statei* (Moskva, 1930).

Forsyth, James. *A history of the peoples of Siberia Russia's north Asian colony 1581–1990* (Cambridge, 1992).

Forth, Aidan. 'Britain's Archipelago of Camps: Labor and Detention in a Liberal Empire, 1871–1903.' *Kritika: Explorations in Russian and Eurasian History*, no. 3 (2015) 651–80.

Frank, Stephen P. 'Emancipation and the birch: The perpetuation of corporal punishment in rural Russia, 1861–1907.' *Jahrbucher fur Geschichte Osteuropas*, no. 3 (1997) 401–16.

Fridman, A. 'Vospominaniia o minuvshikh dniakh.' *Katorga i ssylka*, no. 2 (1931) 150–69.

Frieden, Nancy M. *Russian physicians in an era of reform and revolution, 1856–1905* (Princeton, 1992).

Frierson, Cathy A. *Peasant Icons: Representations of rural people in late nineteenth century Russia* (Oxford, 1993).

Gartevel'd, V.N. *Pesni katorgi: Pesni Sibirskikh katorzhan, beglikh i brodiag* (Moskva, 1910).

Gartevel'd, V.N. *Katorga i brodiagi Sibiri* (Moskva, 1913).

Gatrell, Peter. *A whole Empire walking: Refugees in Russia during World War one* (Bloomington, 1999).

Gaudin, Corinne. *Ruling Peasants: Village and State in Late Imperial Russia* (DeKalb, 2007).

Geifman, Anna. *Thou Shalt Kill; Revolutionary terrorism in Russia, 1894–1917* (Princeton, 1993).

Gentes, Andrew A. 'Roads to Oblivion: Siberian exile and the struggle between state and society.' (PhD dissertation, Brown University, 2002).

Gentes, Andrew A. '"Licentious girls" and frontier domesticators: women and Siberian exile from the late 16th to the early 19th centuries.' *Sibirica: Journal of Siberian Studies*, no. 1 (2003) 3–20.

Gentes, Andrew A. 'Towards a demography of children in the Tsarist Siberian Exile System.' *Sibirica: Journal of Siberian Studies*, no. 5: 1 (2006) 1–23.

Gentes, Andrew A. *Exile to Siberia, 1590–1822* (Basingstoke, 2008).

Gentes, Andrew A. 'Vagabondage and Siberia: Disciplinary Modernism in Tsarist Russia.' In *Cast out: vagrancy and homelessness in global and historical perspective*, edited by A.L. Beier and Paul Ocobock. 184–208. (Ohio, 2008).

Gentes, Andrew A. '"Beat the devil!" Prison Society and Anarchy in Tsarist Siberia.' *Ab Imperio*, no. 2 (2009).

Gentes, Andrew A. *Exile, murder and madness in Siberia, 1823–1861* (Basingstoke, 2010).

Gentes, Andrew A. 'Penal Labor on the Trans-Siberian Railroad.' Unpublished conference paper in *Villains and victims: Crime and punishment in late Imperial and early Soviet Russia* (University of Nottingham, 2010).

Gentes, Andrew A., and Vlas Doroshevich. *Russia's penal colony in the Far East: a translation of Vlas Doroshevich's 'Sakhalin'* (London; New York, 2009).

Gernet, M.H. *Istoriia tsarskoi tiur'mi v piatikh tomakh* (Moscow, 1953).

Glickman, R.L. *Russian factory women* (Berkeley, 1984).

Gol'shukh, G. 'Prizrenie driakhlykh ssyl'nikh v Irkutskoi gubernii.' *Tiuremnyi vestnik*, no. 12 (1910) 1598–1610.

Goncharov, Ivan A. *The Frigate Pallade* (New York, 1987).

Good, Jane. E., and D.R. Jones. *Babushka: The life of the Russian revolutionary E.K. Breshko-Breshkovskaia* (Newtonville, 1991).

Gran, Petr K. *Katorga v Sibiri. Izvlechenie iz otcheta o sluzhebnoi poezdke nachal'nika glav. tiurem. upravlenia P.K. Grana v Sibir v 1913 g* (St Peterburg, 1913).

Gregory, Paul R., and V.V. Lazarev. *The economics of forced labor: the Soviet Gulag* (Stanford, 2003).

Haimson, Leopold J. (ed.) *The making of three Russian revolutionaries* (Cambridge, 1987).

Halfin, Igal. *Terror in my soul: Communist autobiographies on trial* (Cambridge, MA, 2003).

Halfin, Igal. *Intimate Enemies: Demonizing the Bolshevik Opposition, 1918–1928* (Pittsburgh, 2007).

Hartley, Janet M. *Siberia: a history of the people* (New Haven, 2014).

Hartnett, Lynne A. *The defiant life of Vera Figner: Surviving the Russian Revolution* (Bloomington & Indianapolis, 2014).

Hasegawa, Tsuyoshi. *The February revolution: Petrograd 1917* (Seattle, 1981).

Hasegawa, Tsuyoshi. 'Crime, police and mob justice in Petrograd during the Russian revolutions of 1917.' In *Revolutionary Russia: New Approaches*, edited by Rex A. Wade. 46–72. (New York, 2004).

Hasegawa, Tsuyoshi. *The Crowd in the Russian Revolution: Crime, Police, and Mob Justice in Petrograd, 1917–1918* (Harvard, 2017).

Healey, Dan. 'Lives in the Balance: Weak and Disabled Prisoners and the Biopolitics of the Gulag.' *Kritika: Explorations in Russian and Eurasian History*, no. 3 (2015) 527–56.

Henze, Charlotte E. *Disease, health care and government in late Imperial Russia: Life and death on the Volga, 1823–1914* (Abingdon, 2011).

Hetényi, Zsuzsa. *In a maelstrom the history of Russian-Jewish prose (1860–1940)*. (Budapest; New York, 2008).

Hickey, Michael C. 'The Provisional Government and Local Administration in Smolensk in 1917.' *Journal of Modern Russian History and Historiography*, no. 9 (2016).

Holquist, Peter. '"Information Is the Alpha and Omega of Our Work": Bolshevik Surveillance in Its Pan-European Context.' *The Journal of Modern History*, no. 3 (1997) 415–50.

Huey, Meredith P., and Thomas L. McNulty. 'Institutional Conditions and Prison Suicide: Conditional Effects of Deprivation and Overcrowding.' *The Prison Journal*, no. 4 (2005) 490–514.

Hughes, Michael J. 'British Opinion and Russian Terrorism in the 1880s.' *European History Quarterly*, no. 2 (2011) 255–77.

Hutchinson, John F. *Politics and public health in revolutionary Russia, 1890–1918* (Baltimore, 1990).

Iadov. 'Parizhskaia emigratsiia v godi voini.' *Katorga i ssylka*, no 3: 10 (1923) 196–206.

Iadov. 'Iz angarskikh perezhivanii.' In *Sibirskaia ssylka: Sbornik pervyi*, edited by N.F. Chuzhak. 169–80. (Moscow, 1927).

Iadrintsev, Nikolai Mikhailovich. *Sibir' kak kolonii. Sovremennoe polozhenie Sibiri, ei nuzhdy i potrebnosti, ei proshloe i budushchee* (St Petersburg, 1882).

Iadrintsev, Nikolai Mikhailovich. *Statisticheskie materialy k istorii ssylki v Sibir'* (St Petersburg, 1889).

Iakovlev, Dm. 'Ot katorgi k ssylke; okonchanie sroka katorgi.' In *Sibirskaia ssylka: Sbornik pervyi*, edited by N.F. Chuzhak. 109–25. (Moscow, 1927).

Iakubovich, Petr F. *In the world of the outcasts: notes of a former penal laborer* (New York; London, 2013).

Ianson, Ia. 'Iz zhizni Verkholenskoi ssylki 1914g.' *Katorga i ssylka*, no. 4 (1922) 97–103.

'Itogi pereselencheskogo dvizheniia.' *Sibirskii voprosi*, no. 3 (1907) 20–7.

Ivanov, Aleksandr A. *Istoriografiia politicheskoi ssylki v Sibiri vtoroi polovine XIX- nachala XX veka.* (Irkutsk, 2002).

Ivanov, V.N. (ed.) *Istoriko-kul'turnyi atlas Yakutiia* (Moscow, 2007).

Jakobson, Michael. *Origins of the gulag: the Soviet prison camp system, 1917–1934* (Lexington, 1993).

Kaganovich, R.B. *Iz istorii bor'by s tuberkulezom v dorevoliutsionnoi Rossii* (Moscow, 1952).

Kakhovskaia, E. 'Iz vospominanii o zhenskoi tiur'me.' *Katorga i ssylka*, no. 9 (1926) 145–62.

Kalashnikov, A.A., Pavlov, A.A. (eds.) *Istoriia Yakutii v otchetakh Yakutskikh gubernatorov* (Yakutsk, 2007).

Kanatchikov, S.I. *A Radical Worker in Tsarist Russia—The autobiography of Semion Ivanovich Katatchikov* (Stanford, 1986).

Karsch, Stefan. 'Voronezh: Revolutionary violence and Bolshevik victory.' In *Russia's home front in war and revolution, 1914–1922, vol. 3, book 1: Russia's revolution in regional perspective*, edited by Sarah Badcock, Liudmila G. Novikova and Aaron B. Retish. 323–54. (Bloomsburg, 2015).

Kazan, Vladimir. 'Sobol, Andrei.' In *YIVO Encyclopaedia of Jews in Eastern Europe* (Yale University Press, 2010). http://www.yivoencyclopedia.org/article.aspx/Sobol_Andrei.

Kazarian, Pavel L. 'Rol politicheskikh ssyl'nikh v podgotovke trudiashchikhsia mass Iakutii k vospriiatiiu idei klassovoi bor'by.' In *Iakutskaia politicheskaia ssylka (XIX- nachalo XX v.) Sbornik nauchnikh trudov: Chast I*, edited by L.M. Goriushkin and V.N. Ivanov. 65–72. (Iakutsk, 1989).

Kazarian, Pavel L. 'Semeinoe polozhenie politicheskikh ssyl'nikh Yakutii.' In *Osvoboditel'noe dvizhenie v Rossii i Yakutskaia politicheskaia ssylka. Chast 1*, edited by P.L. Kazarian and V.N. Ivanov. 138–43. (Yakutsk, 1990).

Kazarian, Pavel L. *Iakutiia v sisteme politicheskoi ssylki Rossii 1826–1917 gg* (Yakutsk, 1998).

Kazarian, Pavel L. *Iakutskaia politicheskaia ssylka (istorichesko-iuridicheskoe issledovanie)* (Iakutsk, 1999).

Kelly, Catriona. *Children's world: growing up in Russia, 1890–1991* (New Haven, CT; London, 2007).

Kennan, George Frost. *Siberia and the exile system* (Chicago, 1958).

Khaziakhmetov, E. Sh. 'Polozhenie politssyl'nikh Sibiri mezhdu revoliutsionami 1905 i fevralia 1917.' In *Ssyl'nye revoliutsioneri v Sibiri*. 180. (Irkutsk, 1974).

Khrulev, S.S. *Katorga v Sibiri: Izvlechenie iz otcheta nachal'nika glavnago tiuremnago upravlenie S.S. Khruleva o sluzhebnoi poezdke, v 1909 godu, v Irkutskoi gub. i Zabaikalskuiu obl.* (St Petersburg, 1910).

King, Averil, and Isaak Il'ich Levitan. *Isaak Levitan: Lyrical landscape* (London; New York, 2006).

Kleinborg, L. *V tiur'me i ssylke* (Petrograd, 1917).

Klimushkin, P. 'K amnestii 1917 g.' *Katorga i ssylka*, no. 1 (1921) 8–21.

Kliorina, I.S. *Meshcheriakov v Yakutii* (Yakutsk, 1963).

Knight, Amy. 'Female terrorists in the Russian Socialist Revolutionary Party.' *Russian Review*, no. 2 (1979) 139–59.

Koenker, Diane P. *Moscow workers and the 1917 revolution* (Princeton, 1981).

Kolesnikova, Larisa A. *Istoricheskie i istoriograficheskie problemy na stranitsakh zhurnala 'Katorga i ssylka'* (Nizhnii Novgorod, 2001).

Kolonitskii, Boris I. 'The Russian Idea and the ideology of the February revolution.' In *Empire and Society: Approaches to Russian history*, edited by Teruyuki Hara and Kimitaka Matsuzato. 41–71. (Sapporo, 1997).

Kolonitskii, Boris I. *Simvoli vlasti i bor'ba za vlast: K izucheniu politicheskoi kul'tury Rossiiskoi revoliutsii 1917 goda* (St Petersburg, 2001).

Kolpenskii, V. *Yakutskaia ssylka i delo Romanovtsev* (St Petersburg, 1920).

Komkov, V. '"Sukhaia gil'otina". Ocherk sovremennoi politicheskoi ssylke v Rossii.' *Obrazovanie*, no. 8 (1908).

Konstantinov, M.M. and Tochilin, F.M. (eds.) *Politicheskaia katorga i ssylka: Biograficheskii spravochnik chlenov obshchestva politkatorzhan i ssyl'no-poselentsev* (Moscow, 1934).

Korneev, K. 'Iunter-Ofitser Rytov (Vospominaniia ob Irkutskoi peresylnoi tiur'me).' *Katorga i ssylka*, no. 18 (1925) 286–91.

Korochkin, S. 'Istoriia odnoi stolovki.' In *Sibirskaia ssylka: Sbornik pervyi*, edited by N.F. Chuzhak. 156–64. (Moscow, 1927).

Kotsonis, Yanni. *States of obligation: taxes and citizenship in the Russian Empire and early Soviet Republic.* (Toronto, 2014).

Kowalsky, Sharon A. *Deviant women: female crime and criminology in revolutionary Russia, 1880–1930* (DeKalb, 2009).

Kraft, E.E. *Zakony i pravila o ssyl'no-poselentsev i ikh semeistvakh* (Yakutsk, 1912).

Krakovetskii, Arkadii Antonovich. 'Voennoe delo na katorge (Iz vospominanii ob Aleksandroskom tsentrale).' *Katorga i ssylka*, no. 4 (1922) 98–120.

Kramarov, G. 'Iz ssylki na voliu (vospominaniia).' *Katorga i ssylka*, no. 4 (1922) 63–79.

Kramarov, G. 'Nerchinskaia katorga. Doklad, prochitanii na zasedanii Istoricheskoi sektsii Doma Pechati v Moskve 8 Oktiabria 1921 goda. (1907–1910gg).' *Katorga i ssylka*, no. 3 (1922) 57–70.

Kramarov, G. 'Neudavsheiesia ubiistvo na etape (Popytka ubit ugolovnago prozhivnago v 1910g. pri sledovanie avtora iz Gornogo Zerentuia na poselenie).' *Katorga i ssylka*, no. 64 (1930) 121–6.

Krivorukov, E. 'Bor'ba s 'Ivanami' v Aleksandrovskoi katorge (po lichnym vospominaniiam).' *Katorga i ssylka*, no. 47 (1928) 89–95.

Krotov, M. 'Romanovskii protest i proklamatsiiakh yakutskikh politicheskikh ssyl'nikh.' *Katorga i ssylka*, no. 5 (1924) 167–80.

Kudriashov, Vasilii Vasil'evich. 'Men'sheviki v Vostochnosibirskoi ssylke.' (Kandidatskii nauka, Irkutsk State University, 2004).

Kuruskanova, N.P. *Nelegal'nyi izdaniia Sibirskikh Eserov (1901-Fev 1917)* (Tomsk, 2004).

Lansdell, Henry. *Through Siberia* (Boston, 1882).

Laruelle, Marlene. 'Conceiving the territory: Eurasianism as a geographical ideology.' Ch. 4 In *Between Europe and Asia: The Origins, Theories, and Legacies of Russian Eurasianism*, edited by Mark Bassin, Sergei Glebov, and Marlene Laruelle. 68–83. (Pittsburg, 2015).

Leek, P. *Russian Painting* (London, 2005).

Lindenmeyr, A. *Poverty is not a Vice: Charity, society and the State in Late Imperial Russia* (Princeton, 1996).

Lorimer, F. *The Population of the Soviet Union, History and Prospects* (Geneva, 1946).

Lur'e, Grigorii Isaakovich. 'Iz dnevnika "Romanovtsa".' *Katorga i ssylka*, no. 9 (1926) 207–12.

Makarov, E.G. *Ugolovnaia, religioznaia i politicheskaia ssylka v Yakutii vtoraia polovina XIX v* (Novosibirsk, 2005).

Malinovskii, I.A. *Ssylka v Sibir. Publichnaia lektsiia. Chitaniia v Tomske v Noiabre 1899 goda* (Tomsk, 1900).

Maliutina, A. 'Vospominaniia o P.L. Draverte.' *Enisei*, no. 4 (1973).

Margolis, A.D. *Tiur'ma i ssylka v Imperatorskoi Rossii. Issledovanie i arkhivnye nakhodki* (Moscow, 1995).

Marks, Steven G. *Road to Power: The Trans Siberian Railroad and the Colonisation of Asian Russia, 1850–1917* (London, 1991).

Maxwell, Margaret. *Narodniki women: Russian women who sacrificed themselves for the dream of freedom* (New York, 1990).

McGaughey, Aaron. 'The Irkutsk cultural project: Images of peasants, workers and natives in late Imperial Irkutsk province, c. 1870–1905.' (PhD dissertation, University of Nottingham, 2015).

McLennan, Rebecca M. *The crisis of imprisonment: protest, politics, and the making of the American penal state, 1776–1941* (Cambridge; New York, 2008).

Meehan, Brenda. 'From contemplative practice to charitable activity: Russian women's religious communities and the development of charitable work, 1861–1917.' In *Lady Bountiful revisited: Women, philanthropy and power*, edited by Kathleen D. McCarthy. 142–56. (Brunswick NJ, 1990).

Melancon, M. *The Lena goldfields massacre and the crisis of the late Tsarist state* (College Station: Texas A & M University Press, 2006).

Mikhailova, M.G. 'Politicheskaia ssylka i russkaia literatura v Iakutii.' In *Iakutskaia politicheskaia ssylka (XIX- nachalo XX v.) Sbornik nauchnikh trudov: Chast II*, edited by L. M. Goriushkin and V.N. Ivanov. 62–5. (Yakutsk, 1989).

Miller, Vivien M. L. *Hard labor and hard time: Florida's 'Sunshine Prison' and chain gangs* (Gainesville, 2012).

Minaev, P. 'Kak my bezhali iz Aleksandrovsk tsentrale.' *Katorga i ssylka*, no. 6 (1923) 141–53.

Mondry, Henrietta. 'With short cropped hair: Gleb Uspensky's struggle against biological gender determinism.' *Russian Review*, no. 3 (2004) 479–92.

Morrissey, Susan K. *Suicide and the body politic in Imperial Russia* (Cambridge, 2006).

Nadel'shtein, D.S. 'Pobeg Marii Shkol'nik.' *Katorga i ssylka*, no. 2 (1921) 48–58.

Neuberger, J. *Hooliganism. Crime, culture and power in St. Petersburg, 1900–1914* (London, 1993).

Nikiforov, P.M. *Murav'i revoliutsii* (Moscow, 1958).

Nikitin, S.E. 'Politicheskaia ssylka i krest'ianstvo Yakutii (Konets XIX- nachalo XX v.).' In *Yakutskaia politicheskaia ssylka (XIX- nachalo XX v.) Sbornik nauchnikh trudov: Chast I*, edited by L.M. Goriushkin and V.N. Ivanov. 53–65. (Yakutsk, 1989).

Nikitin, S.E. 'Deiatel'nost politssyl'nykh medikov v Yakutii.' In *Osvoboditel'noe dvizhenie v Rossii i Yakutskaia politicheskaia ssylka. Chast 1*, edited by V.N. Ivanov and P.L. Kazarian. 98–101. (Yakutsk, 1990).

Nikitina, E. 'Ssylka 1905-1010 godov.' In *Sibirskaia ssylka: Sbornik pervyi*, edited by N.F. Chuzhak. 10–24. (Moscow, 1927).

Nikitina, S.E. 'Politicheskaia ssylka i krest'ianstvo Yakutii (konest XIX- nachalo XX veke).' In *Iakutskaia politicheskaia ssylka (XIX- nachalo XX v.) Sbornik nauchnikh trudov*, edited by L. M. Goriushkin and V.N. Ivanov. 53–64. (Yakutsk, 1989).

Nikolaev, V. 'Ssylka i kraevedenie; Yakutskii krai.' In *Sibirskaia ssylka: Sbornik pervyi*, edited by N.F. Chuzhak. 88–108. (Moscow, 1927).

Novoe ugolovnoe ulozhenie vysochaishe utverzhdennoe 22 marta 1903 g., s prilozheniem predmetnago alfavitnago ukazatelia. (St Petersburg, 1903).

Otchet po glavnomu tiuremnomu upravleniiu za 1908g (Petrograd, 1910).

Otchet po glavnomu tiuremnomu upravleniiu za 1909g (Petrograd, 1911).

Otchet po glavnomu tiuremnomu upravleniiu za 1910g (Petrograd, 1912).

Otchet po glavnomu tiuremnomu upravleniiu za 1912g (Petrograd, 1913).

Otchet po glavnomu tiuremnomu upravleniiu za 1913g (Petrograd, 1914).

Otchet po glavnomu tiuremnomu upravleniiu za 1914g (Petrograd, 1916).

Otchet po glavnomu tiuremnomu upravleniiu za 1915g (Petrograd, 1917).

Pak, B.B. *Stroitel'stvo Amurskoi zheleznodorozhnoi magistrali, 1891–1916* (Sankt-Peterburg; Irkutsk, 1995).

Pallot, Judith. 'Forced Labour for Forestry: The Twentieth Century History of Colonisation and Settlement in the North of Perm' Oblast'.' *Slavic Review*, no. 7 (2002) 1055–83.

Pallot, Judith, and Laura Piacentini. *Gender, geography and punishment: The experience of women in carceral Russia* (Oxford, 2012).

Paperno, Irina. *Suicide as a cultural institution in Dostoevsky's Russia* (Ithaca; London, 1997).

Penter, Tanya. 'The Unemployed Movement in Odessa in 1917: Social and National Revolutions Between Petrograd and Kiev.' In *Russia's home front in war and revolution, 1914–1922, vol. 3, book 1: Russia's revolution in regional perspective*, edited by Sarah Badcock, Liudmila G. Novikova and Aaron B. Retish, 267–98. (Bloomsburg, 2015).

Petrov, P.U. *Iz istorii revoliutsionnoi deiatel'nosti ssyl'nykh bol'shevikov v Iakutii.* (Yakutsk, 1952).

Phillips, Ben. 'Political Exile and the Image of Siberia in Anglo-Russian Contacts Prior to 1917' (PhD dissertation, University College London, 2017).

Pinnow, Kenneth Martin. *Lost to the collective: suicide and the promise of Soviet socialism, 1921–1929* (Ithaca NY, 2009).

Plekhanova, P.M. 'Stranitsa iz vospominanii o V.I. Zasulich.' In *Gruppa 'Osvobozhdenie truda': Iz arkhivov G.V. Plekhanova, V.I. Zasulich i L.G. Deich*, edited by L.G. Deich. 85. (Moscow-Leningrad, 1926).

Pleskov, V. 'Na Nerchinskoi katorge (iz lichnykh vospominanii).' *Katorga i ssylka*, no. 1 (1921) 80–91.

Pleskov, V. 'Pamiatnie dni.' *Katorga i ssylka*, no. 3 (1922) 45–50.

Polozhenie tiuremnoi chasti i ssylki v Irkutskoi gubernii po dannym dokladov tiuremnago inspektora, 1911–1913gg. (Irkutsk, 1914).

Price, Dorothy C. *Representing Berlin: sexuality and the city in Imperial and Weimar Germany* (Aldershot; Burlington VT, 2003).

Protasov, L.G. *Liudi Uchreditel'nogo sobraniia: portret v inter'ere epokhi* (Moskva, 2008).

Protopopov, K. 'Poslednii s'ezd ssyl'nykh Priangar'ia.' *Katorga i ssylka*, no. 39 (1930) 133–5.

Pyle, Emily E. 'Peasant strategies for obtaining State aid: A study of petitions during World War One.' *Russian History-Histoire Russe*, no. 1–2 (1997) 41–64.

Rabinowitch, Alexander. 'Spiridonova.' In *Critical companion to the Russian revolution*, edited by Edward Acton, V.Iu. Cherniaev, and William G. Rosenberg. (Bloomington, 1997).

Rabinowitch, Alexander. *The Bolsheviks in power: The first year of Soviet rule in Petrograd* (Bloomington, 2007).

Raleigh, Donald J. (ed.) *Provincial landscapes: Local dimensions of Soviet power, 1917–1953* (Pittsburg, 2001).

Randolph, John, and Eugene M. Avrutin (eds.) *Russia in motion: cultures of human mobility since 1850*, (Champaign IL, 2012).

Rashin, Adolf G. *Naselenie Rossii za 100 let (1813–1913)* (Moscow, 1956).

Remnev, Anatolii V. 'Siberia and the Russian Far East in the Imperial geography of power.' In *Russian Empire: Space, People, Power, 1700–1930*, edited by Mark Von Hagen, A.V. Remnev, and J. Burbank. 425–54. (Bloomington, 2008).

Retish, Aaron B. *Russia's Peasants in Revolution and Civil War: Citizenship, Identity, and the Creation of the Soviet State, 1914–1922* (Cambridge, 2008).

Rozental, Pavel I. '*Romanovka*'. *Yakutskii protest 1904 goda. Iz' vospominanii uchastnika* (Yakutsk, 1924).

Rozhkov, N.A. 'Istoricheskii eksiz.' *Sibirskii student*, no. 1–2, Tomsk, 1915.

Said, Edward W. *Culture and imperialism* (New York, 1993).

Sanborn, Joshua A. 'Unsettling the Empire: Violent migrations and social disaster in Russia during World War 1.' *Journal of Modern History*, no. 2 (2006) 290–324.

Savin, A.F. (ed) *Eto ia vinovat ... Evoliutsiia i ispoved' terrorista: Pis'ma Egora Sozonova s kommentariiami* (Moscow, 2001).

Savitskii, F. *Otdel neoffitsialnyi. Aleksandrovskaia tsentral'naia katorzhnaia tiur'ma (ocherki)* (1906).

Savitskii, F. 'Alexandrovskskaia tsentralnaia katorzhnaia tiur'ma.' *Tiuremnyi vestnik*, no. 10 (1907) 751–75.

Savitskii, F. 'Alexandrovskskaia tsentralnaia katorzhnaia tiur'ma.' *Tiuremnyi vestnik*, no. 1 (1908) 62–92.

Schrader, Abby M. *Languages of the Lash: Corporal Punishment and Identity in Late Imperial Russia* (DeKalb, 2002).

Schrader, Abby M. 'Unruly felons and civilizing wives: Cultivating marriage in the Siberian exile system, 1822–1860.' *Slavic Review*, no. 2 (2007) 230–56.

Semyonova Tian-Shanskaia, Olga, and David L. Ransel. *Village life in late tsarist Russia* (Bloomington, 1993).

Seniushkin, F. 'Zavodchiki (vospominaniia iz zhizni Ust-Udinskoi ssylki).' *Katorga i ssylka*, no. 1 (1921) 94–8.

Serebrennikov, P. 'Zaselennost Sibiri Russkimi.' *Sibirskii voprosi*, no. 8 (1908) 31–6.

Seregny, Scott J. 'Zemstvos, peasants, and citizenship: The Russian adult education movement and World War I.' *Slavic Review*, no. 2 (2000) 290–315.

Shapiro, Ann-Louise. *Breaking the codes: female criminality in fin-de-siecle Paris* (Stanford, CA, 1996).

Shcherbakov, N.N. *Vliianiie ssyl'nykh proletarskikh revoliutsionerov na kul'turnuiu zhizn' Sibiri (1907–1917)* (Irkutsk, 1984).

Shul'gin, P.E. (ed.) *Za vlast sovetov: Vspominaet uchastniki bor'bi za vlast v Nizhegorodskoi gubernii.* (Gor'kii, 1967).

Siegelbaum, Lewis H., and Leslie Page Moch. *Broad is my native land: repertoires and regimes of migration in Russia's twentieth century* (Ithaca, London, 2014).

Simanovich, L. 'Ocherki iz zhizni v ssylke (Kirenskoi uezd, Irkutsk gub).' *Katorga i ssylka*, no. 6 (1923) 240–6.

Simonovich, V. *V novom Shlissel'burge* (Moskva, 1934).

Slezkine, Yuri. *Arctic mirrors: Russia and the small peoples of the North* (Ithaca, 1994).

Smith, R.E.F., and David Christian. *Bread and salt: a social and economic history of food and drink in Russia* (Cambridge, 1984).

Smith, Scott B. *Captives of revolution: the Socialist Revolutionaries and the Bolshevik dictatorship, 1918–1923* (Pittsburgh, 2011).

Sobol', Andrei. '"Kolesukha".' *Katorga i ssylka*, no. 3 (1921) 95–120.

Sobol', Andrei. 'Otkritoe pis'mo.' *Pravda*, 23 September 1923.

Sobol', Andrei. 'Otryvki iz vospominanii.' *Katorga i ssylka*, no. 13: 6 (1924).

Sokolov, V.N. 'Sibir i ssylka.' In *Sibirskaia ssylka: Sbornik pervyi*, edited by N.F. Chuzhak (Moscow, 1927), pp. 25–50.

Solomon, S.G., and J.F. Hutchinson. *Health and society in revolutionary Russia*, (Blooming-ton, 1990).

Spiridonova, M. 'Iz zhizni na Nerchinskoi katorge.' *Katorga i ssylka*, no. 14 (1925) 185–204.

Spiridonova, M. 'Iz zhizni na Nerchinskoi katorge.' *Katorga i ssylka*, no. 15 (1925) 165–82.

Spiridonova, M. 'Iz zhizni na Nerchinskoi katorge.' *Katorga i ssylka*, no. 16 (1925) 115–33.

Stanchinskii, A.P. 'Ocherki tiuremnoiu byta; "Politika" i ugolovnyi.' *Katorga i ssylka*, no. 4 (1922) 17–33.

Stanchinskii, A.P. 'V Algachakh.' *Katorga i ssylka*, no. 3 (1922) 74–91.

Strakhov, D. 'V Aleksandrovskoi peresylke.' *Katorga i ssylka*, no. 5 (1923) 184–93.

Sukloff, Marie. *The life story of a Russian exile* (New York, 1914).

Sunderland, Willard. 'Russians into Iakuts? "Going Native" and Problems of Russian National Identity in the Siberian North, 1870s–1914.' *Slavic Review*, no. 4 (1996) 806–25.

Surh, Gerald D. *1905 in St. Petersburg: Labor, society and revolution* (Stanford, 1989).

Sysin, A. 'Ubiistvo konvoinogo ofitsera Sikorskogo.' *Katorga i ssylka*, no. 6 (1924) 190–9.

Takhgochlo, N. 'Ob usloviiakh otbyvaniia nakazaniia politicheskimi zakliuchennymi.' *Pravo*, no. 20 (1907) 1428.

Tarmakhanova, O.D. (ed.) *Pisateli Vostochnoi Sibiri: Biobibliograficheskii ukazanie* (Irkutsk, 1973).

Teterin, N. 'Politicheskaia ssylka i narodnoi poezii Kirenskago uezda.' *Katorga i ssylka*, no. 6 (1924).

Teterin, N.E. ' "Sukhaia Gil'otina" (Ocherk o polozhenie ssyl'nikh).' *Katorga i ssylka*, no. 10 (1924) 178–95.

Thorstensson, Victoria. 'The Dialog with Nihilism in Russian Polemical Novels of the 1860s–1870s.' (PhD dissertation, University of Wisconsin-Madison, 2013).

Tolstoy, Leo. *Resurrection* (Oxford, 1994).

Toth, Stephen A. *Beyond Papillon: the French overseas penal colonies, 1854–1952* (Lincoln, Neb.; London, 2006).

Treadgold, Donald W. *The Great Siberian migration government and peasant in resettlement, from emancipation to the First World War* (Princetown N.J., 1957).

Trigos, Ludmilla A. *The Decembrist myth in Russian culture* (New York, 2009).

Tsingovatov-Korol'kov, E. 'Organizatsiia vzaipomoshchi Eniseiskoi ssylki (Po lichnym vospominaniiam i po pis'mam).' *Katorga i ssylka*, no. 40 (1928) 110–20.

Ul'ianinskii, V. 'Ucheba na katorge (Aleksandrovskaia tsentral'naia katorzhnaia tiur'ma) 1906-1917gg.' *Katorga i ssylka*, no. 54 (1929) 106–26.

Verner, Andrew. 'Discursive strategies in the 1905 Revolution: Peasant petitions from Vladimir province.' *Russian Review*, no. 1 (1995) 65–90.

Vilenskii-Sibiriakov, V. 'Poslednee pokolenie Iakutskoi ssylki (1912–1917gg).' *Katorga i ssylka*, no. 7 (1923) 129–41.

Viola, Lynne. 'Historicising the Gulag.' Ch. 13 In *Global Convict Labour*, edited by Christian G. De Vito and Alex Lichtenstein. (Leiden; Boston, 2015).

Vivdych, M.A. 'Zheleznodorozhnoe stroitel'stvo na dal'nem vostoke v kontse XIX-nachale XX veka.' *Gumanitarnyi vektor*, no. 3 (2011) 40–4.

Vladimirov, V. *Maria Spiridonova* (Moscow, 1906).

Von Geldern, J., and L. McReynolds. *Entertaining Tsarist Russia: Tales, Songs, Plays, Movies, Jokes, Ads, and Images from Russian Urban Life, 1779–1917* (1998).

Vrubelskii, F. 'Vospominaniia ob Amurskoi kolesnoi doroge.' *Katorga i ssylka*, no. 6 (1923) 232–9.

Waldron, Peter. *Between two revolutions: Stolypin and the politics of renewal in Russia* (Illinois, 1998).

Werth, Nicolas. *Cannibal Island: death in a Siberian gulag* (Princeton, NJ, 2007).

Wheatcroft, Stephen G. 'The crisis of the late Tsarist penal system.' In *Challenging traditional views of Russian history*, edited by Stephen G. Wheatcroft. 27–50. (Basingstoke, 2002).

Worobec, Christine D. *Peasant Russia: Family and community in the post-emancipation period* (Princeton, 1991).

X. 'Pamiati L.P. Ezerskoi.' *Lenskii krai*, 4 October 1915.

Yablonskii, P.K., A.A. Vizel, V.B. Galkin, and M. V. Shulgina. 'Tuberculosis in Russia. Its History and Its Status Today.' *American Journal of Respiratory and Critical Care Medicine*, no. 4 (2015) 372–6.

Young, Sarah J. 'Knowing Russia's Convicts: The Other in narratives of imprisonment and exile of the late Imperial era.' *Europe-Asia Studies*, no. 9 (2013) 1700–15.

Zaionchkovskii, P.A. (ed.) *Istoriia dorevoliutsionnoi Rossii v dnevnikhakh i vospominaniiakh; Tom 5, ch. 2; Dopolneniia k t.1–5 (ch. 1), XV v.—1917g.* (Moscow, 1989).

Zenzinov, Vladimir. *Iz zhizni revoliutsionera* (Parizh, 1919).

Zenzinov, Vladimir. *The road to oblivion* (New York, 1931).

Zhbankov, D. 'O samoubiistvakh v poslednie gody (Statisticheskii ocherk).' *Russkoe Bogatstvo*, no. 5 (1908) 126.

Zhukovskaia, N.L. (ed.) *Istoriko-kul'turnyi atlas Buriatii* (Moscow, 2001).

Index